Note: References to Marx's *Capital* are to the Allen & Unwin edition of Volume I, edited by Dona Torr (1946), and to the Kerr edition of Volumes II and III.

PART I

The doctrine that man is the highest being for man; i.e. the categorical imperative to overthrow all conditions in which man is a humiliated, enslaved, despised and rejected being.

Marx

After labour has become not merely a means to live but is in itself the first necessity of living, after the powers of production have also increased and all the springs of wealth are gushing freely together with the all-round development of the individual, then and only then can society inscribe on its banners: "From each according to his capacity, to each according to his need."

Marx

I call revolution the conversion of all hearts and the raising of all hands in behalf of the honour of the free man.

Marx

PART I

The doctrine that man is the highest being for man [is] the categorical imperative to overthrow all conditions in which man is a humiliated, enslaved, despised and rejected being.

Marx

After labour has become not merely a means to live but is in itself the first necessity of living, after the powers of production have also increased and all the springs of wealth are gushing freely together with the all-round development of the individual, then and only then can society inscribe on its banners: "From each according to his capacity, to each according to his need."

Marx

I call revolution the conversion of all hearts and the raising of all hands in behalf of the honour of the free man.

Marx

I

THE MARXIAN ERA

"If a name had to be found for the age in which we live, we might safely call it the Marxian era", is the judgment of one of the most severe of present-day critics of Marxism.[1] The day when Marxism could be treated as of little account is past—if only because, judged by the number of those who regard themselves as his followers and by their political power, Marx must be regarded as an influential figure in human history. And his influence continues, so that it becomes of increasing importance to understand the nature of his ideas and the manner in which they are interpreted.

It is one of the peculiar ironies of history, says Erich Fromm,[2] that there are no limits to the misunderstanding and distortion of theories, even in an age when there is unlimited access to the sources; and there is no more drastic example of this phenomenon than what has happened to the theories of Karl Marx. It is only when such misunderstandings have been removed that serious study of Marx and his thought can be begun. It was Hegel who said that any philosophy may be reduced to empty formalism if one confines oneself to the simple repetition of fundamental principles. It is clear that Marxism needs to be understood for what it is and not for what it has been represented to be if it is to be subjected to critical examination. Above all one must avoid the procedure too common in philosophical controversy: namely, representation of the position of an opponent in the terms it would have if the critic held it; that is, not in its own terms, but translated into the terms of another and opposed theory.

First and foremost, then, it must be understood that Marx himself (and this is equally true of his disciples) was never a speculative theorist interested in ideas for their own sake or a philosopher producing a theoretical system designed to explain the whole course of human history.

"Philosophers," said Marx, "have only sought to interpret the world

[1] Dr. Leopold Schwarzschild, *The Red Prussian*.
[2] Erich Fromm, *Marx's Conception of Man*.

in various ways; the real point is to *change* it." But how is such change to be effected? Not, of course, by the process of discovering the basic principles of a just society and endeavouring to impose them upon the world, but by discovering the laws of historic change by the means at the command of the empirical sciences.

Marx clearly distinguishes the really acting forces in society from the artificial if ingenious reflections of metaphysics. Rational through and through, his aim was not to discover truth by arguments drawn from pure reasoning but by the objective study of things. Scientific theories do not arise in the head but arise from historical and contemporaneous fact, and they are brought to the test in a world of stubborn and irresistible reality which lies outside the thinking process and offers a constant discipline and obligation to the scientific investigator. It was as such an investigator that Marx saw the processes of historic change as arising from the antagonisms which society bears within itself. These antagonisms produce continuous instability, and give rise to social and political movements aimed at overcoming them by radical reorganisation.

This dialectical process, however, by no means implies that the movement of history is independent of the understanding and will of man.

Marx rejected earlier materialism in so far as it regarded man as merely acted upon by external forces; that notion showed no recognition of the part played by men in reacting upon, altering and transforming their environment—and in the process remaking themselves.

The question in every period is not to set the ideal of socialism over against the reality of capitalism and seek by persuasion to win support for its realisation; the question is to recognise or not to recognise in the course of human events the necessity at any given moment for social reorganisation. Is or is not society organised in such a way that the frictions increasing within its economic structure will end by breaking and dissolving it?

What effects social change is the reaction of human consciousness to ripening conditions—the understanding, the decision, and the resulting action. The movement of history is not due to the creative activity of Absolute Mind, nor to the result of a dynamic urge within life and matter; neither is it imposed from without by the irresistible force of economic pressure. It develops out of the *redirective activity of human beings*, trying to meet their natural and social needs by such economic and social changes as are found to be necessary. That necessity arises

from the conditions which develop in the structural pattern of a capitalist society. This, Marx sought to show, is the constant and increasing rebellion of its productive forces against the conditions imposed by that structure, a process maintained and augmented by the laws of its own existence which create the intrinsic conditions of its inevitable death. Marx offered no blueprint of a future society, but indicated how our present society will dissolve by the progressive dynamics of its own forces.

It is now generally recognised that we have here a contribution that represents a truth about the workings of history, a better pattern than the generally accepted view, and one that "offers a corrective of that older view which evaded fundamental problems by seeing history as a field for the activity of disembodied ideas that were treated as irreducible, that is to say, as being the starting-point rather than the consequence of change. Marxism, armed with this historical method, and basing its gospel on Marxist theory, contains a sufficient degree of truth to enable it to stand as a serious challenge to the orthodoxies of the world."[1]

Marxism, however, does not make any attempt to answer the problems of historical enquiry in advance—what it does is to define the right approach to the unimaginably complicated collection of data. "All history", says Engels, "must be studied afresh, the condition of existence of the different formations of society must be individually examined."[2] The Marxist philosophy of history must never become an excuse for *not* studying history.

The necessary reconstruction of society, which Marx envisages, is not, however, the task of society as a whole. For Marx, social change is effected by the coming upon the stage of history of new social classes. For Marx, social structure is defined in terms of economic classes. He sees the end of the capitalist system of production as the dissolution of an industrial society constituted by the economic separation of an owning and a working class; a bold stroke of analytic strategy links the fate of the class phenomena with the fate of capitalism, so that socialism is seen to be the only form of classless society.

Class struggle is not created by propaganda. It is unavoidable where the interests of classes are antagonistic. It necessarily results from a struggle for survival and grows with the development of the contradictions within society. It is the symptom of a disease, of a demonic

[1] Butterfield, *Christianity and History*.
[2] Engels, Letter to Conrad Schmidt. August 5th, 1890.

possession, in the grip of which modern society lives. The Marxist cannot but encourage the fight of the proletariat for its own existence; but his aim is to overcome the system which by its very structure produces and exacerbates class struggle. That there appears to be no way of overcoming it short of socialism is what gives the proletarian fight its universal aim and ethical significance.

For the reconstructive upheaval that alters the economic structure of society there must be not only the action of an organised class but also the ideas and ideals without which no such mass movement is possible—the ideas which arise out of and are relevant to the economic situation and the needs of the class concerned.

This has often been supposed to mean that ideas are secondary in the sense of being themselves ineffectual, merely the ideological reflex of what could happen without them; dismissing the work of the mind as mere superstructure and therefore unimportant. But the fact that ideas have in every case their genesis in the concrete situation and the actual relationships and modes of behaviour of people involved in such relationships, far from disqualifying them, tends rather to guarantee their validity, competence, fruitfulness, and relevance to that reality. So far from denying the power of ideas in life it reveals its origin. Ideas, to be effective and valid, must accurately estimate the objective facts—knowledge is determined by what is known and is not the apprehension of truths existing outside of men and operating as independent powers in history. Ideas must be themselves the result of history before they can start being the cause of anything.

So far from this dispensing with the notion of truth by reducing all ideas to ideology, in the sense of a false consciousness, for Marx truth is the revolutionary thing. Not the abstract truth of metaphysical theory or ethical idealism, but concrete truth, willed, put into operation, maintained and victorious through social struggle by men who work for the liberation of mankind.

Communism, he sought to show, is not the natural and necessary state of human life in all times and in all places; one does not reach communism by fervently preaching it as the social ideal. The chequered history of civilisation cannot be considered as a series of deviations and shortcomings. Communism can be, still more it must and will be, the consequence of the dissolution of our capitalist society—without which, however, it could never have been possible.

In these circumstances the attitude of the working class combines the certainty that the system is doomed and must be replaced by a

system of common ownership, with the feeling of responsibility for its coming. It stimulates the highest degree of activity. Far from giving the workers the right merely to watch the process, it rather makes the demand that the dialectical necessity be materialised by means of revolutionary effort. The most important function of Marxism is to give to the masses, otherwise liable to apathy or despair, an understanding that will awaken them to clear consciousness of their situation, of their historic mission, and will lead them to create a class organisation which will lift the individual out of his solitude into a fighting community.

So far from the transition to socialism being automatic, Marx believed that the promulgation of his illuminating analysis would be instrumental in precipitating the transition, because it would activate the proletariat itself. Not until "the lightning of thought had thoroughly impregnated the yielding popular soil"[1] would the propertyless masses be inspired to appropriate the means of production.

It has sometimes been said that Marx accepted in its entirety the capitalist theory of the "economic man", merely transferring to the worker the role of struggle for self-interest and the motive of individual profit; that Marxim is therefore no more than a working-class version of utilitarianism. How very far this is from Marx's conception both of man and of the economic motive becomes clear when one recalls that his awakening to socialism in 1843 was due not only to his early studies in French socialist theory but to the publication in the *Deutsche-Französischen Jahrbücher*, which he edited in Paris, of Engels' review of Carlyle's *Past and Present*. Here Carlyle furiously attacked the whole capitalist system of economics. "Supply and demand is not the Law of Nature: Cash payment is not the sole nexus of man with man—how far from it! . . . From the pursuit of monetary aims man will utterly fail to achieve happiness." How is this wretched state of affairs to be overcome? By organising work in a co-operative fashion to serve human ends, replied Marx in his first socialist writings. The problem "is to organise the empirical world in such a manner that man experiences in it the truly human. Only in such a community will man find in his relations with others the realisation of his manhood. Society is the necessary framework through which freedom and individuality are made realities."[2]

This clearly is the most complete negation of the concept of

[1] Marx, *Introduction to the Critique of Hegel's Philosophy of Right.*
[2] Marx, *Paris Manuscripts.*

economic man. Nor did Marx ever assert that the motive of individual gain should be the driving force of the working class. True, men necessarily strive for the satisfaction of their basic interests, and those will be the interests of the class to which they belong; but they will see these interests as those of the wider group, and of society as a whole.

For the worker is in the position of serving society as a whole in working for a classless society. What he seeks therefore is not his individual interests but *that common good* in which he hopes to share.

As to Marx's social theory being a form of utilitarianism—the view that human motives are to be explained in terms of desire for pleasure and aversion from pain—Marx derived from his philosophical predecessors Kant and Hegel a scorn for hedonism and related philosophies that always remained with him. The utilitarian ethics of Bentham he regarded as "a flat and hypocritical doctrine", and no more than a philosophical generalisation of the pecuniary relations prevailing in bourgeois society.

In *Capital*, he graciously introduces Jeremy Bentham to the reader as "the insipid, pedantic, leather-tongued oracle of the commonplace bourgeois intelligence of the nineteenth century. At no time and in no country has the most trivial commonplace ever strutted about with such appalling self-satisfaction." To know what is useful for man we must know what human nature is and this cannot be excogitated from "the principle of utility". If this is somewhat unfair to poor Bentham it at least absolves Marx from the charge of being a utilitarian who conceived men as driven by no other motives than individual self-interest.

Was Marx a materialist, then, either in the sense of attributing to man no other motive than the wish for ever-increasing material gain or comfort, or in the philosophical sense of reducing all mental and spiritual phenomena to matter in motion? In fact Marx strongly opposed "the abstract materialism of natural science, that excludes history and its processes". His view as to the nature of life and man we would characterise today as naturalism or humanism, regarding thought as being as real as sight, the one being a function of the eye, the other of the brain. The "materialist method" which Marx speaks of, which distinguishes his view from that of Hegel, involves the study of the real economic and social life of man, and of the influence of man's actual way of life on his thinking and feeling. "In direct contrast to German philosophy," Marx wrote, "which descends from heaven

By the same author

THE OLD TESTAMENT IN THE 20TH CENTURY
A FAITH TO LIVE BY
CHRISTIANITY AND THE SOCIAL REVOLUTION (ED.)
TEXTBOOK OF MARXIST PHILOSOPHY (ED.)
DOUGLAS FALLACIES
THE PHILOSOPHY OF THE SOVIET STATE
THE CASE AGAINST PACIFISM
MARXISM AND MODERN IDEALISM
AN INTRODUCTION TO PHILOSOPHY
MARXISM AND THE IRRATIONALISTS
MARXISM AND THE OPEN MIND
RELIGIONS OF THE WORLD
SCIENCE, FAITH AND SCEPTICISM
ANTHROPOLOGY
SOCIALISM AND THE INDIVIDUAL
A HISTORY OF PHILOSOPHY
MAN AND EVOLUTION

THE LIFE AND TEACHING OF KARL MARX

CONTENTS

Part I

Part II

Part III

Printed in Great Britain by
The Camelot Press Ltd., London and Southampton

THE LIFE AND TEACHING OF KARL MARX

by
JOHN LEWIS

1965
LAWRENCE & WISHART
LONDON

to earth, here we ascend from earth to heaven. That is to say, we do not set out from what men say, imagine, conceive, nor from men as narrated, thought of, imagined, conceived, in order to arrive at men in the flesh. We set out from real, active men, and on the basis of their real life-process we demonstrate the development of the ideological reflexes and echoes of this life-process."[1]

From this we conclude not that man's main desires are materialistic, but that the way a man produces and, in particular, the pattern of social life, the kind of social relations that obtain between man and man at any particular stage of social development, shape the thinking and desires, the ideals and beliefs, which are the guiding light and driving force of his life.

Thus the great difference between Marx and the capitalist theorists of his time was that he does *not* consider capitalism to be the outcome of human nature, nor the economic motives which admittedly operate in capitalism to be universal in man. Indeed, Marx's whole criticism of capitalism is that in making desire for money and material gain the driving force of economic life, capitalism (historically necessary and fruitful though it has been) has now produced a situation which is harmful to human interests and is threatening us with disaster. This situation calls for a socialist society in which not pecuniary interest is dominant but human needs, the interest of the community.

The importance of Marxim lies beyond even its major task, the bringing of socialism into being; it comprises a complete world-view, a *Weltanschauung* in which all human thought and action are related to certain basic principles of interaction and development; for Marx was compelled by his search for a theory of history to enquire into the nature of reality and of man as part of reality, and so create a philosophic basis for his theory of society.

Its existence as the creed of a considerable proportion of the world is of significance in view of the widespread failure of nerve elsewhere and the virtual abdication of philosophy today as responsible for our understanding of man's nature and destiny. As Toynbee has rightly said, "A society cannot maintain its social cohesion unless a decisive majority of its members hold in common a number of guiding ideas and ideals".[2]

But at the moment when the intellectual temper of the West is profoundly sceptical, Marxism offers a map that seems at once to take

[1] Marx and Engels. *The German Ideology*.
[2] A. Toynbee, *An Historian's Approach to Religion*.

in the whole of historical reality, to reveal the working of the capitalist system and the laws of social change. It is a philosophy of history in so far as it is its purpose to account for the development of our civilisation and to offer some guidance as to what we may expect in the future and what is required of us in bringing it to pass. As such it has gained a wider acceptance than any rival explanation advanced in modern times. Engels indeed claimed that it has brought about a revolution in the social sciences comparable to that which Darwin effected in the natural sciences.

It would seem to merit the considered attention of the modern world.

2

THE FORMATIVE YEARS

HOME AND SCHOOL

KARL HEINRICH MARX was born on May 5th, 1818, in Trier (Trèves), an ancient city of Germany in the Prussian province of the Rhine. It is situated on the right bank of the Moselle and lies in a fertile valley shut in by vine-clad hills, the picturesque red sandstone buildings of the old town interspersed with orchards and gardens.

His father was a successful Jewish lawyer who rose to be *Justizrat* and head of the Trier bar. In 1824 he had renounced Judaism even though there was a Rabbinic tradition in both his own family and that of his wife. He and his family were baptised into the Christian faith, thus securing what Heine called "an entrance card into the community of European culture". The young Marx derived no part of his mental heritage from the Jewish tradition, nor did he ever think of himself as a Jew. He was always a European and a German.

In the history of the German intelligentsia the Jews were playing a significant part. Moses Mendlessohn, the philosopher, had brought his people into contact with the German cultural world, and they were becoming of importance to the literature and thought of the day. Four Jews were of exceptional influence—Marx, Lassalle, Heine and Börne. Börne's works are remarkable for brilliancy of style and for a thoroughly French vein of satire. He was regarded as one of the leaders of the new literary party of "Young Germany". Heine too was of "Young Germany", but he combined with his romanticism an intensely matter-of-fact, realistic outlook on life, a withering irony and self-criticism. Marx knew Heine and Goethe by heart and was constantly quoting them.

We have then to think of the Marx household as enlightened and rationalist in outlook, deliberately leaving the narrower Jewish tradition in order to participate fully in both the cultural and national spirit of the times. The elder Marx was indeed passionately Prussian and monarchist in his views and was to have frequent quarrels with his much beloved son, whose university career caused him not a little concern.

The most powerful influence on the young Marx was their next-door neighbour, Baron von Westphalen, a man of the widest culture who knew seven languages, loved Shakespeare, and knew much of Homer by heart. His father, who was regarded as a remarkable figure in military history, had been Chief of Staff to the Duke of Brunswick in his campagin against Louis XV during the Seven Years' War, and had married the daughter of a Scottish nobleman, the Duke of Argyll, who was visiting the General of the British troops participating in that campaign. His son Ludwig von Westphalen was a Privy Councillor, and a typical representative of that section of the German upper class whose representatives were to be found in the vanguard of every enlightened and progressive cause.

What was called in France the Enlightenment was known in Germany as the Aufklärung. Originating in Germany as the rationalism of Leibniz as developed by Wolff and in Britain as the philosophy of John Locke, it culminated in Germany in the philosophies of Kant and Fichte, while the philosophy of Locke became the foundation of French enlightenment as represented by Helvetius, Holbach, Diderot and Voltaire.

This powerful movement of rationalist thought was certainly the dominant influence in that circle of cultural and able Germans among which the young Marx passed his early years. It played a particularly important part in Germany because of Germany's political and social backwardness and authoritarian forms of government. In face of this restricted social, political and industrial life, in which the only public forum was the theatre and the only medium of public discussion the lecture room of the philosopher, Germany experienced a period of intense creative literary and poetical activity, and of philosophical speculation which, though it reflected the weakness of the German middle-class movement, achieved much for the culture of modern Europe.

It was thus the philosophy of Kant and Fichte that first influenced the young Marx before he turned to Hegel. It had undermined faith in religious authority and theology, and tended to reject all those aspects of the social order which embodied a merely traditional feudalism. Further, as Marx said,[1] it developed the *active* side of knowing, in opposition to what Engels called "the simple, metaphysical and

[1] Marx, Theses on *Feuerbach.*

exclusively mechanical materialism of the eighteenth century",[1] though it did so "only abstractly, since, of course, idealism does not know real sensuous activity as such". Thus it made a vital contribution to the ideology of the German revolution of 1848, in which Marx and Engels played a considerable part.

Karl Marx obtained in the Westphalen home a stimulus not afforded elsewhere. His growing interest in Dante, Shakespeare, Homer and Greek tragedy was fostered by his older friend, who lent him books, quoted long passages, took him for walks up the Moselle valley and treated him as his own son. An even more important member of the household as far as the young Marx was concerned was the daughter, Jenny von Westphalen, and the two children grew up together. She was an intelligent and remarkably beautiful girl, and when Marx was but seventeen and she twenty-one they were betrothed. She became his devoted companion through all the long years of exile and poverty, though, as one of the favoured children of fortune, she was not always capable of dealing with the misfortunes of their difficult life as a woman of the people, more inured to hardship, might have done. She copied his manuscripts, and he frequently consulted her on matters of policy. When they lived in Paris, Heine, who was a frequent visitor, expressed his admiration for her penetrating and sensitive understanding of men and events.

UNIVERSITY LIFE

Karl Marx left his school, the Friedrich-Wilhelm Gymnasium, in August 1835 and entered the University of Bonn where it was intended that he should study law. But his father realised that there was in him a demonic spirit, and something at the same time as hard as granite, which was entirely foreign to his own rather conventional ideas. He wrote letter after letter to his son, expressing alarm at his restless energy, begging him to show sobriety and not to be so extravagant. But Karl joined the poet's club and wrote bad verse[2], got into debt, and was the most convivial of students. There is a portrait of him at this time with his head held high under its great mop of black hair,

[1] Engels, *Anti-Dühring*.

[2] Marx's own opinion on these poems was extremely critical. "Feeling stamped flat and formless; nothing natural about them; everything up in the air; utter contradiction between what is and what ought to be; rhetorical reflections instead of poetical ideas." His biographer Franz Mehring, who was himself a literary critic of some reputation, says: "In general these poems breathe a spirit of trivial romanticism, and very seldom does any true note ring through. The technique of the verse is clumsy and helpless."

a look of brooding fierceness in his eyes. Well might his father see in him the Faustian spirit of endless, passionate search for knowledge, that Promethean defiance of all the gods that made him so different from his fellows, even from the ablest of them.

In 1836 his father transferred him to the University of Berlin there to continue his legal studies. He cared little for the set lectures, but worked independently to the point of physical exhaustion—and continued to write bad poetry for Jenny. He read little law and much philosophy, especially the whole of Hegel. But we find him also reading Lessing's *Laocoon* and Winckelmann's *History of Art*, translating Tacitus and Ovid, and learning English and Italian. In 1838 his father died, and in the same year Marx established his friendship with that extraordinary group of philosophers who came to be known as the Young Hegelians.

HEGEL

Hegel's early philosophy was written largely as a response to the challenge of the French Revolution to reorganise state and society on a rational basis, so that social and political institutions might accord with the freedom and interests of the individual. He related the concept of reason to the Revolution with the greatest of emphasis, seeing in it the assertion of reason's ultimate power over reality. As he subsequently characterised this great event: "The idea of Right asserted itself, and the old fabric of injustice broke down. It was a glorious sunrise. All thinking beings celebrated that event. A noble emotion reigned in that epoch; the world was thrilled with spiritual enthusiasm as if the decree had now become a reality in the world."[1]

But while the French Revolution had thus already begun to assert the reality of freedom, "German idealism was only occupying itself with the idea of it. The concrete historical efforts to establish a rational form of society were here transposed to the philosophical plane and appeared in the effort to elaborate the notion of reason."[2]

This was due to the economic and political backwardness of Germany. The remains of feudal despotism still held sway. Serfdom was still prevalent. Princes hired out their subjects as mercenary soldiers to foreign countries. Strong censorship operated to repress the slightest traces of enlightenment; and there was no strong, conscious, politically educated middle class to lead the struggle against absolutism. Hence the educated classes, isolated from practical affairs,

[1] Hegel, *The Philosophy of History*. [2] Marcuse, *Reason and Revolution*.

were impotent to apply their reason to the reshaping of society, and fulfilled themselves in the realm of science, art, philosophy and religion. Hegel's system is the last and most complete expression of this cultural idealism; the last great attempt to render thought a refuge for reason and liberty.

Nevertheless, Hegel saw the possibility of the transformation of ideas into political action in Germany as well as in France. If, he says, the French nation, by the bath of its revolution, has been freed from many institutions which the spirit of man has left behind, and has cast off the fear of death and the life of custom, will not the Germans, once they have cast off their inertia, transcend their present cloudy and undeveloped spirit and "rouse themselves to action, preserving in their contact with outward things the intensity of their inner life, and perchance surpass their teachers"?[1]

Hegel's philosophy is developed through five very different stages, between 1790 and 1830. The earlier and more revolutionary thinking[2] passes by degrees into the more static and systematic thought of his latter years in Berlin; but the whole course of his philosophical progress is accompanied by its political application to concrete historical situations continuing right up to 1831, when he wrote his study of the English Reform Bill. This connection of Hegel's philosophy with the historical development of the time made the political digressions an essential part of his systematic exposition. All his concepts are given historical and political as well as philosophical explanation.

Although the realism of Hegel's position always shows through the idealistic framework and terminology, there is a contrast between the *dialectic*, the great merit of which was that "the whole natural, historical and spiritual world was presented as a process, that is, as in constant motion, change, transformation and development"[3] and the Hegelian *system*, as it came to be formulated, which Engels regarded as "a colossal miscarriage", for which "things and their development were only the images of the idea existing somewhere or other already before the world existed, a system which laid claim to being the very sum total of precisely this absolute truth—a system of natural and historical knowledge which is all-embracing and final."

[1] Hegel, Letter to Zellman, XVII.628.

[2] Hegel's First System is contained in the three volumes of the *Jensener Real philosophie*, which was not published in German until 1931 and has not been translated into English.

[3] Engels, *Anti-Dühring*.

This as Engels well says "is in contradiction to the fundamental basis of dialectical thinking".[1]

As Hegel himself put it: "The consummation of the infinite end consists merely in removing the illusion which makes it seem yet unaccomplished. The Good, the absolutely good, is eternally accomplishing itself in the world; and the result is that it need not wait upon us, but is already by implication, as well as in full actuality, accomplished."[2]

For Hegel, the Idea, which precedes everything, has limited itself in the material world ("Nature is the otherness of Mind"), and is gradually realising itself in the development of man's self-consciousness in history. Here indeed is progress, but the end is already "in full actuality accomplished". Our sole task, therefore, according to one school of Hegelian philosophers, could only be to correct the error that things are other than they ought to be. These disciples of Hegel constituted the more conservative group, among whom one might mention Erdmann and Rosenkranz, and their interpretation of the master appeared to be in full harmony with the doctrine of the Church. Erdmann interpreted him as displaying the whole content of existence as the expression of abstract categories, conceiving the movement of thought as the law of the universe. Rosenkranz held that the real object of the dialectical method was to show that all things are intimately interconnected to form a great totality, as are the thoughts in the mind, and that the essence of existence is: Everything is spirit, and spirit is everything. This made the task of philosophy the reconciliation of man to things as they are.

The Left, which was of far greater importance for the development of thought, drew radical conclusions from the teaching of Hegel, both in the philosophy of religion and in the philosophy of law and society. They were known as the Young Hegelians, and Marx was of their company. They were a most remarkable group of able men who for many years worked closely with Marx, and influenced him profoundly, even though he subsequently came to differ from them. It is impossible to comprehend the development of Marx's ideas unless we can see them as emerging from the philosophical discussions of these Young Hegelians.

Marx understood the *Logic* as showing the movement of thought reproducing the movement of being and bringing it to its true form. Hegel was dealing not with ideas as distinct from reality, for the

[1] Engels, *Anti-Dühring*. [2] Hegel, *Encyclopoedie*.

identity of thought and existence means that he is always dealing with real things. The interplay and motility of the notions reproduce the concrete process of reality.

Hegel also held that every particular existence is essentially different from what it could be if the potentiality were realised. The difference between the reality and the potentiality was the starting-point of the dialectical process.

How radically Marx was to develop these fundamental notions of Hegel remains to be discussed, but the supreme importance of the Hegelian dialectics for Marx's thoughts is unquestionable.

When we think of this group of philosophers, as Marx knew them in those early years, we must see them not as the men of twenty years later, most of them in opposition to Marx, but as young men of talent, even, some of them, of genius, working out their philosophy in endless argument, and learning much from one another. There they were, their views by no means fully developed, good friends, young, vigorous, intoxicated with their theories, alive with gaiety and enthusiasm, more united in their hostility to convention and to the reactionary Hegelians of the Right than they were divided among themselves.

They were all agreed that the idea of progress was paramount. They argued that if, as Hegel had said, the rational was the real then society as they saw it, being far from rational, was not yet the complete realisation of the Idea, and had to be made so. Its development was not complete. This realisation was to be accomplished by correcting the illusions of the mind, and above all by criticising religious error. Those who interpreted Hegelianism in this sense included Bruno Bauer, David Strauss, Arnold Ruge and Moses Hess. It was only when Feuerbach and Marx came on the scene that it was fully realised that the criticism of religion would only be completed by radical social criticism.

Marx as soon as he came to Berlin threw in his lot with the Young Hegelians and joined the famous *Doktor Klub* of vigorous, critical young thinkers, who poured contempt on the church, on the bourgeoisie and even on the state. Marx was only twenty at the time, but he soon became the centre of the group. He enjoyed the rich cultural life of Berlin in company with his friends, attracting all by his audacity and wit, not a little feared as an ironical and bitter controversialist.

In 1839 Bauer went to Bonn as Lecturer in Philosophy, with every prospect of a professorship; and it was the intention of Marx to follow him and teach philosophy there, joining Bauer in the publication of a critical journal. Meanwhile, Marx was busy with his doctoral thesis on the philosophies of Democritus and Epicurus. Bauer was anxious for him "to polish this off" and come and join him in Bonn. He was finding things dull after Berlin and he missed the exuberance and gaiety of Marx. He had never laughed so much in Bonn, he wrote, as he had in Berlin in no more than crossing the street with Marx. But a change in the Ministry of Culture led to vigorous intervention against the Left Hegelians whose attacks on religion were causing great offence, and Bauer lost his promotion. Marx decided not to take his doctorate in Berlin, and submitted his thesis to the University of Jena, which awarded him the degree of Doctor of Philosophy on April 15th, 1841. But all hopes of a career at Bonn and of the radical philosophical journal were at an end.

Nevertheless, it was here that he settled in March 1842, and he "remained to annoy the orthodox" after Bauer's enforced departure. An unexpected opportunity opened up new vistas. In 1842 he became the editor of a new liberal journal, the *Rheinische Zeitung*, which was published in Cologne, and he left Bonn to take up his editorial work there.

When Marx took over the editorship of the *Rheinische Zeitung* he was twenty-four years old. He had already made a great impression on his friends. Hess wrote of him to the author Auerbach, "You will enjoy meeting a man here who also belongs to our group, although he lives in Bonn, where he will soon be holding lectures. He is a character who made an imposing impression on me, though I work in the same field; in short, you can be prepared to meet the only living real philosopher; when he appears before the public (in his writings as well as lectures) he will draw the eyes of Germany upon him. Dr. Marx is still a very young man who is going to give the death-blow to medieval religion and politics; he combines the profoundest philosophical seriousness with a cutting wit."

What sort of man was this young philosopher and editor? We know that he was at all times a tremendously tenacious and thorough worker. His notebooks show how persistently he worked at problems, how insatiable was his thirst for knowledge, how inexhaustible his capacity for research. But he united this with a far from dogmatic attitude. And he was not a dour or over-serious man; on the contrary he was full of gaiety and good humour, delighting in long country walks with his friends and in convivial gatherings.

The editorship of the *Rheinische Zeitung* came to Marx at an opportune moment and in a rather strange fashion. The new journal represented the industrial, Protestant and liberal interest in the rapidly developing Rhineland, as against the more feudal and reactionary Catholic forces, which were considerable. Moreover Prussia, of which the Rhineland was a province, was anxious to further North German interests in the Rhineland, and was resisting the Catholic policy of separatism and of opposition, on purely reactionary grounds, to the development of railways. The Cologne merchants and bankers founded the new journal, and appointed two Young Hegelian lawyers to edit it. Moses Hess also played an important part in its political direction, and the Berlin group of Young Hegelians including Marx, were contributors. The Prussian Government at this time were prepared to put up with a good deal of vigorous liberal writing in order to counteract the Catholic policies of which they disapproved; while the shareholders were impressed by the practical attitude of the most vigorous of the Young Hegelian contributors, Marx. Accordingly, in October 1842 he was made editor of the paper and entered public life. When he assumed the editorship he moved to Cologne and there he was given the opportunity of showing whether a philosophical understanding of actual events, giving society a consciousness of itself, showing it the reason for its conflicts, could actually play an effective part in bringing about radical social change.

The policy Marx adopted was not the advocacy of extreme views, and not general theoretical discussion of liberty and the state, or of religion. Marx always held that theory and practice must be rooted in actual conditions and must contribute to the elucidation of practical problems. He therefore strongly disagreed with the Berlin group of Young Hegelians, whom ill luck with the authorities seemed to have driven into extreme forms of irresponsible literary protest. Bauer was even prepared to advocate that the state, private property and the family were to be dissolved! This appeared to Marx a mere itch for self-advertisement, and a kind of political romanticism for which he had no use at all. He called their contributions to the paper "world-uprooting scribblings, empty of ideas and written in a slovenly style". Nor was he at all impressed by their savage onslaught on religion. "I asked them," wrote Marx, "to criticise religion by criticising political conditions rather than the other way about, because religion, quite empty in itself, lives from earth and not from heaven and will disappear on its own once the inverted reality whose theory it represents is dissolved."[1] In fact, said Marx, this "Berlin gas-baggery deals with

[1] Marx to Ruge, November 1842.

nothing but its own clique concerns, and is of no use to anybody."

Marx saw that the next step was the achievement of constitutional power, and on this he could unite a great number of free-minded and practical men. This was next on the agenda, and he strongly objected to any policy which would split the progressive front into fragments. Ultimate theoretical problems, he said, only become proper for newspaper treatment in so far as they have become practical problems. He calls therefore for "less argumentation, grandiloquent phrases, complacent self-admiration, and more examination of concrete conditions, more factual knowledge".[1] If they want to criticise religion let them do it through the criticism of political conditions rather than criticise political conditions through the criticism of religion; and let them cease playing about with the label "atheism"—behaving "like children who tell everyone they are not afraid of the bogeyman".

But when religion entered the field of politics, in the Catholic opposition to railways, Marx strongly criticised the pretensions of the church to treat such secular matters as if they were spiritual. There was no cowardly compromise, but fearless courage in his editorship, which all too soon brought down upon his head the wrath of the Prussian Government. The paper failed to rally against the threatened censorship a self-confident revolutionary middle-class movement. The liberals were timid in the face of authority and fearful of too much help from the Left and especially from the working class.

Other practical issues of a social character, the peasant and vine-growers' grievances, enlisted his aid and aroused more opposition. Nevertheless the circulation rose from 800 to several thousand. Marx wrote article after article, and the special supplements, containing more theoretical material, which appeared on alternate days, were usually from his pen.

Running through all these articles was the intention of freeing the apparatus of the state from the control of particular class interests; but out of his experience and study there was growing the understanding that the state was itself the organ of a particular class and that constitutional forms were a product of property-relations. It was the injustices inflicted by the Diets on the peasants and vine-growers that aroused him to challenge their claim to speak and legislate for the whole community, whereas in fact they represented definite ruling-class interests.

It was in these articles too that he raised the important question of

[1] *ibid.*

the freedom of the press, a topic on which he had just written a powerful article for Arnold Ruge (which, however, owing to the censorship, was not published until 1843). In this earlier article he severely criticised the new *Instructions* to the Censors of Frederic William IV, which had a specious air of liberalism about them. The Censors were instructed to be generous and tactful in the exercise of their authority, to allow reasonable criticism if it was expressed in serious and modest terms. Candid treatment of political affairs was permissible provided it did not "present in a favourable light any party working for the overthrow of the existing system of government". Religion might be discussed "provided that it was not done in a frivolous, hostile or fanatical manner". Criticism of the government was permissible "if its tendency was well meaning, and if it did not incite suspicion against classes of society or individuals".

This may have seemed liberal in spirit to many of those to whom it was addressed; not so to Marx, who tore it to pieces in a brilliant piece of polemical writing which expressed his belief in the sacredness of the rights of individuals and the inalienable sovereignty of the people. In it he asserts that the end does not justify evil means nor does political authority turn wrong into right. A sound condition of the public mind, he declares, cannot be induced by measures that reduce freedom. Maladies of the press should be left to the natural cure that freedom brings; the censor can but amputate.

Coming to the new concessions allowed to the censors, Marx declared that he preferred precise statements of what was allowed and disallowed to protestations of liberalism which in the last resort depended on what the censor happened to think reasonable. To allow what is written in a "serious" and "modest" style or what is "well meaning in tendency" may mean anything. It is a purely subjective standard, said Marx, and a reactionary censor could exclude more on these instructions (1842) than on those of 1819. And it was absurd to allow "candid criticism" so long as it was not subversive. No affairs can be candidly discussed under such conditions. And then, as to matters of religion, where the treatment must not be frivolous or hostile or fanatical, a frivolous criticism does not touch the essence but any other attack is hostile to the essence; to Catholics all Protestant criticism is both hostile and fanatical, while all Catholic criticism is so to Protestants. So no criticism at all is possible. Then again, all regulations based on "tendency" are anti-political, branding in advance whole schools of thought, and so stifling the reason of the community

Censorship, he concludes, is incompatible with the very essence of law, with public discussion and personal responsibility.

In the *Rheinische Zeitung* of May 1842, he returned to this question. His defence of the rights of the press now went beyond his earlier criticism of the censorship, and raised the question of the hired journalist.

"Is a press which degrades itself to trade, free? A writer must certainly earn money in order to exist and write, but he should not exist and write in order to earn money. The first freedom of the press must consist in its emancipation from commerce. The writer who degrades the press to a material means deserves as a punishment for this inner slavery that outer slavery which is the censorship, or perhaps his very existence is his punishment."

All his life Marx lived up to these principles and to the standard which he demanded from others. And now he was to experience for himself the impossible limitations under which he was trying to work. The censorship had from the first pursued a policy of petty interference which annoyed not only those who worked for the paper but its subscribers. All the hopes that had followed the accession of Frederic William IV to the throne of Prussia had faded. Journal after journal was suppressed, and the *Rheinische Zeitung* came under the strongest condemnation when Marx proceeded to discuss the King's plan for alteration in the Divorce Laws before its actual publication.[1]

The radical movement was not to be intimidated, and opportunity for political expression was found in a series of Yearbooks and Annuals which were edited by Arnold Ruge. These so-called "Annuals" were a device for evading the censorship, which, although it applied strictly to shorter publications, excepted larger works, even when they came out in serial parts. The Annuals appeared, as a rule, as four-page sheets and could subsequently be bound up. The periodicals which Ruge edited contain the most important source material of the intellectual history of Germany during the period of Marx's formative years. The *Hallische Jahrbücher* first appeared in 1838, and represented the rising liberal criticisms of the Young Hegelians. The last of these publications was the *Deutsche-Französischen Jahrbücher* (The Franco-German Yearbook) to which Marx and Engels made important contributions, and

[1] Marx was opposed to easy divorce where children are involved, because marriage was concerned with the welfare of the family. While, therefore, if no children are involved the dissolution of a marriage should no more concern the state than the dissolution of a friendship, the state still has certain responsibilities in regard to marriage.

which was published in Paris in 1843 under the editorship of Marx.

Arnold Ruge was sixteen years older than Marx, and had suffered five years in a fortress for his liberal views. He was Voltairean, secularist, cosmopolitan and saw Hegelianism as the culmination of the rationalism of the eighteenth century. As the editor of the *Halle Yearbooks* he was considered to be the standard-bearer of the philosophical vanguard. When in 1841 his journal was suppressed, he moved to Leipzig and began to issue the *Deutsche Jahrbücher*. In all these publications he brought to mature and vigorous expression not only the views of the younger philosophers but the political aspirations of the rising bourgeoisie. The force behind this literary effort was the dialectical philosophy of Hegel as interpreted by the Left Hegelians, undermining orthodox allegiances to the existing order and its culture. If you reflect on any situation, said Ruge, you find yourself transcending it, passing beyond it into what it must *become*. This will confront you with alternative possibilities and with the demand for decisive action. Ruge began to define those immediate objectives: to demand a legal opposition, to criticise the existing legal theories; but as Marx was to discover later, his understanding of social and economic affairs was inadequate; he failed to discern the importance of the emergent social forces and dismissed such an important event as the revolt of the weavers in Silesia as of no significance. In the end he saw political activity within the framework of the existing state as the sole instrument of social reform. Against Ruge, Marx was to formulate his very different theory of the state. But these differences only emerged later.

Until Marx took the post of editor of the *Rheinische Zeitung* in Cologne, his acquaintance with the practical politics and economic realities of capitalism, with industry and agriculture in Germany, was of the slightest. The Young Hegelians indeed had not come to grips with politics and social problems. Only Ruge was beginning to see that when philosophy works from abstractions to historical realities it is putting things the wrong way round. "The alliance of philosophy and politics is the only way in which modern philosophy can become truth."

Before the journal fell under the axe of the censorship it was beginning to consider wider aspects of social reform than those which concerned only the Rhineland. Hess had written an article in which he declared that new problems were everywhere emerging. England at least had reached a stage at which liberalism had no adequate answer to the question of poverty. Three more articles appeared describing the consequences of English industrial development—unemployment and political unrest amongst the workers. Hess also wrote on French conditions and Marx must have read Hess's brilliant description of the socialist and communist movement in Paris in the *Augsburger Zeitung*. Before any further advance could be made in this direction the government decided at the end of 1842 to suppress the paper and it ceased publication at the end of March 1843. This was felt as a personal insult by the whole population of the Rhineland. Petitions with thousands of signatures were sent to Berlin, but in vain. Marx's opinions were, according to the Berlin officials, "in utter contradiction to the principles of the Prussian state".

Marx himself was not sorry to go. He wrote to Ruge: "The atmosphere was becoming too oppressive for me. It is a bad thing to work in servitude and to fight with pin-pricks instead of with the sword. I am tired of the hypocrisy. Now the government has given me back my freedom. There is nothing more I can do in Germany. One debases oneself there."

Driven from the public stage by the suppression of the *Rheinische Zeitung* Marx "retired to the study". If his journalistic responsibilities had interfered with the intellectual work he was eager to engage in, he had greatly profited by his close acquiantance with the real condition of men and the actual functions of the state. His attention had been turned from abstractions to realities. This meant great theoretical progress, for he had now to link these practical problems to his philosophy, and then to remould his philosophy as the theory of his practical policies.

Marx first considered Switzerland as the home of his future activity. But Ruge, who was already planning a revival in a new form of the Annuals which had been appearing in Germany, favoured Paris, where there was a large German colony and living was cheap. Marx was to be married in June and after that was to settle down with his wife in the same house as Ruge and the poet Herwegh, and share a kitchen and a cook.

The young couple were married on June 12th, 1843, and spent their honeymoon in Kreuznach where Jenny and her mother had been living. They went to Paris on November 11th.

3

THE FOUNDATIONS OF MARX'S THOUGHT

THE giants of German philosophy and poetry, Hegel and Goethe, had passed from the scene in 1831 and 1832. The spirit of the times underwent a change. The new watchword was emancipation—moral, intellectual and political. The influences that went to the making of the mind of Marx have been indicated; it remains to show how his thought developed, and the part played in this development by his young Hegelian friends.

The key to his thinking is contained in a letter which he wrote to his father in 1837, in which he says: "I went on from idealism—which, by the way, I equated with Kantian and Fichtean idealism, since I drew it from that source—to search for the Idea in reality itself. If previously the gods dwelt above the earth, now they were at the centre of it."

Kant's great contribution to philosophic thought was his insight into the essential activity of mind, as Marx explains in his first *Thesis on Feuerbach*. Materialists like Feuerbach conceived the human mind as passive, simply reflecting as in a mirror the external material world. There was no adequate recognition of the part which men played in reacting upon, altering and transforming their environment. They regarded the mind as simply reflecting the external world and moulded by it. This leaves man impotent to affect the course of things, and does not therefore account for the redirective activity of mind, for the fact that man was not merely a product of his environment but the creator of it, first in the form which went to his own making, and now, in *remaking* it, so that the new world of his creation in turn remakes man yet again.

Marx never accepted the naïve materialism which regarded thought as mere ineffectual reflection of the external world. His approach was dialectical, recovering "the active side" of knowing as "developed by idealism",[1] and showing how in man knowing and acting go together.

Fichte, Kant's great disciple, exerted a powerful influence on Marx

[1] *Theses on Feuerbach*, No. 1.

and all the Young Hegelians. He went beyond Kant, asserting that man does not merely comprehend things with the activity of mind, but realises himself in willing and working. It is the practical faculty which lies at the root of the ego. In the process of self-actualisation, the ego creates an objective, resistant world over against itself.[1] This implies an obstacle whose resistance has to be overcome. We realise our liberty and independence through the successful overcoming of this resistance.

But Fichte extends the field of actualisation from the life-history of the individual to the life-history of the human race. Man's self-realisation thus became the theme of a philosophy of history. Hegelianism was the high point of this development.

It is clear how much of Fichte there is in the activism of Marx, and in his fundamental idea of the self-realisation of man, not in the pure realm of mind, but in changing the world.

When Marx had turned to Greek philosophy for his doctoral thesis, it was the idea of self-realisation that was in his mind. The theme was the opening up of new and wider horizons to the human intellect, beyond the intellectual limitations of Hellenism and the social limitations of slavery; the reaction against "a demoralised age in which its passions were without truth and its truth without passion". It was at the same time a parable for his own times, pointing to a new task for human thought—not the contemplative understanding of things, but their radical transformation, a new phase in human history in which a man should at last begin both to think his life and live his thoughts.

Marx turned to the later Greek philosophers because, rejecting the idea that in them Greek philosophy like a bad play had come to a tame ending, he believed that the three great closing phases, Epicureanism, Stoicism and Scepticism, represented the final achievement of self-consciousness, coming after the theoretical achievement of Aristotle in accounting for the universe in a comprehensive system of thought, and completing philosophy's task by applying it to actuality. These philosophies sought to achieve that victory over the external world which vindicates the freedom and security of the mind and makes us equal to the gods. We can see in this assertion of the will and

[1] It is in this process of the ego bringing into existence a world over against itself and then overcoming the limitations with which it is confronted that Fichte finds the sequence of thesis-antithesis-synthesis. This is of course a Fichtean, not an Hegelian, formula.

the self, confronted by all the powers of the external world, the influence of Fichte. It was to inspire Marx's Promethean defiance of the powers that be.

The completion of thought is the awakening of the will, and the realisation of the ideal in action. When the philosopher has created his rational ideal, and we understand how far the world falls short of it, what is to be done? There are two possibilities. We may accept the irrationality of the world and alter our philosophy accordingly, arriving at the philosophy of irrationalism in the service of reaction; or, on the other hand, we may set to work to change the world. But by thus bringing philosophy into the realm of action we change its character.

We have arrived, says Marx (in the preliminary studies for his dissertation), at one of the key points in its development at which philosophy assumes a practical attitude towards the world and as "subjective consciousness" revolts against reality. "That which was an inner light becomes a consuming flame, turned outward." Thus the philosophical idea is transformed into a will to revolt against a world not yet shaped in the image of that idea. As Prometheus, in revolt against the gods and defying them, steals fire from heaven and comes down among men to make a new world, so does philosophy in this day and age.

But this is the end of philosophy. "By liberating the world from the unphilosophical condition, men at the same time liberate themselves from philosophy, which in the form of a definite system has held them in fetters."

At first sight these reflections would appear to have little to do with Democritus and Epicurus, but in fact they are the key to Marx's understanding of those philosophers. Democritus, the first atomist, he shows to be involved in a fatal dualism. The ultimate reality is the atom—but we never see it or know it. What we know is only the object of perception, appearance, which is not the ultimate reality. Thus the atom, the truth, is not brought into any relation with what we actually know. Moreover, since the atoms act upon one another in a strictly mechanical way, the world is revealed as subject to a complex of iron laws determining every event.

Epicurus introduces an important modification into the materialistic scheme of Democritus. The atom possesses a capacity for self-determination. Atoms in association behave differently from atoms conceived in mechanical interaction. What appears, therefore, is not a mathematical resultant but differentiation, originality, new qualities. The scientific value of this theory is found in its escape from the eternal regress of causality. The natural world is in a perpetual process of dissolution and rebirth. This opens up an immense field of possibility—*whatever is could be otherwise*. Here is the vindication of man's power to assert his own freedom and attain his own ends.

Much was yet to be worked out, but it is clear that Marx is interpreting both the materialism of the atomists and the philosophy of Hegel in an entirely new way. They do not involve us in a finished, rational whole in which everything is determined, but direct us to an unlimited war against the existing world, a united effort to change it, to reorganise it. It is a demand to make the world philosophical. It is a sweeping indictment and rejection of earthly reality on the ground of its "unphilosophical condition".

Between his resignation as editor and his arrival in Paris, Marx had spent five months of quiet retirement at Kreuznach, which was also inevitably a period of intensive study. He was already planning with Arnold Ruge, who had financial means, the new *Deutsche-Französischen Jahrbücher* which were to succeed the earlier Yearbooks or Annuals which had appeared and disappeared during the past few years. (The *Deutsche Jahrbücher* had been suppressed in January 1843.) The intention of Marx was to produce something new in philosophical thinking, something in harmony with life and humanity (here speaks Feuerbach). The heart must be French and the head German. The head must reform and the heart revolutionise. Only where there was movement, emotion, passion and feeling could there be vitality. So said Marx in his letter to Ruge of March 13th, 1843.

They eventually decided to publish the Yearbook in Paris, as being closer in touch with German life than any other likely centre. Marx at once began to plan his own articles and to push vigorously ahead with reading and reflection which marked the next stage in his development.

We have the record of these months of research in the notebooks which he made at the time.[1] He was reading a great deal of history, especially that of England and France. He studied with special care the French Revolution. It was now, for the first time, that he made a thorough and critical study of Rousseau, Montesquieu and Machiavelli.

Rousseau had taken precisely the critical line towards the existing structure of society which Marx was taking to the Hegelian state. Society did not in its present form reconcile the interests of its

[1] Photostats are preserved in the Marx-Engels Institute, Moscow.

members; it left them incompatible. The problem was to reform and reconstruct society until it did in fact defend and protect the person of each member. Only in such a society can the individual both accept the demands of society and still obey himself alone. Helvetius, who was highly thought of by both Marx and Engels, said very much the same thing and had asserted that if the so-called "general interest" was actually inconsistent with individual interests then the laws of society would inevitably be broken and crime would break out. The wise legislator is he who overcomes this separation, and establishes a society in which the interests of the individual and the community coincide.

Montesquieu showed Marx that there was no absolute system of law governing man's social activities. All laws are relative and changeable, and develop with direct reference to particular environments, by which he meant not only geographical differences and economic resources, but the level of industrial development, commerce, customs and political institutions. Their nature was variable and their essential characteristic adaptability. Particularly as regards the theory of the state, Montesquieu broke away entirely from the idea that its authority was from above, and bore no special relation to actual conditions of social development. The state was itself a natural growth subject to the law of change.

From Machiavelli Marx learned a great deal about the autonomy of politics, which owes no allegiance to moral rules outside the law of social necessity. The only criterion of action is within society and is the correct evaluation of the actual forces which must be employed to achieve the good of society at that historical moment. This holds with special force in times of political change, when institutions and rules must not dictate to statecraft, but must be adapted to serve man's needs. There is no general principle of morality overriding the good of society. If the statesman holds by existing moral rules he will do far more harm than good. Here was the first clear-headed advocate of the application of conscious systematic realism to political affairs, showing that reality is obedient to its own stern necessity and that all mere ideas are powerless when faced with its relentless logic—but not, of course, the ideas that are relevant to the actual demands of society. Like Montesquieu, Machiavelli was also conscious that there was no constant pattern of society, that all things are in continual motion. Therefore, new situations are constantly arising in which, since men themselves are the only judge of their needs, they must also be the only judge of the means to satisfy them.

It was during this period too that Marx discovered from his

comparative study of political constitutions that social and political structures are dependent upon property relations. He had followed with close attention the development of democracy in the United States and especially Hamilton's argument on the danger of revolution arising from the universal franchise. It was clear that Hamilton's primary concern was to guarantee the rights of property owners against the majority of the people. Those with no property, it was argued, could not be regarded as having a will of their own. The common people indeed, are unjust, tyrannical, brutal, barbarous and cruel, and we should be ruled by the natural autocracy of the wise, the rich and the good—from which it appeared that the rich might be regarded as necessarily possessing the other qualifications.

These notebooks are an important indication of the growth of Marx's thought during these months. He retained from Hegel the dialectical historical approach, but in the place of the Absolute he had now placed human society as the reality. The "first mover", as Aristotle had called it, was society itself, which had become its own moving spirit. It is often supposed that Marx began his philosophical career as an Hegelian idealist, but gradually changed or developed his views in a materialistic direction. But there is no evidence that Marx ever thought that world history was an expression or incarnation of the unfolding of the Absolute Idea, or that he hypostasised abstractions by treating as self-subsistent entities general ideas, or principles, as if they could have an existence in themselves not derived from experience of the concrete world. The rational whole which Hegel believed in was, for Marx, not a truth about reality (Hegel had only imagined its realisation) but a programme. The existing world was far from being philosophical. It was not a world in which man could come to experience himself as a godlike being, as Hegel declared it to be.

Nor is it the case that Marx took from Hegel the idea of the inevitable progress of thought and reality through the succession of *thesis*, *antithesis* and *synthesis*. Hegel's *Logic* cannot possibly be reduced to this simplification.

It is just such a use of the so-called "triad" by Proudhon that Marx ridicules in his *Poverty of Philosophy*. Proudhon had attempted, to use his own words, to "make history not according to the order of time but according to the succession of ideas". But as Marx says: "He thinks to construct the world by the movement of thought, while all that he does is to reconstruct systematically and range under the absolute method the thoughts which are in the heads of everybody."

This mystical theory, which reveals an immanent process of development in history as merely the embodiment in reality of a logical process, is utterly foreign to the thought of Marx, who never attempted to draw patterns for history out of logic. "Nor", as Plekhanov says, "does it at all play even in Hegel's work the part which is attributed to it by people who have not the least idea of the philosophy of that great thinker. Not once in the eighteen volumes of Hegel's works does the triad play the part of an argument, and anyone in the least familiar with his philosophical doctrine understands that it could not play such a part. . . . It was not at all a distinguishing feature of his philosophy."[1] Nor when we turn to Hegel's *Philosophy of History* do we find any such mechanism of development exemplified. Hegel shows us history as the development of freedom, which in his view is identical with the moral reason in man, as a cosmic process in which the world comes to realise itself "in self-consciousness".

When Alexei Mikhailovich Voden, Russian man of letters and translator, asked Engels whether Marx was ever a Hegelian, Engels declared emphatically that he never was. This, said Engels, is clearly shown in the doctoral thesis of 1841, which reveals the fact that although Marx had already completely mastered Hegel's dialectical method, he had completely emancipated himself from it. In the doctoral thesis he was applying it in a very different manner from Hegel, and that in the very sphere in which Hegel was strongest—the history of thought. The conclusions Marx arrived at with regard to the later Greek philosophy were in fact opposed to Hegel's estimate of this school of thought. Engels adds that Marx had a high opinion of the dialectics of Plato and Aristotle, and, in modern philosophy, of the dialectics of Leibniz and Kant, and had intended to continue his study in the history of Greek philosophy.

Marx developed his criticism of Hegelian idealist dialectics on the basis of Hegel's *Phenomenology* in the 1844 essay entitled *Critique of The Hegelian Dialectic and Philosophy as a Whole*.

Marx arrived in Paris towards the end of October 1843, his notebooks full of materials and with the manuscripts of the *Critique of Hegel* and at least two articles in draft form for the *Deutsche-Französischen Jahrbücher* which he was to edit for Arnold Ruge.

It was his first intention to continue his studies in economics and French socialist literature; and it was at this time he became a Socialist. Evidence of the change is to be found in his letter to Ruge, subsequently

[1] Plekhanov: *The Development of the Monist Theory of History*.

published in the *Jahrbücher*, in which he says: "This system of acquisition and commercialism, of possession and the exploitation of mankind, is leading even more swiftly than the increase in population to a break within the present society, which the old system cannot heal, because it has not the power to heal or create but only to exist and enjoy." This was the first step, but in the following months he made rapid progress towards the clarification and consolidation of his position. In one of his letters from Kreuznach (September 1843) he had already revealed his acquaintance with Fourier, Proudhon and others. In contradiction to the utopian tradition of French socialism he was beginning to see his task as a new interpretation of the struggles and aspirations of the age. There were forces already at work, but they needed to be brought to a clearer self-consciousness. "We only make clear to men for what they are really struggling, and to the consciousness of this they must come whether they will or not." The thinker propounds no fresh problems, brings forward no abstract dogmas, but awakens an understanding for the growth of the future out of the past, inspiring men with the awareness of their task and its necessity. "We must not say to the world: stop your quarrels, they are foolish, and listen to us, for we possess the real truth. Instead we must show the world why it struggles."

The double number of the *Jahrbücher* was to prove its one and only issue. But among those who contributed to the new publication were Heine, Herwegh, the revolutionary poet, Hess, Ruge and Marx, and also Friedrich Engels, the youngest of them all, who wrote an important article entitled *Outlines of a Critique of Political Economy*, and reviewed Carlyle's *Past and Present* in a second article describing the situation in England. Engels declared that Carlyle's volume of essays was the only book worth reading out of the literary harvest of a whole year.

But disheartened by the defeat of liberalism in Germany, Ruge and his friends were confused and disillusioned. Marx on the other hand was studying the social forces which were giving rise to conditions incompatible with the existing state of affairs. He declared that they would either compel the reaction to become even more reactionary, which would be suicidal, or would set in motion new forces within the culture of reaction itself. Far from despairing of the people of Germany, he says that even here, where reaction was strong, and social development backward, in protest against injustice and exploitation men will inevitably resist in order to preserve their existence. Two things are necessary for revolutionary activity—the objective conditions and the feeling of self-respect, the desire for freedom. Only this feeling, arising when social forces are ripe for change, can transform society into a community of free men. A feeling mankind which thinks, and a thinking mankind which feels, will know where to find the instruments of social liberation.

Though the venture thus came to a premature conclusion, the essays contained in the *Deutsche-Französischen Jahrbücher* are of the greatest importance. They include Marx's *Introduction to the Critique of Hegel's Philosophy of Law*, and *The Jewish Question*.[1] The former, together with the *Critique* itself, which was never published, must have been written much earlier, since Marx offered it to Ruge in March 1842 for publication in his *Anekdota Philosophica*.

Marx's fundamental criticism of Hegel, however, is to be found in a later essay, which was written in 1844 and not published until after his death.[2] It is entitled *Critique of the Hegelian Dialectic and Philosophy as a Whole*. It is in fact an examination of Hegel's *Phenomenology of Mind*. This is one of the most difficult and yet the most interesting of Hegel's works, and Marx finds in it the key to the science of society. But Hegel presents the cause of social change as an activity of pure thought, reflecting itself or manifesting itself in history. Marx reconstructs the theory in terms of the origin and development of capitalist society. But, far from rejecting it, he regards it as invaluable—when it has been restated in the terms of social history instead of pure thought.

In the Preface to the second edition of *Capital* he repeats the key conception of this critique. He says: "For Hegel, the thought process (which he actually transforms into an independent subject, giving to it the name of 'Idea'), is the *demiurge* of the real, and for him the real is only the outward manifestation of the Idea. In my view, on the other hand, the ideal is nothing other than the material when it has been transposed and translated inside the human head." Here he abruptly finishes, and the statement in this highly condensed form is not sufficiently enlightening. But he tells us immediately where to look for the full exposition of this criticism. "Nearly thirty years ago," he says, "when Hegelianism was still fashionable, I criticised the mystifying aspect of the Hegelian dialectic." As this Preface was written in 1873, that would indicate the *Critique* of 1844.

In Hegel's *Phenomenology* the process of self-realisation of the

[1] See Chapter V.

[2] Karl Marx, *Der historische Materialismus*, ed. by Landshut and Mayer, Leipzig, 1932, and later in the Marx-Engels *Gesamtausgabe* and in English translations.

Absolute manifests itself in historical reality as exhibiting a dialectical form and rhythm, as involved in self-development. It is a merciless criticism of whatever is regarded as permanent and invincible. Nations, systems, creeds—they are all unstable and doomed to be fugitive. Science and religion, morality and art, logic and history—they are all shown in process of inevitable change, through the contradictory elements within them and their resolution. It is precisely this internal opposition which sets things in motion, which is the mainspring of development, which calls forth the latent forces of whatever we are considering. In every case when the contradiction reveals itself, evolution or revolution to a higher level of existence begins.

This process of change involves not only a dialectical way of understanding the changing world, as though it were dialectical thinking which was responsible for the world being apprehended as developing, but the realisation that reality possesses an independent nature not conforming to static ways of thinking, but rather exacting submission from the mind and compelling us to think dialectically. The world itself is in process of endless change. Hegel's world considered in its totality as the universal, is evolving in this way, but this universal is not, as it is for most forms of idealism, a transcendental reality lifted above the actual world of experience. Hegel's universal is *in* the concrete. There is only one world not two, not a world of spirit and a world of matter, not even a world of moral ideals and a world which fails to come up to it—the conflict of what *ought* to be and what in fact *is*. Hegel sought to transcend all the dualisms that have plagued the history of thought—between mind and matter, consequence and law, individual and society, *thought* and the *is*, by presenting them all as equally objective aspects of continuing process. Thus in his philosophy Hegel brings thought and being, reason and the universe, into the closest connection and agreement, as inseparable from each other. The task of philosophy is to comprehend what is. Hegel was no abstract thinker, divorced from actuality, and speculating at large. Rather he set himself to give material content to the Idea, to make it concrete. The idea without reality, or reality without the idea, seemed to him absurd. Accordingly, his logic could not deal merely with the laws of thought, but must at the same time take account of the laws of social and cosmic evolution. He therefore created a science of thinking, which formulated not only the laws of thought, but also the laws of evolution. Unfortunately, he did so in a language which offered immense difficulties to his readers.

One can now see why Marx was so powerfully influenced by Hegel; why the *Phenomenology* is the work with which Marxism is immediately affiliated. But where did he disagree with Hegel? This is most clearly seen in the *Critique*. Hegel had tried to show that the very nature of man is the result of human productive labour, which has the effect of confronting man with estranged objects hostile to himself. But it is really *abstract* thought with which Hegel is concerned. It is the opposition within thought of thinking and the object thought. Nevertheless, he sees in this process the secret of the creation of civilisation and of the development of history.[1] In this sense man makes himself. But this externalisation of himself in what he creates is, says Hegel, a loss; man is drained of himself in creation, it is a process of deprivation, alienation. The world which man creates stands over against him as an enemy, so that he is ruled and destroyed by his own creations. Then Hegel tries to show that man can repossess himself by coming to *understand* that the whole process is the way in which the Absolute Idea realises itself. But Hegel, says Marx, has got the whole thing upside down. Hegel's conception of a self-alienated God is really a portrait of man as an economic producer. In the *Phenomenology* Hegel had shown man as creating himself in productivity—"labour is the self-productive act of man". But Hegel considered all productivity as no more than an expression of the thought process. As a consequence, says Marx, "he has only discovered the abstract, logical and speculative expression for the movement of history, but not yet the real history of man". In fact, what Hegel sees as spirit producing itself in work and finding itself confronted with an alien world, is man producing himself and finding himself in an alienated condition. Thus the history of production is not anything so mystical as the process of spirit's becoming in terms of knowledge. The dialectic stands on its head. "You must turn it right way up again if you want to discover the rational kernel that is hidden away within the wrappings of mystification."

This Marx proceeded to do, taking Hegel's theory of alienation as the model of his own philosophy of history, the model which, in spite of the inverted form which Hegel gives it, is the indispensable key to the actual sequence of events in economic and social development.

[1] It is impossible in a few words to do justice to "the secret of Hegel". But however complex the theory (and it is extremely complex), it is, as Marx saw, much more than a metaphysical speculation. It is the actual course of history stated in mystical form. Every step in the argument reflects some real aspect of human life and development.

4

MARX IN PARIS

WHEN Marx left the Rhineland in 1843 he had not arrived at any clear understanding of socialism. He had still an open mind about whatever was called "communism". His philosophy was still in process of reconstruction. He was working critically through the legacy of Hegel, profoundly influenced by Feuerbach's materialism, but also by the social and political struggles in which he had vigorously participated. He had learned much from Fichte and Hess of the philosophy of action as the completion of the philosophy of understanding. He had already repudiated the utopian programme of realising an ideal created solely by the imagination. Above all, a new feeling of passionate indignation and sympathy for the struggle of the dispossessed was deepening and inspiring his spirit of revolt. He had fought the battle of the forest-dwellers and the vine-growers, and now, in Paris, he was to meet for the first time the revolutionary elements of the working class. "Among these people," he says (1844), "the brotherhood of man is not a phrase, but truth, and from their faces hardened by affliction, the whole beauty of mankind looks upon us."[1] And a year later, "one must experience what are the studies, the mental hunger, the restless impulse for development in the French and English workers, in order to be able to form a notion of the human nobility of the movement."[2]

The Paris in which he arrived was utterly different from anything that he had known before. The Revolution of 1789 had been followed by the restoration of the Bourbon monarchy, which was in turn overthrown by the revolution of 1830 and replaced by the rule of King Louis Philippe, the son of the Duke of Orleans—Citizen Equality, who had taken part in the great revolution. In four years' time the third revolution of 1848 was to replace the monarchy by the republic and give a powerful impulse to the bourgeois transformation of Europe.

The monarchy of Louis Philippe represented and defended the interests of the wealthiest section of the big bourgeoisie, the aristocracy of finance. In Paris there was evidence of vigorous financial

[1] Marx-Engels, *Gesamtausgabe III.* [2] Marx and Engels, *The Holy Family.*

and industrial progress, but also of ruthless corruption, in which fortunes were being rapidly made and suddenly lost. Against this background there was the seething activity of *émigrés*, socialist reformers, poets and writers, among whom were some 85,000 Germans. There was an atmosphere of intellectual excitement and passionate protest against injustice and political tyranny. There was condemnation of reaction, of commercialism, of philistinism, and a warm defence of human rights. Argument and discussion went on continuously, pamphlets were written, journals published, debates raged, and committees were formed. The mood was exalted and optimistic.

Marx and his wife had arrived in Paris at the end of October 1843, and his first task was to complete and publish his two contributions to the *Deutsche-Französischen Jahrbücher*; this was accomplished by January 1844. He then quickly established contact with the French democrats and socialists, the leaders of the German revolutionary society, the League of the Just, and many other societies and groups. We must picture him not shut up in his study, not merely discussing affairs with leading intellectuals, though his studies were varied, exhaustive and continuous, and he met everybody of importance, but as attending meetings and immersing himself in a more vigorous and lively workers' movement than anything he had seen in Germany. Ruge says of him at this time that Marx was reading a tremendous amount and working with unusual intensity, often not going to bed for three or four nights in succession. He was studying the French Revolution, and also the French liberal historians of that period: Mignet, Guizot and Thierry.[1] It was in their work that he obtained a new and fundamental insight into the driving force of historical development which became fundamental to his whole position and which he had never understood before.

[1] Guizot, the most distinguished of these historians was a remarkable man—historian, statesman and orator, he was the master spirit of Louis Philippe's administration for eight years, the longest administration and the last which existed under the constitutional monarchy of France. He was a liberal of the extreme right and eventually a conservative. A considerable scholar, he wrote histories of the English Revolution, a study of Cromwell, and a history of the civilisation of Europe and of France. As a statesman he was the opponent of Thiers and confronted his political enemy with indomitable courage and eloquence.

Thierry was a disciple of Saint-Simon and supported the July revolution. His historical work deals with the *Third Estate*, the rise of the *French Commune*, the *Norman Conquest* and the English parliamentary struggle against Charles I.

Mignet, the friend of Thiers, wrote a *History of the French Revolution* in support of the liberal cause.

The French historians, looking at the history of Europe, both empirically and as liberals who supported the Revolution of 1789, found something far more concrete, understandable and convincing than Hegel's development of the Idea in a sequence of historical epochs—*the conflict of class interests*. When in the course of history the bourgeoisie were struggling to assert their supremacy they had no reluctance in explaining in such terms what was happening. They spoke of the class struggle with enthusiasm; they were not horrified at the thought of revolution: "God gave justice to men only at the price of struggle", said Thiers in his *History of the French Revolution*.

Thierry reached the same conclusion in his essay on *The French Revolution*. The war was started and maintained, he argued, "for positive interests; the rest was only pretext or appearance". Political revolutions, he argued, are the consequence of the struggle of classes fighting for their positive economic interests. Property relations are the bases of political movements.

Marx always insisted that the economic basis of historical change was not his discovery, but that he learnt it from Guizot's theories which threw a flood of light on the problem which had been engaging him in his essays on Hegel and his reflections on the rising revolutionary movement in Europe. It was not the appearance of a new idea in the political form that inspired revolutionary change, as if dialectical logic could itself produce it, but the actual struggle of masses of people against misery and oppression. Nor was this enough, for there had been such misery in every age. When does such a movement actually arise in a form so effective as to bring about a revolutionary change in society? Of course the conditions must be such as to provide the opportunity and constitute the necessity; "ripeness is all". But what are these conditions and how do they ripen?

To this question the French historians had no answer. If political and revolutionary struggle depends on property relations and a clash of interests, on what do these in their turn depend? The answer that Marx was to give depended on what he was now to learn about the development of industrialism from Friedrich Engels and from his profound study of French socialism.

Arriving in Paris with no knowledge of socialism at the time that Engels was turning to communism, Marx admits that he was following in Engels' footprints when the overwhelming importance of the doctrines of the great French socialists Saint-Simon and Fourier dawned upon him.

EARLY FRENCH SOCIALISM

The founders of French socialism grew up under the influence of the too-confident optimism which characterised the early stages of the Revolution of 1789. They had excessive faith in the possibilities of human progress and perfectibility; they knew little of the true laws of social revolution. "To crude conditions of capitalist production and the crude class conditions corresponded crude theories. The solution of the social problems, which as yet lay hidden in undeveloped economic conditions, the utopian attempted to evolve out of the human brain."[1] But it is foolish to treat their work with derision. "For ourselves," says Engels, "we delight in the stupendously grand thoughts and germs of thought that everywhere break out through their covering of fantasy." What were these illuminating thoughts?

Comte Henri de Saint-Simon (1760-1825), the founder of French socialism, saw the whole course of history as the progress of mankind in the satisfaction of its various needs through the development of technology. Human institutions arise to correspond to the requirements of a particular stage of invention and production, therefore the institutions of past ages must not be condemned out of hand, since they came into existence to function under particular historical conditions.

Society is in constant change; periods of consolidation give place to periods of criticism and destruction. And in every age there are the people who matter, who represent what is coming, and the people who don't, who represent what is dying away. In our day we are entering a new scientific age, which will mean a new industrial age, and to correspond with it we shall see new people arising, scientifically qualified and equipped, created by the advance of technology.

This demands a total reorganisation of society: politics will give way to economics and the government of man will be replaced by the administration of things. All idlers, parasites, speculators and swindlers will be eliminated—"All men ought to work". The waste of competition will give way to planning and co-operation, and the new society will look after the welfare of its people.

The system of François Fourier, born in 1772, was in many respects different from that of Saint-Simon. If the latter represents the principle of authority, Fourier stressed the importance of local and individual freedom, and advocated a delightful but impracticable system of

[1] Engels, *Anti-Dühring*.

decentralised utopian communities, with co-operative output and individual choice of labour. Fourier regarded with dismay "the frenzy of speculation, the spirit of all-devouring commercialism", which the reign of the bourgeoisie had introduced, belying all the promises of the revolution. The new abundance provided by the machines had led only to an increase in poverty. But in the poverty of the working class he saw only poverty, he did not see the revolutionary possibilities in it.

For the last ten years of his life he waited in his apartment at noon every day for the wealthy capitalists who should supply the means for the realisation of his scheme.

In England this form of utopian socialism was represented by Robert Owen, a successful cotton manufacturer, philanthropist and educational reformer, who believed that the way to make people good was to give them a good environment and education. This he proceeded to do for his own 2,500 employees in New Lanark (1800-29). The machine, said Owen, now makes it possible for my 2,500 workers to produce as much as 600,000 hand workers. Where does the surplus go? It should raise the standard, physical and spiritual, of the whole working population. Owen fought for the new Factory Acts. He was President of the First Congress of Trade Unions. He advocated consumers' and producers' co-operatives and Labour Banks in which the currency consisted of cheques for the amount of work each man had done. Finally, disappointed at the failure of the authorities to accept his scheme, he set up model communist societies, which inevitably failed. His great contribution to socialist thought was the realisation that the factory system must be the root of the social revolution. Engels describes him as "a man of almost sublime, childlike simplicity of character, and at the same time one of the few born leaders of men. . . . Every social movement every real advance in England on behalf of the workers links itself to the name of Robert Owen."

FRIEDRICH ENGELS

It was through Engels that Marx became acquainted with Robert Owen's work and the political and industrial struggles of the British working class. Engels was the son of a wealthy textile manufacturer, who owned mills in Barmen and Manchester—the first in the Rhineland to install British machines. His son was intended to enter the business and it was proposed that after his military service he should go to Manchester where the firm of Ermen and Engels had established their British branch. The young Engels was a man of great natural charm, with a wide range of friendships. Musical, a lover of literature and the arts, he combined these accomplishments with a considerable grasp of philosophy.

He came to Berlin in the spring of 1841 to serve his year in the Army. The Young Hegelians welcomed him, and he became one of the boldest radicals among them. When the *Rheinische Zeitung* was launched he became a contributor, and it was in the offices of the journal in Cologne that he first met Marx. Their first meeting was not particularly cordial. Marx, who was at that time at odds with the Young Hegelians in Berlin, may well have thought that Engels shared their views. It was not until they met in Paris after the suppression of the paper that they came thoroughly to understand one another.

When his term of military service was up in 1842, Engels was duly despatched to Manchester. He did not neglect his business there, but he became deeply interested in British industrial conditions and very quickly reached the point of associating himself closely with militant trade unionism and the advanced political movements of the time. He became familiar with the work of Robert Owen; he read the revolutionary journals *Northern Star* and *The New Moral World*, and he knew the Chartist and socialist leaders, John Watts and George Julian Harney. He made a thorough study of the political economists of the day, particularly Ricardo. He was thus in a position to acquaint Marx when he next met him in Paris with the picture of an advanced industrial economy.

It is not surprising that when he met Hess, who was a fervent socialist, on his next visit to Cologne, he left Hess "a passionate communist".

When he came to Paris in 1843 he had reached very definite conclusions. He was shocked by "the brutal indifference, the unfeeling egotism" of his business acquaintances, "each concentrated on his own private interests".[1] He believed that all real social progress in England could be attributed to Robert Owen and the Chartists. But while he admired the Chartists, he found them too confident of the effectiveness of politics and insufficiently aware of the importance of economics and the trade union movement.

Before he left England[2] he wrote two important essays for the *Deutsche-Französischen Jahrbücher*. The first was his *Outline of a Critique of Political Economy*, and is an introduction to the theories of Ricardo

[1] Engels, *The Condition of the Working Class in England in 1844*.
[2] Late 1843 to January 1844.

and Adam Smith, which attempted to explain the contradictions of bourgeois economics from their source in private property. He pointed out the inhuman effects of competition and the failure of advancing industrialism to emancipate humanity, so that "the people starve from sheer abundance". As a result, he declares, we have that "hideous blasphemy against nature and humanity", the Malthusian theory of population, which argued that poverty results from over-population.

It was this essay that opened the eyes of Marx for the first time to the economic structure of capitalism and the contradictions which arise in an acquisitive society based on private property.

Engels' second contribution to the *Jahrbücher* described the social situation in England on the basis of Carlyle's *Past and Present*. He draws attention to Carlyle's caustic comments on the paradox of over-production and under-consumption; but is amazed that so powerful a mind cannot see that all these evils are rooted in the institution of private property. Engels sees clearly that the only solution of the economic problem is for men to produce consciously as men and not as atomised individuals without social consciousness. "The community will have to calculate what it can produce with the means at its disposal, and in the light of the relationship of this productive power to the mass of consumers it will determine how it has to raise or lower production, how far it has to give way to, or curtail luxury."[1]

Engels returned to Germany in August 1844, travelling home through Paris. It was now that he really came to know Marx, and their friendship was never afterwards broken. The two men complemented one another—Marx was more profound and searching in his thoughts; brilliance and obscurity are often fused together in his writing. Engels wrote rapidly and lucidly, his phrases run unhesitatingly, but he always acknowledged that Marx had the master mind. Yet at this time it was Engels who taught Marx the importance of economics, showed him on what battlefield the decisive struggle was to be fought out, and helped him to know the living realities of the world of industry.

When Marx left Germany for Paris he had declared that his aim was "to make the petrified conditions dance by singing to them their own tune". He meant that within the conditions which appeared incapable of movement were actual forces maturing and developing; but something was necessary to make them effective. They must be brought to consciousness and to the recognition of the significance

[1] Engels, *Outline of a Critique of Political Economy*.

of their own movement. Engels showed Marx how this was to come about. None of the French socialists could conceive of the workers themselves acting as an independent force. Most socialists looked upon the workers as a sore or as a pitiful mass whose sufferings were to be alleviated by appeals to benevolence, or reason, or such denunciations as Carlyle and Ruskin made so eloquently. They even thought of stopping the development of industry, of doing what was possible to turn the wheel of history backwards so as to abolish the proletariat. Marx and Engels now began to base all their hope on its continuous growth. Their aim was "to teach the working class to know itself, to be conscious of itself and to put science in the place of dreams".[1]

Engels wrote *The Condition of the Working Class in England* in Barmen in the winter of 1844-45. He was perhaps the first man in the centre of modern industry who had opened his eyes to the significance of these conditions. Most of the book is taken up with a description of the working class in its various strata—factory workers, miners, agricultural labourers. There is a chapter on the great cities, and an important section on the effect of competition on the proletariat. The book concludes with an enquiry into the attitude of the bourgeoisie to the proletariat. He now saw the inevitability of revolutionary struggle if the effects of commercial crisis were allowed to drive the workers to action; "if the bourgeoisie does not pause to reflect".

Fifty years later (1892) he wrote a new Preface in which he was able to judge how far his diagnosis had proved correct. He may be forgiven if at the age of twenty-four his enthusiasm sometimes overcame him, but as he says, "The wonder is not that a good many of these prophecies proved wrong, but that so many of them have proved right." Once again he declared that a worsening of conditions and immediate collapse of the system was by no means inevitable. There can be temporary improvements which are lost, however, when unemployment worsens, and even permanent improvements for factory workers and trade unionists; but for those outside the unions things are bound to get worse.[2] In fact, during the period of England's industrial monopoly, the working class has shared in its benefits, hence the slow growth of socialism. But what will happen when that monopoly breaks down? Then we shall see socialism in England.

[1] Lenin: *Friedrich Engels.*

[2] Marx also in later years, contrary to what is often stated, qualified his anticipation of "increasing misery" by making due allowances for countervailing tendencies such as trade union pressure.

He doubted, however, whether the bourgeoisie would ever go farther than futile middle-of-the-road reforms. "The prejudices of a whole class cannot be laid aside like an old coat." But if the revolution must come, its pains may be mitigated to the extent that the proletariat has absorbed socialist and communist elements. "If, indeed, it were possible to make the whole proletariat communists . . . the end would be very peaceful"; meanwhile, he anticipated "enough intelligent comprehension of the social question among the proletariat, to enable the communist party, with the help of events, to conquer the brutal elements of the revolution and prevent a 'Ninth Thermidor'."[1] This is so because communism goes far beyond the mere bitterness and exasperation which are the feelings of the enraged but uncomprehending populace. The communist, while fully aware of the cruelties of capitalism, knows perfectly well that the individual capitalist cannot act otherwise under existing circumstances than he does act; moreover, in a sense, the communist "stands above the strife between bourgeoisie and proletariat", in the midst of which there may be recognised "only its historic significance for the present, but not its justification for the future", since the aim of communism is not to create class antagonism (that does not have to be created by communists since it is created, fostered and fomented by capitalism), but to do away with it, by going forward to socialism. Of course communism is now the essential instrument for social change, but its aim is the deliverance of humanity, the emancipation of society at large, and it is not a mere party doctrine of the working class. In his later preface Engels points out that however true this is, it has little chance of convincing the wealthy. Although therefore (as Marx and Engels were to repeat in *The Communist Manifesto*), some few of the better elements will join the workers, the revolution will have to be prepared and fought out by the working class itself.

Marx was never a utopian; his Hegelian outlook made him immune to all eternal truth and final social forms. But there was utopian thinking in Engels until Marx explained to him the meaning of political and social conflicts. His early writing on economics and his *Condition of the Working Class*, powerful and important though they were, are in the same category as the writings of Proudhon and Robert Owen. They all sought to expose the contradictions of the economic system, not in order to discover in them the hidden force making for the progress of society, but to condemn them in the name of justice. But

[1] Ninth Thermidor, the fall of Robespierre, July 27, 1794.

Engels found the solution of the social problem in Marx, whom he rewarded with a lifelong friendship and devotion. Marx for his part had been thinking in too philosophical, too general terms. Now the various concepts with which he had been working, even the concept of the proletariat, are filled with the content of experience, the actual blood and tears of the working-class movement. "Theory without practice is empty, and practice without theory is blind." Now theory and practice had found one another. Marx now saw clearly that the Hegelian system as he understood it was working itself out before his very eyes in the most actual and dramatic fashion. At this moment Marxism comes to life, Marxism is born.

Marx believed that what was desirable and historically possible could be significantly determined only when it was thus related to the actual. The advent of socialism depends upon the gradual emergence of the objective conditions of its feasibility. These are bound up with the development of the economic system. Man can realise his aims only with the material that society provides him with. Marx now knew how, when and under what conditions socialism could be realised.

It is his conception of human emancipation that inspires him. He hates the fetters that pervert the practical and spiritual life of man and is seeking always how to overcome the barriers that lie in the way of achievement of "human society or social humanity". This passionate belief in the dignity of man was the abiding inspiration of his life.

The two years Marx spent in Paris were fruitful. Not only did he write some of the most searching and constructive of his theoretical works, but he was fortunate in being able to meet on terms of equality and friendship a number of distinguished figures who were in a certain sense his equals. This was not to last. The counter-revolution on the continent broke up these progressive circles and disheartened all but the most convinced. Among those he met and knew in Paris were Proudhon, Bakunin, Herwegh, Hess, Heine and, of course, Arnold Ruge. The intellectual world in Paris was dazzling, almost confusing in its richness of ideas and pregnant with the socialist ideal. In London Marx was unable to find any group among whom he could move in this way, exchanging views, discussing theories.

Marx had a great love for the poets and he became the warm friend of Heine, encouraging him while during the year 1844 he was writing his *Winter Fables*, the *Song of the Weavers*, and his famous satires on the German Government. He knew Heine for a fighter, whereas so many other literary figures were to collapse in the face of opposition and persecution. Heine for his part glories in the fact that the working-class movements could claim great philosophers like Marx as leaders.

Heine's satires had appeared in the Paris *Vorwärts*, to which Marx had also contributed a reply to a scurrilous article by Ruge attacking him; and the Berlin Government, stung to fury, then intervened and persuaded Guizot to expel the editors and contributors from France. Guizot secured the exception of Heine, but Marx and Bakunin had to go.

Marx was expelled from Paris in January 1845. He packed his bags, and, with his wife and his one-year-old daughter Jenny, set out for Brussels. There Engels joined him and they lived next door to each other in a working-class suburb. Never again did they work in such close contact as in these years before the revolution of 1848, when they were working out their final position in economics, in philosophy and in practical politics.

5

THE PARIS MANUSCRIPTS

MARX arrived in Paris at the end of October 1843 and was expelled on January 16th, 1845, reaching Brussels with his family in February of the same year. During these months, Marx wrote not only his articles for the *Deutsche-Französischen Jahrbücher* (the Franco-German Yearbooks), but a number of contributions to the German paper *Vorwärts*, the actual occasion of his expulsion, and a series of important *Economic and Philosophical Manuscripts*,[1] known under this title or more shortly as the 'Paris Manuscripts'. These essays cover three closely interrelated topics: firstly we see him grappling with the economic problem in a series of studies of Wages, Profit, Competition and Rent, which almost certainly followed his reading of Engel's *Outlines of a Critique of Political Economy* (late 1843): secondly, his thinking centres around the problem of estrangement or alienation, of the depersonalisation of man under the wage system: finally he relates this topic to Hegel's study of *The Phenomenology of Mind*, being particularly moved by the idea that estrangement is a phase of the dialectical process, and that by experiencing and overcoming it man creates his own self and then fulfils himself as man. But Marx parted company with Hegel. He was not concerned with alienation in the strictly Hegelian sense but with its role in the contemporary world, especially in relation to man's economic and social position under capitalism. It should be remembered that during this period he began those studies of economics which continued until 1853. His notebooks are filled with excerpts from and commentaries upon the works of the principal writers upon economic subjects in England, France and Germany. We have already mentioned his *Introduction to a Critique of Hegel's Philosophy of Law* and his article on *The Jewish Question*, which was really a study of the Hegelian doctrine of the state. These works, taken together, mark the first creative phase of the work of Marx.

[1] The early writings of Marx were published as early as 1912 in the four volumes of Mehring's *Nachlass*. The first English translation of the *Economic and Philosophical Manuscripts* appeared in 1959.

It is important to note that during this time Engels was writing his *Condition of the Working Class in England* and contributed his essay-review on Carlyle's *Past and Present* to the *Jahrbücher*. The first of Marx's Paris Manuscripts follow immediately from his conversion to the economic field of study, and it is from a new and intense realisation of the situation of the wage-earner under capitalism that he passes over to the study of alienation. If we wish to find the link, it will of course be Carlyle's fierce denunciation of the reduction of all human relationships to that of "the cash-nexus" to which Engels had drawn attention in his review. Carlyle had launched a forthright and eloquent attack on "the dismal science" of political economy as it was then presented by James Mill, MacCulloch and other leading economists. "Supply and demand is not the Law of Nature: Cash Payment is not the sole nexus of man with man—how far from it!" From the pursuit of monetary aims man will utterly fail to achieve happiness. "Perpetual mutiny, contention, hatred, isolation, execration shall wait on his footsteps, till all men discern that the thing which he attain, however golden it look or be, is not success, but the want of success . . . We, with our Mammon Gospel have come to strange conclusions. We call it a society; and go about professing openly the totalest separation, isolation. Our life is not a mutual helpfulness, but rather, cloaked under due laws of war named 'competition' and so forth, it is a mutual hostility."[1]

It was the purpose of Marx to show that the normal operation of the economic system necessarily produced an impersonal mechanism, which, created by man, now became his master. Hegel had long pondered the fact that men seemed to have been bereft of their personality—"Spirit estranged from itself"—and his whole philosophy sought to explain it and the ultimate resolution of the contradiction. Marx ridiculed all attempts to explain it in these terms. His concern was not with alienation as a process within an abstract conceptual system but with the actual and concrete conditions of economic life under capitalism; not as idealistic socialists would make it out to be, but as the capitalist economists themselves insisted that it was.

The money economy was a system in which above all things labour is bought and sold and embodied in a commodity that man has produced, which therefore contains something of himself, and becomes an alien power opposed to him, which enslaves him. Even the instruments of labour, machines, confront the worker as

[1] Carlyle: *Past and Present.*

mere mechanism that dominates and pumps dry his living labour power.

In his later work Marx completed his study of the labour process of which this is but the beginning. When in the exposition of his developed system he describes labour-power as a "commodity" that its possessor, the worker, surrenders up to capital and declares: "The exercise of labour-power, labour, is the worker's own life-activity, his own life expression. Thus his life-activity is for him only a means to enable him to exist. He works in order to live. He does not even reckon labour as part of his life, it is rather the sacrifice of his life."[1] This is but the picture of alienated labour in the Manuscripts of 1844. This splitting of man, he points out, we also see in the separation of the interests of the individual from those of the community, and in the separation of intellectual and manual activities. Moreover, this economic process brings into existence destructive economic forces of the market, of overproduction, of economic crises, which men can neither understand nor control—"an utterly alien power, an inhuman force" that holds sway over the whole of human existence.[2]

It has sometimes been stated that in his later work Marx abandoned this criticism of the destructive effect of capitalism on human personality: a view that suggests lack of familiarity with *Capital*. Here what was originally described as the passion of greed is not denied but emphasised and expanded. The inhumanity of capitalism is drawn with a descriptive power far surpassing that shown in the Paris Manuscripts. The only difference is that he speaks of wage-labour instead of alienated labour—the latter term having lost its currency. *Capital* shows with even greater force, because it is now set before us concretely with a great mass of factual data, man being dehumanised and destroyed by a tyrannical force of acquisitiveness that is part of his nature as capitalist man.

How is this to be overcome? In the Paris Manuscripts, as in all his later work, he declares that the problem is "to organise the empirical world in such a manner that man experiences in it the truly human, becomes accustomed to experience himself as a man, to assert his true

[1] Marx, *Capital*, Vol. I.

[2] Professor Hayek in his defence of the economics of capitalism in a free society, declares that men must discipline themselves to accept "the anonymous and irrational forces of society. . . . Craving for intelligibility produces illusory demands which no system can satisfy", and he deplores "the increasing unwillingness to bow before any moral rules whose utility cannot be rationally demonstrated" (*Individualism: True and False*).

individuality". This will only be possible where the means of production are communally and not privately owned, which provides the basis for genuinely co-operative human relations and a society that is really human.

Nor is it the case, as has frequently been alleged, that in his later writings Marx abandons his early concern for the full development of the individual—"the unfolding of man". On the contrary he continued to believe that only common ownership can restore the human relations in industry so that "all the faculties and powers of the individual are developed". It is in *Capital* that he speaks of "the self-realisation of the person" and of "fully developed human beings".[1] One could without difficulty find hundreds of statements in *Capital* which express Marx's deep concern for the value of the individual and his consistent determination "to overthrow all conditions in which man is a humiliated, enslaved, despised and rejected being".[2]

It is not individualism that fulfils the individual, on the contrary it destroys him. Society is the necessary framework through which freedom and individuality are made realities, but not, as Hegel thought, society as such, as found in the state, but only a socialist society. Marx emphatically declared that "above all one must avoid setting 'society' up again as an abstraction opposed to the individual" (as Hegel had done). "The individual is the social entity. His life is therefore an expression, a verification of social life."[3]

It was in his article on *The Jewish Question*[4] that Marx raised once again a question he had first dealt with as editor of the *Rheinische Zeitung*. In his defence of the rights of the Rhineland peasantry he had severely criticised the governing authority known as the Diet which represented the "state" and claimed to represent the good of society and its members, standing as an impersonal authority above the interests of any particular section of the people. This is the Hegelian conception of the state. This is "a great organism in which legal, moral and political freedom receives its realisation, and in which the individual citizen obeys, in obeying the laws of state, only the natural laws of his own reason".

But as Marx saw clearly at this time, the privileged classes, who held all real economic and political power in their own hands, had no diffi-

[1] Lenin also speaks of socialism as not merely "the method of adding to the efficiency of production, but the only method of producing fully developed human beings" (Lenin, *Karl Marx*).

[2] Marx, *Introduction to the Critique of Hegel's Philosophy of Law*.

[3] *Paris MSS.* [4] *Deutsche-Französischen Jahrbücher*.

culty in persuading themselves that the state, which was in fact serving their interests at the expense of the workers, really represented the interests of "the community". Now he takes up the same question on the basis of his wider experience and deeper knowledge.

The aim of his essay was to deal with Bruno Bauer's contention advanced in a book he had just published on the Jewish question, that if both Christians and Jews would give up their religious prejudices, then political emancipation would follow because Christians and Jews would then be free men and at last able to establish a free political system.

Marx was not interested in Jewish questions as such. His father had early emanicpated himself from Jewish orthodoxy and became nominally a Christian. The elder Marx always regarded himself as a German rather than a Jew, as did Marx himself. His whole upbringing and education was moulded by the German liberal and intellectual tradition. It is in vain that we search his works for traces of any specific Jewish attitude or sentiments. Therefore when Marx replied to Bruno Bauer the problem he dealt with was not primarily a religious but a social one. "We do not turn secular questions into theological questions: we turn theological questions into secular ones." Religious prejudices remain even where, as in the United States, political liberty is found. Why is this? It is because of the *nature* of the state. Religion flourishes as a manifestation of *social* defects within a democratic state. "We explain the religious backwardness of free citizens in terms of their social narrowness in order to abolish their social fetters. We assert that they will abolish their religious narrowness as soon as they abolish their social fetters. . . . The limits of political emancipation are evident in that the state can free itself from its fetters without men getting really free of it. The state can be a *free state*, without man becoming a free man."[1]

The emancipation of us all, Christians and Jews alike, depends on our emancipation from the rule of money, of the commercial spirit, and the twisted ideas and irrational prejudices it gives rise to.[2] It is never enough to argue against religion. Deep at the heart of society is quite another god than that of religion itself—money has dethroned all the gods.

But if "the state can be a *free state* without man becoming a free

[1] Marx, *The Jewish Question.*

[2] Marx hastened to add that of course we are right in advocating the immediate extension of civil rights to Jews.

man", what is the cause of this contradiction? It lies in the double existence of man. In his real life, in his work, his practical relations, man is a member of "civil society", he is governed by private interest, by egoism. It is only in his political aspect, as a member of the state, that he *appears* as a social being. But these two aspects are governed by opposite principles. This state in which theoretically, ideally, abstractly, he is an integrated member of a society in which he can fulfil himself, is only a dream, an imaginary heaven. There remains a basic contradiction within man in society as a competitive individual, estranged from others and from himself, the victim of inhuman pressures, so that he is only the abstract citizen. Human emancipation has not yet been achieved even though a constitutional state exists, nor will it be finally achieved until man becomes in his economic relations not a warring atom but a social being. His private resources must become social forces. Of course, "Political emancipation is a great step forward. It is not, indeed, the last form of human emancipation, but it is the last form of human emancipation *within* the existing social order." But it is the existing order itself that must now be changed.

Marx again makes clear the importance he attaches to the rejection of all forms of society where man is subject to conditions which he cannot control and which do not express the common interest of humanity. He had yet to discover how the transition is to be effected, what state of economic development prepares the ground and make necessary the advance to socialism, and above all what human forces, what sections of society, will be called upon to effect this revolutionary change. He was to move nearer to an answer in his second article in the *Deutsche-Französischen Jahrbücher*, "The Introduction to the Critique of Hegel's Philosophy of Law".[1] Here the central problem is the relation between theory and practice, ideas and reality; and in it for the first time Marx defines the alliance between the philosopher and the proletariat. The article sparkles with phrases which have become some of the most precious jewels of Marxism.

He begins by raising once again the question of religion. This was by no means a secondary question for Marx, because religion was the inevitable creation by the troubled mind of man in a topsy-turvy world

[1] Marx had already written a critical review of Hegel's *Philosophy of Law*, commenting paragraph by paragraph on the sections dealing with the state (this was published in 1927, but there is no English translation). In 1842 Marx wrote an essay on it, but this has been lost. All that we have is his *Introduction* to such a Critique.

"All the mysteries which drive thoughts towards mysticism find their rational solution in human practice and in the comprehension of this practice."[1]

Hegel had made man and the world the emanation of pure Idea. Feuerbach had declared that man had depersonalised himself by projecting his essential manhood onto the deity. He contended that thought does not create man, but proceeds from man, who creates God in his thoughts by attributing to God all that he could be but is not. To enrich God he becomes poor. Bereft of all the ideal attributes that are conceived to belong not to him but to God, man has nothing left of value in himself. It seemed to Feuerbach that the only escape from this deprived condition would be the emancipation of man from religion. Thus man would bring back the qualities he had projected into heaven and actualise them in himself as a human being.

This is where Marx takes up the argument. Is man's unhappy condition really the result of an intellectual or psychological error? Or is the truth that, finding himself impoverished, deprived, estranged for quite other reasons—social and economic—he consoles himself by creating an imaginary world of his lost happiness?

It is *man as exploited* who is bereft of his manhood, of his personality. And he will continue to console himself with the idealisation of his own humanity in God so long as he remains in servitude. Therefore, to start with removing the religious illusion, which has always been the aim of rationalists and secularists, hoping that by so doing man will recover his full human personality, is to put the cart before the horse.

It is not religion that makes man a degraded being; it is because man is degraded that he consoles himself with religion. "Religion", said Marx, "is precisely the self-awareness and self-consciousness of man who has not achieved himself, or has lost himself." Society produces religion, "the topsy-turvy world consciousness of a topsy-turvy world". It is the *imaginary realisation* of human perfection, necessary because in our world the fulfilment of human personality is not possible. The struggle against religion is therefore the struggle against the world. Religion is man's protest against his condition in society. "It is the sigh of the oppressed creature, the kindliness of a heartless world, the spirit of unspiritual condition. It is the opium of the people."

By this Marx does not mean that man's oppressors provide him

[1] Marx, *Theses on Feuerbach*.

with religion to drug him into acquiescence, but that oppressed man turns to religion to enable him to endure life's ills. It is not even a consolation for his poverty; it is a consolation for his non-humanity, it is a substitute for being a fully developed man.

Marx goes on: "The removal of religion as the illusory happiness of the people is the demand for its real happiness. The demand that it should give up illusions about its real conditions is the demand that it should give up the conditions which make illusion necessary. Criticism of religion is therefore at heart a criticism of the vale of misery for which religion is the promised vision. Criticism has torn away the imaginary flowers with which his chains were bedecked, not in order that man should wear his chains without the comfort of illusion, but that he may throw off his chains and pluck the living flowers."

What Marx calls for, therefore, is not primarily the emancipation of man by critical thought, but the reconstruction of society. Feuerbach had failed to realise that human relationships, the community, is not characterised by love and friendship but by the antagonism of classes. Feuerbach could envisage a perfected humanity resulting from an intellectual deliverance from error which would permit man to find himself in comradeship—society being seen as a happy family just waiting to receive him. Marx, on the contrary, saw a society in which men are exploited, in which the very source of their being is corrupted, in which they are stripped of their full personality. Revolutionary reconstruction of society was necessary at one and the same time to establish a truly human society, and banish the illusion of religion.

In the political revolutions which had taken place hitherto, *one class*, raising itself to a dominant position, at the same time undertakes the general emancipation of society. This requires the acceptance of the values of this class by the rest of society. It feels itself the representative of the whole of society. At the same time all the defects of society will be felt to be concentrated in the class that is now to be overthrown so that liberation from its rule is felt to be general self-emancipation.

Will any class fulfil this task in Germany? Not until its actual situation forces it to do so; but when this is the case that class will be the emerging proletariat, the class which claims no historical right but a human right, a class which cannot emancipate itself without revolutionising the entire structure of society.

Here is that element in society that is tending towards practical-critical activity; and insofar as its aim is a conscious one, the aim of the proletariat is the philosophical aim of the thinkers. But once it is realised it ceases to be a programme, a plan, a philosophy, since it is a fact. Thus do we liquidate philosophy by realising it.

As philosophy finds its material weapons in the proletariat, so the proletariat finds its intellectual weapons in philosophy. Theory itself becomes a material force when it takes hold of the masses; but theory is realised by a people insofar as it is the realisation of the people's needs.

In the thought of Marx this is the working out of the philosophy of Hegel, who had conceived of the embodiment of reason and freedom in concrete reality, the *realisation* of philosophical truth, that is to say its embodiment, its manifestation in history, so that it no longer remains a distant, unattained idea or ideal.

All the works of Marx in this period look forward to sociological studies of modern capitalism and the strategy of revolutionary struggle, not backwards to philosophical reflections upon religion or human history. Therefore, the question immediately arises in his mind: What are we to do, here in Germany, to change these social conditions? A further question, which is more closely linked with the political problem, may also be asked: What is the importance of philosophy in relation to the social and political struggle?

There is a peculiar situation in Germany, Marx replies. Conditions are backward, they are "beneath the level of history". Only in philosophy has Germany moved forward; but this is because "the Germans have *thought* in politics what other people have done". Nevertheless, this philosophising is by no means without significance. It is the "theoretical consciousness" of the other peoples. German history, broken off fifty years ago in politics, has in philosophy continued up to the present. "German philosophy is the ideal prolongation of German history." If Germany has to pass beyond her backward political and social position, she certainly possesses that advance already in her philosophy. The task now is not, as the philistines vainly declare, to abandon philosophy and continue German political existence from where it is, but to see in contemporary philosophy the living reality of Germany and the programme for the future. It has to be *realised* not abandoned—and that is the way in which philosophy will be abolished.

But how are we to realise this philosophy, seeing that the German bourgeoisie has long since missed the occasion for political advance seized by the French bourgeoisie in 1789 and by the British before that? The German bourgeoisie can no longer genuinely represent humanity.

But there has been born another class which can—the proletariat.

Thus Marx arrives at his programme for emancipation. The proletariat is already there, and alone can now claim to represent humanity and bring to its own redemption that high sense of the justice of its claims which is necessary for a successful revolution.

"The proletariat is the *actual* dissolution of the old world order. For when the proletariat demands the abolition of private property, it only establishes as the principle of the whole society what is *its own* social principle."[1] But how was it that Marx came to understand the political role of the proletariat? Undoubtedly, an important contribution to his thinking came from Lorenz von Stein, a conservative Hegelian, who had been commissioned to study the new French doctrines of socialism and communism. His study[2] commenced with Babeuf and at once drew attention to the emergence of a new and 'dangerous class' in the French revolution, the propertyless mass, which bore within itself the seeds of the total overthrow of European society founded on the principle of property. Marx's concept of the role of the proletariat undoubtedly derives from Stein. He endows this class with the very attributes Stein had seen in it. It is proud, resentful and defiant, possessing that "revolutionary valour which hurls in the face of the adversary the insolent challenge—I am nothing but I shall be everything".[3]

Von Stein had been quite right in tracing the proletarian movement back to Babeuf, who stands at the divide between primitive and modern socialism, not charting the details of an ideal society but devising and organising the means for winning and maintaining power. Babeuf appealed directly to the working class of Paris: he developed an elaborate propaganda machine; he formed secret cells in the Army and the police. Since the rich will never voluntarily surrender their power, he said, it must be taken from them by force. Babeuf actually launched his revolt. It failed and Babeuf himself died on the guillotine; but he left an enduring legacy; and it was Marx who inherited it, even though he profoundly modified it. Babeuf's immediate follower, however, was Blanqui, another conspiratorial socialist, who placed his faith in a putsch accomplished by a small disciplined group of professional conspirators. This surprise assault was to be launched without any

[1] Marx, *Introduction to the Critique of Hegel's Philosophy of Law.*

[2] Lorenz von Stein, *Der Socialismus und Communismus des heutigen Frankreichs* (1842).

[3] Marx, *Introduction to the Critique of Hegel's Philosophy of Law.*

preliminary attempt to educate or prepare a large number of workers to support it. Blanqui marks the transition stage from utopian socialism to revolutionary Marxism. Marx and Lenin both thought highly of him and learnt much from him, which Lenin was to make effective use of in Russia in 1917; but they totally rejected his idea of fighting the class war without the support of an informed and organised working-class movement.

For this a radical theory is needed. Just as the theory is useless without the rise of a class to grasp it and embody it, so that class is impotent unless inspired by the idea. "Theory becomes a material force as soon as it lays hold of the masses."

Thus philosophy and the proletariat come together. Both drive to the same results, both have the same interests. "As philosophy finds in the proletariat its material weapons, so the proletariat finds in philosophy its intellectual weapons, and as soon as the lightning of thought has struck deep into the virgin soil of the people, the Germans will emancipate themselves and become men."[1]

[1] Marx, *Introduction to the Critique of Hegel's Philosophy of Law*.

6

THE YOUNG HEGELIANS

THE original division of the Hegelians into the more conservative and the more radical wings, which we may call Right and Left, was followed by a division of the Left into a group which followed Feuerbach, and among these was Marx, while another group consisted of the three Bauers: Bruno, Edgar and Egbert—the "Holy Family" and their friends. A third tendency was represented by Kaspar Schmidt, who under the name of Max Stirner wrote a book entitled *The Ego and His Own* (*Der Einzige und sein Eigenthum*) which was a statement of philosophical anarchism. This was fiercely and exhaustively criticised by Marx in part of the two-volume work known as *The German Ideology*, which was not published in Marx's lifetime.

The original left-wing group were known as the Young Hegelians. Instead of emphasising the rationality of existing institutions they adopted a more revolutionary interpretation of the master. If history is the logical, progressive unfolding of absolute reason, all that exists must be incessantly superseded. They emphasised, therefore, the element of process in Hegel's thought.

Three outstanding Young Hegelians played an important part in the development of Marx's thought: David Strauss, who regarded Spirit as the unconscious myth-making power of the collective mind and interpreted Christianity in this sense; Bruno Bauer, one of Marx's best friends for many years, who concentrated his efforts on changing the minds of men by criticism, holding that all social evils were due to the failure to grasp essential truth. He held that existence depends on consciousness, and that it was the function of criticism to purge the mind of error; Feuerbach, was the third. He regarded himself as a naturalist and a humanist, reversed Bauer's position and held that the spiritual world is a creation of the imagination, a projection of human needs or their compensatory fulfilment.

MOSES HESS

One of the close friends of Marx whom Feuerbach profoundly influenced was Moses Hess; a Rhinelander of Jewish descent. It was

Hess who threw open the world of socialism to Marx and Engels. Deeply influenced by Spinoza and Fichte, as well as by Hegel, his philosophy was eclectic, with ever-changing emphasis. When Feuerbach showed him that man created an imaginary world of the spirit, and thus reduced himself to a deprived or alienated condition, Hess realised that the French socialists, Saint-Simon and Fourier, had in their turn revealed the fact that this deprived condition was due to exploitation. Thus Hess sought to complete the philosophical revolution of Feuerbach with the social revolution which alone could make Feuerbach's restoration of human self-consciousness a reality.

It was this idea that Hess passed on to Marx and Engels. Man, said Hess, had robbed himself of his humanity by turning his labour, his very self, into money-profit for his master. Money is externalised man. In this process of exploitation both employer and employed are placed in a non-human relationship which can only be changed when men are associated in a co-operative way in production. In our world, said Hess, money has become the practical object of worship for us all. "God is only idealised capital and heaven only the theoretical commercial world."

Hess was closely associated with the *Rheinische Zeitung* and later, in Paris, with the *Deutsche-Französische Jahrbücher*, and he it was who converted Engels to communism. His influence on Marx is plainly seen in the Paris Manuscripts and *The Jewish Question*. "The god of practical need and self-interest is money. Money dethrones all the gods of man, turns them into commodities. Money is the universal and self-sufficient *value* of all things. It has, therefore, deprived the whole world, both the human world and nature, of their own proper value. Money is the alienated essence of man's work and his being. This alien being rules over him and he worships it."[1]

Although Marx later found it necessary to criticise the socialism of Hess, which was called 'True Socialism', the latter long remained a close associate of Marx and was active in the First International. Personally, he was a man of singular purity of character—sensitive to every form of injustice, passionate in in his devotion to principles, and almost saintly in his everyday behaviour. He found himself unable to hate even those who had harmed him.

The theme of the power of money took hold of Marx. It appears again in the essay in the Paris Manuscripts on *The Power of Money in Bourgeois Society*, and it occupies an important place in *Capital*. Here

[1] Marx, *The Jewish Question*.

he repeats the argument of the 1844 essay in briefer form. The theme is so basic to Marx's thought that it deserves some attention. He relates it to the position of women in society. The relationship of the sexes shows how far man has become really human. Love is not love if it relies on anything other than the power to evoke a real response. You can only exchange love for love, trust for trust. You cannot buy them with gold. Unless you make yourself a loved person through a living expression of yourself, your love is impotent and the relationship you attain is a meaningless one and a tragedy.

He quotes the passage in Shakespeare's *Timon of Athens*,[1] a play which shows money as the destroyer of social order, beginning:

> Gold? yellow, glittering, precious gold? No, Gods,
> I am no idle votarist. . . .
> Thus much of this will make black white, foul fair,
> Wrong right, base noble, old young, coward valiant.

Marx expounds it thus: My power is as great as the power of my money. Money transforms my incapacity into its opposite. I may be unintelligent, but I can buy other peoples' brains or win honour by my wealth, I may be a coward, but I can buy men to fight for me. But this is utterly destructive of real social bonds. Every one of your relationships to men must correspond to something real and tangible in yourself, otherwise we are left with a system of society divorced from morality, an authority without responsibility, a power animated solely by self-interest.

TRUE SOCIALISM

"True Socialism" was a somewhat vague political tendency among a group of literary men who had all been greatly influenced by Feuerbach. The two most influential were Hess and Grun, who each developed his philosophy in his own way. Hess had been a close collaborator with Marx, who thought very highly of him. He had gone much farther than Feuerbach by tracing man's deprived condition to the evils and injustices of the commercial system and he had derived from Fichte the notion that the philosophy of spirit must become a philosophy of action, that not only human thinking but the whole of human life had to be lifted onto a plane on which all radical oppositions would disappear. Fichte had energetically repudiated the barren enlightenment of merely rational criticism interested only in

[1] Act 4, Scene 3.

its own sapless concepts, and had called attention to the spirit working with us, an infinite force, a life, a light, leading towards a new age, a revolutionary age.

Hess saw this revolution historically, from the point of view of socialism. All the great civilised nations appeared to him to be moving towards the overthrow of reactionary authority and the liberation of mankind. In England, he saw the promise of the Chartist movement, in France the rising power of the socialist ideals of Saint-Simon and Proudhon, and now in Germany, with its bourgeoisie already striving for the defeat of political absolutism and a democratic constitution, there arose the demand for something more than a liberal revolution, the great ideal of philosophical communism.

But from this position he went on to preach the elimination of all conflict between man and man, and class and class. His guiding principle was the conception of the true nature of man, man viewed as humanity. But man cannot live as man until all institutions based on money and private property are swept away and replaced by the co-operative activity of all individuals for common ends. Therefore, the socialist movement would not appeal to the proletariat for material ends, but to all men in terms of every kind of ideal good.

Marx believed that this position was mistaken and had disastrous political consequences. Karl Grun, who largely agreed with Hess, differed from Marx on another, a purely political, issue. Marx saw clearly that in Germany the next item on the agenda of politics was constitutional reform demanded by the bourgeoisie. He urged all socialists to support this demand even though after it had been conceded the conflict would inevitably break out between the workers and the bourgeoisie. Marx held that the main enemy of the movement was the feudal Prussian Government and that a victory for liberalism would represent a partial and temporary gain in the immediate interests of wide strata of the people. Not to fight for this democratic advance, argued Marx, is political madness and aids reaction. What then was the alternative policy of the True Socialists? It was to explain to the workers that the real cause of social distress was economic and that to fight for political rights was a waste of time. What the workers needed was education as to their real situation; it was to proclaim the ethical ideals of socialism on the basis of true human nature. Socialism was the only system which was in harmony with human nature as it ideally was. The economic facts which were opening the way to socialism were ignored, the whole emphasis was on spiritual enlightenment.

All the assumptions behind these positions were challenged by Marx.

In the first place, on the political issue, it was a mistake to follow political principles as if they were true under all conditions. Principles are not derived from eternal truths but from actual experience and must be modified as changes occur. The principle of fighting the bourgeoisie at that moment held for France but not for Germany, where the bourgeoisie was the most dangerous foe of the reactionary government. To attack it was to play the game of the Prussian monarchy and disrupt the popular movement.

In the second place, Marx criticised their appeal to very general moral ideals as meaningless and ineffectual. A morality that is timeless and placeless does not reflect the urgent, actual needs of people and ignores the immediate, concrete means of alleviating their actual condition. General ideals of freedom, brotherhood and the like can be readily accepted by the bourgeoisie and interpreted to suit their interests—not hypocritically but quite naturally. The concrete needs of the working class must be the point of departure for its morality. Is this a purely selfish class interest if it wins a decent life first for the whole working class, and ultimately for everyone?

Marx strongly criticised their appeal to "human nature". This, he said, is not something permanent, as they believed, but changing. It is not abstract human nature which determines the form of society. How could that be so, if human nature were always the same, for the form of society changes radically? On the contrary, it is society and the position one occupies in it that determines human nature. It is our task to remake human nature by changing society.

The political consequences of this view Marx saw as disastrous. The appeal was to be wholly to ideals above all class interests, whereas Marx was convinced that the proletariat must be the agent of social transformation, since the advance to socialism was entirely in their interests, though it was also in the interests of society as a whole.[1]

THE HOLY FAMILY

In February 1845, Marx published a book of 300 pages which he entitled *The Holy Family*. It was the first work in which Marx and Engels collaborated. Engels wrote his part before leaving for Germany in September 1844. During their separation, Marx, who had not yet left Paris, continued to work on it and turned it into a work of con-

[1] Marx's criticism of "True Socialism" is in *The German Ideology* and *The Communist Manifesto*.

siderable size. The whole was published in February 1845, in Frankfurt.

Its target was the Bauer family, an influential group among the Berlin Hegelians, who had decided that criticism was the really important weapon in changing the world and had launched an attack on Marx in their journal the *General Gazette for Literature*. Now this view was itself subjected to criticism.

Bruno Bauer placed his entire emphasis on purging the mind of error as the way not only to clarification of thought but the overcoming of social evils. He objected to agitation among the working classes, and came to regard their participation in events as a source of confusion. Only ideas make history, and these must never be allowed to be affected by class interests, because this could only concern itself with particular evils, whereas the real task concerned principles. Let history take care of the crisis bound to follow the success of the critical onslaught.

Marx replied that this was a profound philosophical error, bound to lead to the acceptance of a world of ideas with an independent existence of its own. This could only open the door to supernaturalism and a return to religion—hence he described the Bauers as *The Holy Family*. Marx accuses them of failing to see the close relation of ideas to facts, of history to industrial development, as though ideas developed in a world of their own and then made their impact on the world. "The great historical movements have always been determined by mass interest, and only in so far as ideas represented these could they prevail." Thus the principles and ideas behind the French Revolution were effective because they corresponded to the class interests of the bourgeoisie. They were of no avail to the masses, although they had been dressed up as eternal principles and identified with universal human interests. The disappointment of the masses was inevitable, for "the real conditions of their emancipation are radically different from the conditions within which the bourgeoisie can emancipate itself and society". There is only one way in which masses can be emancipated and that is when the proletariat abolishes its own poverty, abolishes itself, and abolishes private property.

The Bauers had also criticised the French Socialist, Proudhon. Marx sprang to the defence of Proudhon's book *What is Property?* to which he attributed great importance. Proudhon not only foreshadowed Marx's theory of surplus value but developed a theory of conflicting classes and an economic interpretation of history, and he reached the conclusion that "in the multitude of secret causes by which people are agitated, there is none more powerful, more regular and more unmistakable than the periodic explosions of the proletariat against property". Marx declared that Proudhon was the first to criticise private property, the basis of all developments of political economy, even though he tried to solve its problem within the system of private property itself.

EUGENE SUE AND "THE MYSTERIES OF PARIS"

If Bruno Bauer had deduced human action from independently existing ideas, ideals and principles, much popular thinking follows the same unphilosophical course. An immensely popular novelist in Paris at this time was Eugene Sue, who had a reputation for being a progressive and even a revolutionary writer, and regarded himself as a socialist. His *Mysteries of Paris* (10 Volumes, 1842-43) narrate the adventures of Rudolf of Geroldstein, who defends the poor against injustice and misery and attacks the wickedness of capitalism.

The book had been warmly praised by a friend of Bruno Bauer who wrote an enthusiastic interpretation of it—a singular example of the way life can avenge itself upon abstract thought. The hero shows how idealism and benevolence uplift and redeem the fallen. Marx criticises the philosophy behind these volumes because it attributes all effective human actions to principles of humanity which are abstractions from experience. As with Bauer and the Hegelians, first the abstractions are created from experience and then the abstractions are treated as transcendental realities from which experience is derived. Marx points out that the characters in Eugene Sue's novel thus become puppets of words, abstractions, principles and moral ideals, and have no integrity, no authenticity.

If, like these philosophers, says Marx, we reduce concrete things which we know well, real fruits—apples, pears, grapes—to the *concept* of fruit, and hold that this concept, existing apart from them, constitutes their essence, we make this concept the substance of the real fruits, and make the real fruits mere modes of existence of the concept. From now on what is essential in the apple or pear is not its real being but the concept or abstract idea we have substituted for it. It is however, not as easy as some philosophers suppose to show how abstractions can bring into existence actual fruits in their particular variety. This is to try to conjure real rabbits from metaphysical top-hats.

In other words, philosophical speculation first converts real objects into concepts and then recreates them as expressions of the concept, performing the miracle of eliciting concrete objects from abstract terms. This is to put an imaginary world in the place of the real world. Everything real is made a mystery, and the mystery arbitrarily incarnates itself in real things which are copies of itself.

So Eugene Sue's characters are not real people at all, but only the puppets of a moral lesson or idea.

Both the novel and the philosophy lend themselves to a mode of criticism highly congenial to Marx, a mixture of fantastic and exuberant satire with an iron and inflexible logic, the whole exposition richly illustrated from history.

LUDWIG FEUERBACH

Feuerbach, the son of an eminent Bavarian jurist, came to Berlin in 1824, seven years before the death of Hegel, and became his disciple. By 1830 it was clear that in certain important respects he was in disagreement with the master of German thought. His first books marked him as a radical, but his *Essence of Christianity* was the occasion of a philosophical revolution and changed the entire outlook of the Young Hegelians. He met Strauss, Ruge, Marx and Engels. His reputation grew and his influence spread. He carried on a voluminous correspondence with leaders of thought in all domains.

It has been said that Feuerbach was "Hegel's fate". Hegel had to have a Feuerbach; his whole system needed its completion and correction. Feuerbach's criticism of the philosophy which had fascinated the ablest minds in Germany at that time was that Hegel was mistaken in holding that the world was an emanation of the unfolding Idea. On the contrary, the primary reality was the world of man whose frustrations and struggles compelled him to project his essence into the realm of religion and philosophy. Man was not an emanation of the Idea—the Idea, the Absolute, God, was an emanation of man. In other words, Feuerbach reduced the metaphysical Absolute Spirit to "real man on the foundation of nature". His book produced a shock effect upon the Young Hegelians: "enthusiasm was general; we all became at once Feuerbachians," said Engels. "There is no road to truth and freedom other than the road through this 'brook of fire' " (*feuer-bach*), was the emphatic judgment of Marx himself.

The importance of Feuerbach can hardly be overestimated. In him began that reaction from Hegel which found expression not only in Marxism but in all those movements in philosophy which broke away from the block universe of Absolute Idealism and the paralysing conception of a predetermined historical process. "Who", said Marx, "has put an end to the dialectics of concepts, to the war of the Gods, that the philosophers alone knew? Feuerbach. Who placed man in the stead of the former rubbish, driving away with the same stroke the infinite consciousness? Feuerbach, Feuerbach alone."[1]

How much Marx owed to Feuerbach we realise when we remember that according to Feuerbach, God is the image of man; according to Marx, the sentiment and ideas of men are the reflections of their conditions of existence. According to Feuerbach, the history of the gods is the celestial repetition of the earthly progress of man; according to Marx, human history is a reflection of the conditions of production. We see here both the initial idea, the revolution in thought whereby "in total contrast to German philosophy, which descends from Heaven to earth, we here ascend from earth to heaven", and the advance far beyond that original idea.

In the spring of 1845 Marx had written down the first draft of his criticism of Feuerbach in the eleven theses only discovered by Engels after Marx's death.[2] In the *Theses*, having pointed out the defects of Feuerbach's undialectical materialism—that is, the mistake of treating the mind of man as the passive recipient of sense-impressions whereas in fact man constantly interacts with his environment and apprehends the external world in terms of his present intentions, knowledge, basic needs and level of technological development—Marx proceeds to criticise his conception of the nature of man. Feuerbach seems always to consider man in the abstract, as a manifestation of the "essence of humanity"; but man is never abstract but always actual man, at a particular stage of technological development and constituted by it, always in a particular historical form of social relationships. Feuerbach, considering "man as such", can only see man as an isolated individual, and as the same at any time and under whatever conditions.

Also, since Feuerbach never sees man's actual life, which is one involving exploitation and alienation, he has no real explanation of the alienated condition and therefore no remedy but the purely mental one of dispelling the religious illusion which he imagines to be its

[1] Quoted in F. Mehring's *Nachlass von Karl Marx, etc.*

[2] Feuerbach was for many years hardly known, apart from Engel's essay of 1888. Marx's *Theses on Feuerbach*, which although written in 1845 were not discovered by Engels until 1885, were appended to Engels' book on Feuerbach. They were not in a finished form and Engels published them in a more polished shape. Engels describes them as "invaluable as the first document in which is deposited the brilliant germ of the new world outlook".

cause. But once we see that it is in a class-divided society that man is robbed of his humanity, we can see that the way to restore his humanity is to overcome the class division of society. Thus the present condition of man "must be theoretically criticised and radically changed in practice". If we consider the true nature of man as constituted by his social activity and social relationship, we have risen above the notion of the isolated individual as he exists in society today and arrive at the true conception of socialised humanity.

Marx concludes his *Theses* by pointing out that hitherto "philosophers have only sought to *interpret* the world in various ways: the point, however, is to change it". Thus both Feuerbach and Hegel provide explanations of the human condition which offer us no consolation except that of removing the illusions which conceal reality. With that reality, as seen correctly, we have to be satisfied. The alteration is in our attitude to the situation. Marx, on the other hand, points out that the evils of human life have to be removed in reality by changing the world, that is to say, by changing the pattern of social relationships.

Feuerbach never investigated the actual pattern of social relationships to discover to what extent the qualities of man, the "essence of the species", were historical; nor did it occur to him that the emancipation of man, his deliverance from alienation, the achievement of communism, laid upon him a programme of action. In failing to do justice to the historical elements in culture, he missed the factors which constitute the levers of social change. He writes as if the demonstration of truth and the exposure of error came to the same thing as passing sentence of death upon the actual human condition. Thus Marx shows us Feuerbach, like so many other philosophers, as confining his philosophical activity to thinking about ideas. He identifies philosophy with passionless thought, thought unrelated to practice. Marx, on the other hand, conceives of philosophical activity as action on behalf of human interests; such thought itself leads to that action which alone makes it possible to achieve a world in which alienation is overcome.

7

THE GERMAN IDEOLOGY

AFTER Marx and Engels had settled in Brussels they proceeded to deal in yet another work with a series of theoretical problems which included not only the philosophical errors of the young Hegelians and especially Feuerbach, but the socialism of Moses Hess, and the individualism of Max Stirner. It is an enormous book of some 800 pages. "It was composed by Engels and me in common," says Marx, "and that for the sake of settling accounts with our former philosophical conscience." Thus its aim was to clear up in its writers' minds all the remaining uncertainties on their position with regard to the existing German philosophies and their own fresh outlook. Marx continues: "The manuscript was already in the hands of a Westphalian publisher when we were informed that altered circumstances rendered publication impossible, whereupon we abandoned our manuscript to the gnawing criticism of mice. We did so with little regret because our main object had been achieved—we had come to an understanding with ourselves." As a matter of fact, the mice did get at the manuscript, but its remnants are sufficient to explain why its authors were not too depressed at the misfortune.[1]

Yet this is perhaps the most pregnant theoretical work that Marx and Engels ever wrote. For the rest of his life Marx worked out its theories in his exhaustive analytical studies of contemporary history and economic development, illuminating and systematising in magnificent fashion a world of complex and significant facts. But this was all the elaboration and explication of the basic principles first comprehensively set down in *The German Ideology*.

MATERIALISM AND IDEALISM

The first part, entitled *Feuerbach: Opposition of the Materialistic and Idealistic Outlook*, is not a detailed criticism of Feuerbach, but a clear exposition of the philosophical basis of Marxism in a positive form,

[1] First published in the *Marx-Engels Gesamtausgabe* 1.5 (1932). The English translation of Parts I and III appeared in 1938.

beginning with the conditions of all thought and all history. Marx and Engels proceed to sketch the development of human society through the growth of private property, working out at each stage the relations between the economic structure and the accompanying and dependent political and theoretical forms.

This exposition is concisely summarised in the well-known two pages in the Preface to the *Critique of Political Economy* (1859), but invaluable though that is, the full treatment of this basic theory in *The German Ideology* is indispensable for the understanding of Marx's position.

In the first part Marx and Engels develop the criticism of Feuerbach in the *Theses*. They see man not as the passive subject of perception, acted upon by an external world, but as continuously making and remaking the external world. Nature, for man, does not exist in isolation from him. Everything that we handle and alter and use, that enters our social life, must be understood subsequently as self-externalisation of the creative subject at a particular historical moment.

Man wrestles with nature to satisfy his basic needs; and whenever we find him doing this he is operating a particular technique—the stone axe, the loom, the steam engine—and operating it in a particular social form; and as he thus puts himself into his creations, into what he makes, so at the same time he makes himself. Man makes his environment and his environment makes him. How does social development come about? Because man improves his techniques, discovers new sources of power, invents machines. These not only revolutionise production but demand new methods of work-organisation, new relations between the men engaged in production. Thus a new social and material external world or environment is brought into being; and into that environment the new generation enters and by it it is made.

Thus does Marx replace Feuerbach's man, the passive, abstract man, by the active social man whose reality consists in social activities historically conditioned. It is this man-made form of production, this man-made world, that determines the "essence" of man; and the "essence" of man is not therefore as idealists imagine, something constant, but is constantly changing. And in this sequence of changes we have the source of historical development.

COMMUNISM

They then proceed to develop under the title *Communism: The Production of the Form of Intercourse Itself*, the only comprehensive exposition of the Marxist philosophy of history. Marx conceived of the succession of historical forms or societies as following a definite pattern, each one being marked by a characteristic attitude towards the instruments and forces of production. It is the *relations of production*, the "forms of intercourse", the way people are associated together in the production of their material means of life, which condition the general character of cultural life. As Marx subsequently put it in the Preface to the *Critique of Political Economy*: "The sum total of these relations of production constitutes the economic structure of society—the real foundations, on which rise legal and political institutions and to which correspond definite forms of consciousness."

Marx is at pains to make it inescapably clear that this basis is not the technology, skills, tradition, is not the natural conditions which provide materials, not climate, race, geographical factors, but the way in which productive forces and productive conditions are organised by the social activities of man. Property relations are their legal expression. The relations may be those of serfs to manorial lords, of individual hand-workers and peasants to one another, of wage-earners to a capitalist class which owns the factories. The particular patterns of intercourse in work constitute the economic basis of the institutional processes which govern the production and distribution of wealth, like the systems of slavery, feudalism and capitalism. And the capitalist structure involves the production of commodities for a market by workers who are formally free to work or not, and who are themselves not the owners of the instruments they use. These commodities are produced for purposes of profit to those who own the instruments of production and not for the use of those who produce them.

This, then, constitutes the analysis of the social form. But from this we pass to the dynamic analysis which shows how the economic foundation changes and how this changes the superstructure of ideas, culture, law, institutions. "According to this conception, the ultimate causes of all social changes and political revolutions are to be sought, not in the minds of men, in their increasing insight into eternal truth and justice, but in changes in the mode of production and exchange; they are to be sought not in the *philosophy* but in the *economics* of the epoch concerned."[1]

When Marx says that the origin of social change is not in ideas as such, ideas derived from speculative thought, from metaphysical

[1] Engels, *Anti-Dühring*.

reflection, he does not mean that social change takes place automatically, apart from ideas, but that the ideas that are effective arise out of actual situations, as the result of thinking about the problems that arise, and striving to understand the dangers and possibilities involved. Marx is not saying that thought is impotent in shaping history, but that fundamentally it is a seeking answers to questions set by the conditions of contemporary society. Once it reaches a correct understanding of the situation and what needs to be done, thought becomes the force which reshapes the economic basis.

The ideas which change the basis of society arise when the existing economic structure definitely hampers the full use of the productive forces existing within it and fails to realise the possibilities of the new productive forces which are emerging. Such is the state of affairs in contemporary capitalist society. Where great masses of human beings are confronted with the fact of economic stringency, a class is called forth which has borne all the burdens but does not enjoy the advantages of the production of wealth, and it becomes clear to the most enlightened that they must appropriate the existing totality of productive forces to safeguard their very existence, for at this stage the productive forces have become destructive forces. Then there arises the consciousness of the necessity of a fundamental revolution.

Thus the social and economic forms which production assumes become increasingly less adequate for the satisfaction of the needs of men, and the discrepancy between the productive forces of society and the capitalist mode of production becomes greater and greater.[1] There is an increasing conflict between the forces and the forms which restrict them. The forms, however, are rigid and resent modification because they are artificially preserved beyond the point at which they are economically useful by the owning and ruling class whose interest they represent.

Change, therefore, must be brought about by new social groups which have been brought into existence and developed by the existing order and whose interests are linked with the most advanced productive forces. It is they who take charge of the reorganisation and institute it. "Thus all collisions in history have their origin in the contradiction

[1] It was in *Capital* that Marx showed how the capitalist system itself fostered the immense development of the productive forces, concentrating them in fewer and fewer hands and immensely increasing productive capacity, until the very conditions which at first released and expanded these forces become an obstacle to their full utilisation and further expansion. Thus, one thing can, in the course of its own development, turn into its opposite.

between the productive forces and the forms of intercourse. But this contradiction need not necessarily come to a head in this particular country. The competition with industrially more advanced countries, brought about by the expansion of international intercourse, is sufficient to produce a similar contradiction in countries with a backward industry."[1]

It is important to recognise that Marx is not saying that social change is uniquely determined by technological advance. The same technical forces, the modern machine, may be operated under different economic systems. And it is not the economic techniques which produce effects like monopolies and unemployment. These are consequences of the use of such techniques in an economy devoted to the quest for private profit. In the first place it is the mode of production itself that stimulates the development of techniques, but beyond a certain point further advance in efficiency demands a new mode of production, a new and more appropriate economic system to suit the now enlarged and developed productive forces and carry them forward to a higher and more fully productive stage. There is thus a dialectical relationship between the forces of production and the relations of production and neither can be considered as operating in isolation.

The movement of history is not imposed from without by the creative fiat of an Absolute Mind, nor is it the result of a dynamic urge within matter. It develops out of the re-directive activity of human beings trying to meet their natural and social needs. Human history may be viewed as a process in which new needs are created as a result of material changes instituted to fulfil the old.

Equally important to Marx's theory of history is the relation of the economic system to human nature and to the individual. This is worked out nowhere but in *The German Ideology* and it is basic to Marxism. When man makes history he makes himself—here is the fundamental idea which Marx derived from Hegel's *Phenomenology*. Man has no original human nature. Least of all is that nature the competitive individual of Hobbes, Bentham and Adam Smith, for ever engaged in the "war of all against all", nor is he the egoistic hedonist of Max Stirner. Marx repudiates the "economic man" of contemporary political economy as the essential human type. The type in any particular period is explicable, not by man's original nature, but

[1] *The German Ideology*. This little-noticed statement of Marx throws light on the frequent assertion that he saw revolutionary change as necessarily occurring in the first place in the most advanced industrial countries.

ultimately by the economic structure of society. When he *has* to change this in order to go on living, in order to overcome the obstruction which limits his life, he *has* to reconstruct society and it is the reconstructed society that changes the man and his ideas and moral principles and institutions. If man has imagined that in society he found his real freedom (as Hegel believed), he is forced to realise that a class society makes this impossible, so that the community he thinks he belongs to is "a completely illusory community", and a fetter as well, something standing over against men to enslave them, and to deny their free activity. It is only when man is compelled to end the class structure of society that he achieves "the real community in which individuals obtain their freedom in and through their association. . . . It is just this combination of individuals which puts the conditions of the free development and activity of individuals under their own control." Thus the sequence of economic systems, of forms of intercourse, of social relations—"the definite conditions under which men produce" —is a progress towards human emancipation and individual freedom. "These various conditions, which appear first as conditions of self-activity, later as fetters upon it, form in the whole evolution of history a coherent series of forms of intercourse, the coherence of which consists in this: that in the place of an earlier form of intercourse, which has become a fetter, a new one is put, corresponding to the more developed productive forces and, hence, to the advanced mode of the self-activity of individuals—a form which in its turn becomes a fetter and is then replaced by another. Since these conditions correspond at every stage to the simultaneous development of the productive forces, their history is at the same time the history of the evolving productive forces taken over by each new generation, and is therefore the history of the development of the forces of the individuals themselves."[1]

Human existence then partakes of the nature of the pattern of social relations, the way in which men are associated together in their daily life and work, belonging to any particular system. All social life follows the pattern of basic human relations; in a pattern constituted by individual ownership, competition, profit seeking, the purchase of labour as a commodity, the institutions, the law, the morality, the ideas, the art and the religion will all tend to move into conformity with this pattern. All this Marx describes as "the superstructure". This falls into two parts—the institutions and principles which are determined *directly* and *immediately* by the characteristic economic relations—the

[1] Marx-Engels, *The German Ideology*.

law, the state system and the moral code—and all those creations of the mind and imagination: art, literature, music and philosophy itself, which are determined *indirectly* and *mediately*.

It would be a complete mistake to imagine that this superstructure is merely a reflection of the basis and is itself powerless and ineffective. On the contrary it consists of those institutions which form the coercive and defensive state power; and every system of law protects the interests of which it is the expression.

Thus the superstructure serves the purpose of maintaining the class system and resisting its supersession. The political institutions embody the rule of the class which is predominant in the economic field. The values and the moral code, equally with the law, help to uphold and sanction conduct in harmony with the needs of the established order.

But if this is so, it is also the case that the interests of a rising class determined to overthrow the existing economic order and construct a new one, will bring into existence a rival ideology, and the ideas and institutions which play a creative role in history will be those which are identified with living and growing social forces. And when victory is won, the new ruling class must at once begin the long and difficult task of reconstructing the whole superstructure to express, maintain and develop its own new system of social relationships. Its new institutions, moral code, legal system and forms of culture will be indispensable forces for the making and moulding of the new society and the new man of the socialist world.

Marx and Engels were not unmindful of the fact that the superstructure necessarily attains a considerable measure of independence once it has come into existence, and that there is of course no one-to-one correspondence between the particular forms of the cultural system and the underlying basis; nevertheless, by and large there is a real correspondence and reciprocal interconnection, and each plays an immensely important part in determining the other.

This important insight into the basis of culture, therefore, cannot be taken as an answer to every question. "All history must be studied afresh, the conditions of existence of the different formations of society must be examined in detail, before the attempt is made to deduce from them the political, civil-legal, aesthetic, philosophic, religious, etc. notions corresponding to them."[1]

Nor must it be forgotten that long after basic change has occurred relics of the old superstructure linger on; well-established institutions,

[1] Engels, Letter to C. Schmidt, August 5th, 1890.

like churches, run for centuries on their own momentum; philosophical ideas are derived from the intellectual heritage and tradition and are not so much swept aside as modified in the course of development by social changes, new conditions, and new human demands for a meaningful philosophy.

MAX STIRNER'S INDIVIDUALISM

The second part of *The German Ideology* contains an elaborate, lengthy refutation of the anarchist individualism of Max Stirner's *The Ego and His Own*. Satirical and hilarious, exuberant and extravagant, it is none the less a work of considerable importance.

Stirner's book *Der Einziger und sein Eigentum* (*The Ego and His Own*) was a Nietzschean defence of the absolute independence and the right of self-fulfilment of the individual. In so far as it was directed against the contemporary vogue of sentimental and idealistic philanthropy which sought to solve the social problem by moral appeals, it had point; his criticism of natural rights was also valid and helped to undermine the rights of property; finally his criticism of the emptiness of abstract freedom and of the formal freedoms of democracy was important. Freedom, he argued, is not mere absence of constraint but having the positive means to achieve your aims. You can have in a capitalist society plenty of freedom from constraint and none to satisfy your needs, while political freedom which does not satisfy our basic interests may be little more than the freedom to talk.

But Marx strongly criticised Stirner's conception of "the ego" as completely abstract. The real ego is a social product and achieves its fulfilment in co-operation with others. The rejection of social responsibility does not fulfil the ego, but stultifies it. By throwing in his lot with his fellow workers a man's whole personality is fulfilled in a way which would be impossible if he were to stand aside and alone. Marx concludes by pointing out that this egoism has social rather than ideological roots. From the latter point of view, indeed, it is quite indefensible; but its real strength is that it reflects the ideas of the small shopkeeper or craftsman. "Stirner offers us an additional proof of how the most trivial sentiments of the petty bourgeois can borrow wings from a high-flown ideology."

This, then, is *The German Ideology*. Taken as a whole it provides the basis on which Marxism arose. The theories which were in turn discussed and criticised were well chosen to allow the full and symmetrical exposition of a new interpretation of history and a new economic and political science.

The first part, dealing with Feuerbach, corrects the vague idealisation of humanity by establishing the social character and development of the individual. The second part, dealing with the Hegelian philosophy, furnishes a powerful criticism of the idealistic philosophy of the time, then generally regarded as final and conclusive. Stirner's individualism gave the opportunity to ground an historical theory on a principle of development which seeks to explain and unify the multiplicity of social and historical facts in a manner which is reminiscent of the Newtonian treatment of astronomy, though the field investigated obviously lends itself to less exact treatment. Finally, in the criticism of the "True Socialist", Marx and Engels draw the practical and ethical conclusions of the new socio-economic philosophy. All these formed part of one remarkably consistent, comprehensive and articulate conspectus of sociological theory.

The work of Marx as a socialist theorist began in Paris in 1843 and reached the completion of its general formulation in Brussels in the summer of 1846 with *The German Ideology*.

PART II

As soon as the lightning of thought has struck deep into the virgin soil of the people, they will emancipate themselves and become men.

Marx

The whole of history is nothing but the progressive transformation of human nature. By acting on the world and changing it man changes his own nature.

Marx

Only through years of struggle can the class which overthrows cleanse itself of the mire of the old society and become fit to create a new society.

Marx

8

MARX IN BRUSSELS

It was in February 1845 that Marx arrived in Brussels with his family. That same spring Engels joined him, and the two friends shortly afterwards went together to England and stayed there for six weeks. It gave Engels immense pleasure to bring his friend for the first time into contact with British life and industry, the trade union movement and his Chartist friends. Engels, who was well known to George Julian Harney, the Chartist leader and editor of *The Northern Star*, became a regular contributor to that journal and in the articles he wrote for it revealed a waning confidence in the middle class and a new faith in the workers. It would be they alone, he now believed, who would carry through the impending revolution. Marx had already come to the view that radical change in the social order was dependent upon the proletariat, which, he said, was not only a suffering class but a fighting class that, by the very conditions of its existence, was being converted into a revolutionary force. He and Engels found ample support for this conviction in the British working-class movement.

The defeat of the Chartists in 1839 had been followed by the Newport uprising under John Frost in which a number of Chartists had been shot before the military suppressed it. It was the period of the hungry forties, and the idea of a general strike was revived. All over the country there was much unrest and violent repression of the workers' movement; and yet in spite of all setbacks it still had high hopes of coming victory.

Engels worked energetically to establish contacts between the revolutionary elements in Britain and the socialists of the Continent. In this he was helped by Ernest Jones, a poet and reformer whose youth had been spent in Germany and who found it easier than the other English labour leaders to understand Engels and Marx. Jones strove to transfuse the new blood of class conflict into the declining Chartist movement, while Engels became a contributor to his *Notes to the People*.

Revolution was certainly in the air and in 1848 was to sweep through

Europe from one end to the other. Marx had given an undertaking to the authorities to have nothing to do with Belgian politics, but Brussels was something of an international centre and there was plenty to do. Not only was there a considerable colony of German workers, but there was much coming and going between Brussels and Paris and London. Marx and Engels on their return to Brussels at once got in touch with the German colony, many of whom were communists in exile like themselves.

Insurrection had broken out in Germany, among the Silesian weavers, and in 1845 and 1846 socialism spread rapidly through the country and socialist periodicals and even socialist novels began to appear. France too was seething with socialist ideas. A spectre of communism was abroad in Europe. Engels' economic studies had shown him that with the rapid expansion of industry periods of prosperity were invariably followed by slumps in which the workers fought with ever increasing bitterness against the iron law of wages, the bare subsistence, and the hopeless unemployment that was their lot.

When they returned to Brussels, Marx and Engels at once began to establish connection with the workers' movement which they found there. They proceeded to penetrate every organisation they could find.

The steps that Guizot had taken against the radical writers living in Paris made Belgium the chief meeting-place for German communists. Besides Marx and Engels, there were about twenty others. In Brussels as in Paris, London and Switzerland there were also groups of German tailors, cabinet-makers and leather workers who were spending the usual years abroad to complete their training.

Brussels was at that time a transit station between France and Germany. German workers and intellectuals making their way to Paris usually passed through the city, and it was not difficult for Marx to establish contact between communists in all three countries. Many of these were loosely organised in revolutionary societies like the League of the Just, which had played an important part in Blanqui's abortive insurrection of 1839; and Marx realised the importance of gaining influence in such groups—not always an easy task, since they had a deep distrust of intellectuals.

The most prominent of the French socialists at this time was Louis Blanc, who came to the fore in 1848 and was then given the opportunity of starting the National Workshops. Blanc was convinced that his schemes could be put into operation within bourgeois society. He was very soon to be bitterly disillusioned. Then there were the followers of the utopian, Cabet, who had written a popular book describing the civilisation of the future, *The Journey to Icara.* Within the ranks of the workers themselves there was Proudhon, the most influential of them all.

In London, Engels found three able Germans leading the League: the watchmaker Joseph Moll, the shoemaker Heinrich Bauer and Karl Schapper, now a teacher of languages. They were all to be closely associated with Marx in later years. Marx was also on good terms with the many Russians he found in Paris, some of them liberals, or even revolutionaries—the most important being Bakunin. We have an admirable account of Marx as he then appeared from one of these Russians, Annenkov. "Marx belonged to the type of men who were all energy, force of will and unshakeable conviction. With a thick black mop of hair on his head, with hairy hands and a crookedly buttoned frock coat, he had the air of a man used to commanding the respect of others. His movements were clumsy but self-assured. His manners defied the accepted conventions of social intercourse and were haughty and almost contemptuous. His voice was disagreeably harsh and he spoke of men and things in the tone of one who would tolerate no contradiction, and which seemed to express his own firm conviction in his mission to sway men's minds and dictate the laws of their being."[1]

Marx certainly aroused some opposition by his attitude to Weitling, a German tailor who had made a great reputation as a socialist propagandist, and had written a book entitled *Guarantees of Harmony and Freedom* (1843) which was very highly thought of. Weitling was one of the most active and popular of itinerant agitators of that time. Marx himself had praised him as the "fiery and brilliant" propagandist who was the first to arouse the German workers.

But Weitling was to prove a bitter disappointment; Marx soon realised that he was doing little more than playing with fancy pictures of the future socialist society, which he expected to be realised by violent insurrection in the near future. To this end he believed in the disruption of society by every form of agitation among those most likely to be aroused—the lowest stratum of the proletariat. He was a man who regarded himself as the appointed leader of German proletarian communism, carrying in his pocket the recipe for establishing heaven on earth and under the delusion that it was the intention of Marx to steal it from him.

That he was an able propagandist, gifted with a certain talent, Marx

[1] P. Annenkov, *A Wonderful Ten Years.*

did not deny; but he was equally aware of his lack of education, of any historical sense and of his inordinate vanity and fundamental irresponsibility. All this came out when a meeting was arranged in Brussels for Marx and Weitling to work out a common plan. It was a total failure. Weitling enraged Marx beyond endurance by his endless stream of varied rhetoric, his scorn of theory, the lack of any considered basis for his revolutionary proposals. Marx abruptly stopped him: it was reckless of him to arouse the workers, to endanger their safety, without any conception of what line of social development was being worked out. Weitling retorted that his speeches had aroused enthusiasm everywhere. Marx replied that enthusiasm without scientific thought was folly. "It is simple fraud to arouse the people without any social and considered class basis for their activity." Then losing his temper he struck his fist on the table with great violence and leaping up he shouted, "Ignorance never helped nor did anybody any good." All those present rose too. The conference was at an end. As they left, Marx still furiously angry was striding up and down the room. This outburst was characteristic of Marx. He appeared domineering, arrogant and dogmatic, but such boldness and ruthlessness were required to demolish the delusions of the age. His judgment certainly developed a searing trenchancy which wounded many. It often seemed as though the sharpness and force of his mind could best manifest itself in controversy, and that in overthrowing the errors of others he clarified and brought to birth his own ideas. There were times when he and Engels went on at enormous length, with a certain sardonic humour, knocking the philosophers' heads together; but then indignation would supervene, as if the force of Marx's argument would be dissolved and enfeebled if diffused by too much urbanity.

Marx was determined to rid the movement if he could of muddle-headed and irresponsible leaders. He was equally determined to have done with any more preaching of goodwill as the way to socialism, which was made clear by his devastating criticism of the "True Socialists" Grun and Hess, even though Hess had been a close friend of Marx and had been of great help in developing his ideas. Engels went to Paris and debated furiously with the followers of Grun and Proudhon, but found the German workers who had fallen under their influence more petty-bourgeois than proletarian, anxious indeed to become, not employees, but independent master craftsmen.

The Paris communists were in constant touch with similar groups in London, Brussels and other cities and thus some sort of beginning had been made of an international communist organisation. Marx in Brussels worked steadily at the task of linking up these scattered bands of communists. He had influenced the London Corresponding Committee by means of a series of pamphlets mercilessly criticising the theories of the French and German communists, and the views of this group were in process of reconstruction. In 1847 Joseph Moll, a German watchmaker, arrived from London to clarify the position of the London organisation in relation to Marx's ideas. Whatever form of organisation actually existed at the time in London[1] was now reorganised as The Communist League and Marx and Engels were invited to join. Their first Congress, which was attended by Engels, was held in June 1847, when the aims and methods of the League were revised and it was resolved that it should cease to be something of a secret society and become an open propagandist society.

There had been a good deal of activity in London. In 1844 refugees from many countries formed a society of Fraternal Democrats which met at the German Communist Working-men's Club in Drury Lane. This Society was active in discussing international affairs, and the Chartists who also joined found their understanding of continental affairs considerably widened. A similar organisation was later started in Brussels.

The Fraternal Democrats called a meeting in November 1847 to commemorate the Polish insurrection of 1830. It was held in the Drury Lane premises and was addressed by Marx himself, who had come to London with Engels to attend the Congress of the Communist League, and also by Engels and the Chartist leaders, Harney and Jones. The meeting did not only concern itself with the Polish business. In his speech, delivered in German, Marx declared that the Fraternal Democrats in Brussels had instructed him to ask the London organisation to convene a Congress of Nations, "a Congress of working men to establish liberty all over the world. Effect this grand object you workmen of England, and you will be hailed as the saviours of the whole human race."[2]

Immediately after the meeting, and in the same room, the Second Congress of the Communist League took place, to adopt new statutes

[1] There is some doubt whether the original group, which consisted of Schapper, Moll, Bauer and other German communists, was a branch of the League of the Just. It appears that the Paris group of the League also became a branch of The Communist League under the influence of Engels, who represented it at the Congress of 1847.

[2] *Northern Star*, December 4th, 1847.

and to consider an altogether new socialist programme which Marx and Engels had put before them after they joined the League. From these debates, after their second Congress at the end of November 1847, *The Communist Manifesto* was to emerge in 1848.

The year 1847 had been busy for Marx. Not only had he prepared many articles and lectures, but he had read with increasing impatience Proudhon's *Philosophy of Poverty*, and written a forceful reply which contained the clearest and most developed statement of his present position. He and Engels now had at their disposal a journal which appeared twice a week called the *Deutsche-Brüsseler Zeitung*. They were suspicious about the reliabilty of the editor, who might well have been an agent of the Prussian Government, but Marx scoffed at the reluctance of the socialists to make use of the paper. "An opportunity for doing something, is nothing but a source of embarrassment for them," he said. He and Engels had no such qualms and plunged into political controversy, writing a number of vigorously worded articles in the journal. It was the German political situation that was under discussion, and they pursued their usual tactics of supporting the bourgeoisie against reactionary feudalism and the monarchy and scornfully criticised the socialists who wanted to attack only the bourgeoisie, on the grounds that however radical the ultimate aims, the next step was to support the bourgeoisie in their struggle for constitutional rights. But Marx made no secret of his conviction that the rule of the bourgeoisie would be of brief duration and would be followed by the socialist revolution. Addressing the liberals in the issue of the *Deutsche-Brüsseler Zeitung* in January 1848, Engels makes no attempt to conceal his aims: "Fight on bravely, then, gentlemen of capital! We need your help, we even need your rule on occasions. You must clear from our path the relics of the middle ages. . . . Your factories must lay the foundations for the liberation of the proletariat. Your reward shall be a brief time of rule."

Marx also attacked in the same journal a curious form of socialism which emanated from religious quarters and was becoming influential. What it amounted to was the belief that if the ruling class could be persuaded to show Christian benevolence and practise social justice a better world for the poor would appear. Marx replied in the *Deutsche-Brüsseler Zeitung*:

"The social principles of Christianity have had eighteen hundred years in which to develop and they need no further development at the hands of the Prussian Ecclesiastical Commissioners. The social principles of Christianity justified slavery in the classical world and they glorified medieval serfdom, and if necessary they are quite willing to defend the oppression of the proletariat even if they should wear a somewhat crestfallen appearance the while. The social principles of Christianity preach the necessity of a ruling and an oppressed class, and all they have to offer to the latter is the pious wish that the former may be charitable. The social principles of Christianity transfer the reparation of all infamies to the realms of heaven and thus they justify the perpetuation of these infamies on earth. The social principles of Christianity declare that all the villainies of the oppressors against the oppressed are either the just punishment for original or other sin or tribulations which God in his own inscrutable wisdom causes the elect to suffer. The social principles of Christianity preach cowardice, self-abasement, resignation, submission and humility—in short all the characteristics of the *canaille*; but the proletariat is not prepared to let itself be treated as *canaille*, and it needs its courage, confidence, pride and independence even more than it needs its daily bread. The social principles of Christianity are sneaking and hypocritical, whilst the proletariat is revolutionary."

THE POVERTY OF PHILOSOPHY

The revolutionary activity of Marx and his ceaseless practical role in the working-class movement demanded on the one hand the investigation and exposition of his theory of social development, and, on the other, endless polemics directed against rival theories. "To leave error unrefuted," Marx used to say, "is to encourage intellectual immorality." His refutation of the theories of Proudhon is a particularly interesting and important example of a presentation of Marx's ideas which derives its force and clarity from the critical exposure of a position which he regarded as wholly erroneous.

Proudhon was a worker. Coming up from the country to Paris he became a printer and then a proof-reader. Deeply concerned at the misery he saw around him he became acquainted with the socialist ideas which were then fermenting in the capital. In his capacity as a proof-reader he read widely and taught himself several languages. Marx got to hear of him and was at first extremely hopeful of the young and vigorous socialist, as he was then regarded. He tried to teach him philosophy and sat up all night explaining Hegel to him. Self-educated, however, Proudhon never really comprehended half what he read and his outlook never rose above his peasant background.

And he was not really a socialist. He was fundamentally an individualist and an idealist, objecting to injustice and inhumanity, denouncing the rich and proclaiming the brotherhood of man.

Proudhon's first book of any importance was entitled *What is Poverty?* and his answer: "Property is theft", had a revolutionary ring. But although he was opposed to the misuse of property when used to accumulate riches he still believed in it and wanted the peasant and the artisan to possess it. What he objected to was the rich taking the money from them and thus obtaining the power to exploit them.

Marx gave generous praise to this work and recognised the great impetus it gave to the working-class movement, an impetus, which, in fact, undoubtedly affected him also. He regarded it as a pioneer achievement in the economic field and the first scientific manifesto of the modern proletariat.

In 1846 Proudhon expounded his views in two substantial volumes entitled *The System of Economic Contradiction or The Philosophy of Poverty*. Like all his work it is forcefully written and wins attention by its paradoxes and antitheses. These he now advances in a philosophical form, which he claims to be Hegelian. His book swarms with philosophical formulae and such expressions as "thesis", "antithesis", "antinomies", "synthesis", "dialectics", "induction". Proudhon had learned one thing from Hegel—that contradictions are involved in every concept. He saw in the contrast of riches and poverty the basic contradiction of contemporary society. But wherever he looked he found contradiction—property is theft, the division of labour increases wealth but impoverishes the worker, in any system of economic relations there is a contradiction between the good side which affirms equality and the bad side which affirms inequality. How are such contradictions to be overcome? The conflict, said Proudhon, must be resolved in the synthesis of this antagonism between thesis and antithesis which will eliminate the evil side and retain the good. It is the errors and the evils in the system which have to be removed, while the elements which seem just and right must be retained and strengthened. He therefore appeals to the ideals of justice and brotherhood which will inspire the struggle to eliminate the evil side of the contradiction. Then exploitation will cease and capital will no longer be accumulated.

What sort of social order would result? One in which production would be organised by societies of workers who exchanged their goods among one another according to their equivalent in labour. To aid the formation of such co-operatives he advocated the establishment of credit banks which would lend them money without interest. In such a society, concluded Proudhon, government would no longer be necessary. "The highest perfection of society is found in the union of order and anarchy."

Marx was moved to fury when Proudhon submitted his book to him for criticism. He realised that Proudhon's ethical standpoint, his eloquence and sincerity, were likely to win wide support. Yet for ten workers who might be awakened by such a book and find the way to real understanding, ninety might be entirely confused and remain in darkness. This is in fact what happened. For many years the French socialist movement accepted these ideas. Twenty years later, at the Geneva Congress of the International, Marx had the utmost difficulty in defeating the Proudhonists who were advocating a policy of Co-operative Production Associations, no strikes and no revolutionary action, and no support for the Polish Revolution. Later the influence of Proudhon was seen in the emergence of French syndicalism and of anarchism. The syndicalists believed that socialism would be achieved by industrial unions embracing all the workers in a particular industry.

Marx at once recognised the basic individualism in this anarchist tendency and in the whole of Proudhon's programme. Indeed, he saw in his ideas a veritable compendium of basic errors, well calculated to confuse and mislead the workers. Marx had no patience with Proudhon's garbled version of the Hegelian dialectic, the muddled economic theory, the florid, bombastic way of writing. He sat down and immediately wrote a devastating reply in French, so that it might reach those for whom Proudhon had intended it.

In the Preface to his critique Marx declared that Proudhon had been doubly misunderstood. In France they forgave him his bad economics on the strength of his German philosophy. In Germany they thought he was one of the best French economists and therefore overlooked the weakness of his philosophy.

He undertook to correct both errors. His reply was entitled *The Poverty of Philosophy*. It is clear and forceful. The essential arguments are expressed with perfect lucidity and much of Marx's sardonic humour. Written in 1847, two years after his first formulation of what is now known as Marxism, it might well be regarded as the first exposition of his developed theories, giving full weight to the economic understanding which he had spent many months in developing.

Marx detected behind Proudhon's argument the assumption that the basic structure of society, with the categories of property, competition and so forth, is unalterable. Therefore all that we can do is to reconcile the contradictions that arise within it. Marx replied that once we accept this pattern of society its conflicting aspects are an inherent and necessary part of it. The good and evil at any particular stage in historical development originate from the system of social relations belonging to it, and the evil cannot be eliminated without introducing a new social system. But how does the social pattern change?

It is because as the forces of production develop, the classes into which society is divided find themselves more and more opposed. One of these classes, the working class, which in fact represents the "bad" side of capitalism, its exploitation, its poverty, grows unceasingly along with the development of the material conditions for its own emancipation. But simultaneously the inner contradictions are intensified and a period of crisis supervenes.

The consequence is that the very contradictions that Proudhon lamented are the sources of social progress. It is what he called the "bad side" which calls into being the movement which makes for change, in that it brings the struggle between "good" and "bad" to a head. What happens is that the oppressed class which feels the brunt of the growing contradictions finds it necessary to bring into being an entirely new system of social relationships, in which the contradictions recognised by Proudhon have no place. What has gone wrong is that the old system is no longer appropriate to the developed productive forces but obstructs them, throws them into disorder, and disrupts society with crises and wars. Therefore, a pattern of society appropriate to these productive forces must be brought into existence. This will be effected by the class which suffers under the old system taking the initiative in its own interests.

The type of society demanded by the economic situation is in fact a classless one—that is to say, a society in which the private ownership by one class and the wage labour of the other both disappear in the social ownership of the means of production.

The reason why the victory of the proletariat produces a classless society is not that the proletariat are more faithful to utopian ideals than other classes, but because the elimination of classes is the necessary condition of their liberation, of bringing into being an economic system which can satisfy their needs and the removal of the obstacles to security and prosperity which a class society creates and maintains.

"The condition of the liberation of the working class is the abolition of all class."

Marx adds an important word on the relation of his theory of social change to utopian socialism, the importance of which, in the immediately preceding historical period to his own, both he and Engels recognised.

When the productive forces are not sufficiently developed for the conditions necessary for the proletariat's liberation to have arrived, the theories of reformers will necessarily be utopian—taking the form of devising ideal societies. It is only when the conditions of the struggle ripen and the situation becomes clear, that theory ceases to be utopian and becomes scientific, practical and revolutionary.

Proudhon's *Philosophy of Poverty* has fallen into the limbo of forgotten treatises, but Marx in his reply brought together and welded into a unity the ideas which had occurred in the whole sequence of his writing up to that time. Here they are developed systematically and with the convincing clarity which marked his polemical writing. It represented a milestone both in the life of its author and in the history of social science.

WAGE LABOUR AND CAPITAL

It was in Brussels that Marx wrote his important *Theses on Feuerbach*; and at the end of May 1845 Engels' *Condition of the Working Class in England* was published in Leipzig. In the last chapter, Engels had predicted that the next great economic crisis would start in England in 1852 or 1853 (unless delayed by the repeal of the Corn Laws). By the time it arrives, he declared, "the English people will have had enough of being plundered by the capitalists and left to starve when the capitalists no longer require their services. If, up to this time, the English bourgeoisie does not pause to reflect—and to all appearances it certainly will not do so—a revolution will follow with which none hitherto can be compared."

In January of 1848 Marx addressed the Democratic Association on Free Trade and his speech was well received. While defending himself from the charge that he was a protectionist, by pointing out that the German bourgeoisie at the time needed a high tariff wall behind which to develop their industries, and as a weapon against feudalism, he attacked the Free Traders for pretending that they were primarily concerned with the welfare of the workers by providing cheaper commodities. Free Trade favoured the capitalists, and to their benefit it was proposed to pull down the tariff barriers within the expanding area of modern industry; as soon as German industry was strong enough it would need too the world market as well as that of Germany, and would therefore demand free trade. Free trade must, in the long run, aggravate the contradiction between the bourgeoisie and the proletariat and increase international competition. The whole problem was thus examined purely from the revolutionary standpoint.

The German workers in Brussels were well organised, and one of their more important societies was the German Workers' Association with its social evening, library and educational classes. Moses Hess was one of the chairmen of this organisation, which numbered over a hundred. In spite of the immense amount of study and writing which occupied him, Marx was always ready to play an active part in such activities. He was no recluse.

Marx delivered his first series of lectures on economics to the Workers' Educational Society in Brussels. We are told by those who heard them that he showed a surprising gift for popularisation. He made full use of the blackboard and used a method of exposition of his own. He would formulate a proposition as briefly as possible, and then explain it at length, being careful never to use words which his students would not understand. Then he would invite questions and would himself ask them of the class, working over the material until every point was thoroughly grasped.

These lectures were subsequently published in April 1849 in the *Neue Rheinische Zeitung*, and were reprinted and published in London as the pamphlet *Wage-Labour and Capital*, with an Introduction by Engels, in 1891.

In these lectures Marx first set forth his own labour theory of value and the method of capitalist exploitation. The view that value is constituted by the amount of labour used in production had been held by Adam Smith, Sir William Petty, Ricardo and others, and was at that time generally accepted. It was not at all clear, however, how this could lead to any form of exploitation. It was generally agreed that commodities exchanged at their labour value, but if so, how could profit be obtained? Was it that the capitalist added his profit on to the cost of production, its real value? Or was it that the worker was paid far less than the value of his own labour?

Proudhon had made an effort to explain this, which won the warm commendation of Marx, but his explanation was incomplete. The problem was not solved until Marx showed that although the worker receives as wages the value of the labour he gives, he does not receive the value of the product of his labour. How can that be?

It is, argued Marx, because since the value of a commodity is the amount of labour it takes to produce it, the value of labour (or rather, according to Marx's subsequent correction of the terminology, of labour power[1]) is not what it produces, but what it costs to produce the labour, i.e. the subsistence wage of the worker. The cost of keeping the worker is very much less than the value of the commodities which he produces. If you can feed and clothe a worker at 10*s.* a day, that is the value of his labour (power) and that is what he gets for a fair day's wage; but what he produces in the course of the day may be five times that amount. This, explained Marx, is *surplus value*, the source of all profit; and it reveals how the worker is exploited. Labour power, as Engels said, in his Introduction to the 1891 edition, "is quite a peculiar commodity". It is a value-creating source as well as having its own cost of production value. It is the source of more value than it possesses itself.

Bakunin, the Russian anarchist, who had been expelled from Paris along with Marx, was now living in Brussels and was a friend of Marx. His temperament, however, would not allow him to appreciate the kind of theoretical work that Marx was doing. Impatient with scientific theory, Bakunin derided these lectures on economics as a vain activity "spoiling the workers by making logic-choppers out of them". He declared that he could not breathe freely in the company of Marx and Engels. The two men nevertheless had a great regard for one another at this time, although their characters and attitudes were incapable of any real reconciliation.

The Brussels lectures were given towards the end of 1847. *The Communist Manifesto* was published in London, in German, in February 1848. Only a few days later, on February 24th, the bourgeois monarchy of Louis Philippe was overthrown by a revolution. The revolutionary impulse spread rapidly through Europe and was not long in reaching Belgium. The King ordered the arrest of all foreign *émigrés*. Marx and

[1] At this time Marx had not yet evolved the concept of "labour power" as distinct from "labour", and the word he actually used in these lectures was "labour". Later he was to point out that "the value of labour" is a meaningless expression. This distinction is an important one, because it lies at the basis of Marx's theory of surplus value.

In editing the edition published in 1891 Engels corrected the text, and substituted "labour power" for "labour". As he explained in his Introduction, "I therefore tell the reader before hand: this is not the pamphlet as Marx wrote it in 1849, but approximately as he would have written it in 1891. . . . My alterations all turn on one point. According to the original, the worker sells his *labour* to the capitalist for wages; according to the present text he sells his labour *power*."

his family were apprehended, but they were detained for only one night. On March 4th he was expelled from the country. Marx had already been making his preparations to leave for Paris; the Provisional Government having invited him in the following terms:

Paris, March 1st, 1848.

Brave and Faithful Marx,

The soil of the French Republic is a place of refuge for all friends of freedom. Tyranny has banished you; France, the free, opens to you her gates—to you and to all who fight for the Holy cause, the fraternal cause of every people. In this sense every officer of the French Government understands his duty. *Salut et Fraternité.*

FERDINAND FLOCON
Member of the Provisional Government.

Flocon, Louis Blanc and Ledru-Rollin were the leaders of the Democratic Socialist Party in France—Flocon edited *Réforme*, the organ of the party. It was in fact the speeches of Ledru-Rollin and Louis Blanc that heralded the revolution, and all three entered the Government.[1]

When Marx arrived in Paris he set to work immediately to establish a new headquarters for the Communist League.

With Engels, he elaborated the political platform of the League in relation to the German revolution which broke out on March 18th, but he showed his good sense in strongly opposing the organisation of a revolutionary contingent which would march into Germany and join the uprising there—an enterprise which nevertheless was carried out but ended in ignominious failure.

By April events in Germany had moved so fast that Marx and Engels left Paris for Cologne to take their own part in the struggle.

[1] How speedily their influence was overborne by the bourgeoisie is apparent from the fact that by August 1849 Marx was again expelled from Paris and emigrated to London.

9

THE COMMUNIST MANIFESTO

In *The Poverty of Philosophy* Marx set forth with admirable clarity his whole analysis and programme. What was now needed was its forthright expression in a form which would bring the working class to a consciousness of its historic mission, something trenchant, illuminating, imaginative and yet strongly scientific in its basic theory. This Marx effected in *The Communist Manifesto*.

When Marx returned to Brussels from London in December 1847, after attending the Convention of the Communist League, it was with explicit instructions to prepare a booklet or pamphlet setting forth the socialist principles of which he had at last convinced them. Marx and Engels had been planning something of the sort for some time and a draft document by Moses Hess had been discussed by the Communist League in Paris in October 1847. Engels' severe criticism led to its withdrawal and he was commissioned to draft a new one with the idea of sending it to London. This he terms a "confession of faith"; it consisted of a series of questions and answers in the form of a catechism. Marx received a copy and was no doubt considering it while preparing his own document preparatory to going to London early in December.

Engels wrote to him from Paris on November 24th, suggesting that the catechism form should be abandoned and the thing be called "The Communist Manifesto", and that "more or less of it will consist in historical narrative". He brought his new draft with him when he joined Marx in London.[1]

The London debates were vigorous and lasted for several days, and it cost Marx some labour to convince the delegates of the correctness of the new programme. But Marx went back to London commissioned to prepare the *Manifesto* and no doubt consulted Engels' draft when he came to write it. But the finished work bears in every line the stamp of Marx himself. Engels himself notes this in his own

[1] This was edited by Edward Bernstein and published by *Vorwärts* in Berlin in 1914 under the title *Gründsatze des Kommunismus.*

excellent summary of the theme: "The basic ideas of the *Manifesto*: that in every historical epoch the prevailing mode of production and the social organisation necessarily following from it, form the basis upon which is built the political and intellectual history of that epoch; that consequently at the different stages of social development (since the dissolution of the primitive community of property in the soil) the history of mankind has been a history of class struggles, the struggle between the exploited and the exploiters, oppressed and ruling classes; that this struggle has however reached a stage where the exploited and oppressed class—the proletariat—cannot attain its emancipation from the exploiting and oppressing class without, at the same time, and for all time, emancipating society as a whole from all exploitation, oppression and class struggles—these fundamental ideas belong entirely and solely to Marx."

Marx wrote it and revised it with his usual meticulous care—we have one page from the first draft which shows how painstakingly he laboured over each phrase. The Central Committee in London wrote a peremptory letter on January 26th, 1848, declaring that if the *Manifesto* which Citizen Marx had promised to draw up had not arrived by February 1st, "further measures will be taken against him". The letter is signed by Schapper, Bauer and Moll.

The *Manifesto* was finished only a few days before the Revolution in Paris on February 24th, 1848, and was published in London in German. It did not reach Germany, however, before May or June, and it first appeared in English in a journal known as *The Red Republican*, in 1850. By the end of the century it had been published in all the important European languages; since then there can hardly be a written language in which it has not appeared. Engels wrote a special Preface with Marx for the German edition of 1872, and after the death of Marx the Preface for the revised and authorised edition of 1888 translated by Samuel Moore, the translator of the greater part of *Capital*.

Both the style and the content of the document are unique. It is a work of genius and, with the possible exception of Rousseau's *Social Contract*, there is nothing comparable with it in eloquence and power, in dramatic force, and ruthless argumentation. Marx could irradiate theoretical matter with the lightning of his own energy, and with a vivid imagery in which blood, spectres, storms and cataclysms occur again and again.

In the *Manifesto* we have a sense of bold, arresting historical generalisation, moving phase by phase to demonstrate the destruction of the present class society by the forces, economic and human, which the system itself has brought into being. "What the bourgeoisie produces, above all, are its own gravediggers." Strong emotion and extraordinary intellectual power are united in it. Years of study of one of the boldest and most fertile minds are here welded together in the glowing heat of an intensely perceived understanding of the whole course of human history and its present outcome.

It is almost impossible to summarise the *Manifesto* without destroying the sweep and eloquence of its argument. Its mere forty pages are already a compact and lucid condensation of a vast mass of material. And yet it is essential to indicate the nature of its theme. Today no other comprehensive and ordered system of socialist thought exists;[1] all earlier brands of socialism have disappeared, while Marxism is a world-wide movement, more numerous and more powerful than any form of socialism has ever been.

The first section, entitled *Bourgeois and Proletarians*, is the core of the *Manifesto*. It describes how capitalism came into being through the breaking of the crippling bonds of feudal society, and, having established the bourgeoisie as the ruling class, developed the productivity of human labour to previously undreamt-of heights. The achievements of capitalism are set forth in glowing terms. "It has created more powerful and more gigantic forces of production than all past generations put together", and at the same time it has changed the whole structure of society to bring into existence a social system of capitalist property, wage labour and economic law, which the new industrialism demands for its efficient working.

So much for its positive achievements. There is a negative side to this: capitalism for all its accomplishments, has not done away with poverty. It has brought about uncontrollable anarchical economic conditions disturbed by periodical crises and flawed by areas of extreme poverty. Nor has it done away with exploitation. It has merely substituted a new form which disguises its nature as a system of wage labour, in which the worker is "free" to accept or reject the remuneration offered him.

But even more serious is the fact that when capitalism had developed

[1] Continental socialism today hardly goes beyond a moderate degree of national ownership and such measures of economic control of a mixed economy as will preserve and improve the welfare state. Hugh Gaitskell declared that the central idea of British socialism was "the brotherhood of man. It is this rather than public ownership which surely inspires all our aims in social and economic policies alike."

to a certain stage it revealed a more and more glaring contradiction between the enormous powers of production which it had created and the narrow consuming base provided by the exploited and impoverished proletariat. It is this contradiction which is in the last resort the cause of economic crises.

Thus capitalism engenders of itself and in itself the constant and increasing rebellion of its productive forces against the conditions of production, and as it struggles to overcome these difficulties it only succeeds in augmenting the intrinsic conditions of its inevitable death. Whatever the concessions in the direction of higher wages or better conditions that are forced out of it, it always remains true that the necessity for profitability if industry is to continue, upon which the whole present order rests, imposes limits beyond which capitalism has no more reason for existence.

The *Manifesto* did not confront the evils of capitalism with the brighter picture of an alternative and ideal system; it explained how our present society will eventually dissolve by the progressive dynamics of its own forces. Having reached the stage at which the system can produce more goods than it can profitably distribute, the hampered forces of production press upon the limits imposed upon them by private ownership. The system has clearly become obsolete. Society now demands reorganisation. Capitalism has created possibilities and awakened hopes which can only be fulfilled by transcending it.

MARXISM AND HISTORY

Marx sets the contemporary situation against the background of historical development which reveals the significance of the capitalist dilemma.

We are shown the course of history as a continuous process of social development through successive forms of production—technological and social—and through successive forms of class domination. Each transformation marks the rise of a new pattern of economic life, more productive and controlled by a new social group linked with the new productive forces and the new system of human relationships. Thus the dominant class in feudal times corresponds to the simple-method of guild and individual craft production, and the corresponding way in which men were associated in their work. Quite different is the new class of industrialists with machine industry, and the employment of wage-earners who no longer own their means of production but work for the factory owners.

Marx then shows how each transition involves a struggle between the old ruling class and a new class, determined to reorganise society in forms appropriate to new methods of production. Thus change becomes urgently necessary because the older forms now constitute a fetter on the productive forces, nor will such forms give way. They resist modification because they are artificially preserved beyond the point where they are economically useful by the ruling class whose interest they represent. If the transition to a more advanced stage of social organisation were left to the capitalist class it would never be carried into effect, because it is contrary to their interests, their rights and indeed their very existence.

But capitalism has itself brought into being the class whose historic mission it is to effect the transition to socialism. The proletariat is the special and indispensable creation of capitalism: as capital expands so must the proletariat. Moreover, the proletariat's condition of life is such as to force it to organise to fight for its own interests. Marx sees the proletariat not as an excrescence, an evil which can and must be eliminated from capitalist society. It is its essential condition, its inevitable product, the cause which preserves and maintains society itself.

It is the proletariat alone which can realise that there is no way out of the difficulties of capitalism within the framework of that form of society. "Society can no longer live under this bourgeoisie, in other words, capitalism's existence is no longer compatible with society." The change, therefore, will be introduced by the class whose interests are imperilled by capitalism's continued existence and are identified with the further expansion of the forces of production, only possible under social ownership and planned production for use and not for profit.

"The advance of industry, whose involuntary promoter is the bourgeoisie, replaces the isolation of the labourers, due to competition, by their revolutionary combination, due to association. The development of modern industry, therefore, cuts from under its feet the very foundation on which the bourgeoisie produces and appropriates products. What the bourgeoisie therefore produces above all, are its own grave-diggers. Its fall and the victory of the proletariat are equally inevitable."

SOCIAL STRUGGLE AND IDEOLOGY

It would be a complete mistake to imagine that this transition is automatic and that all that is asked of man is to acquiesce in the inevitable.

The pressure of exploitation compels the workers to organise, but this, while an important and necessary step, is not enough. Marx emphasises the role of communists in giving understanding and leadership to the working class. But this requires the rejection of the ideas, economics, legal codes and moral principles of the bourgeoisie. "Your very ideas are but the outgrowth of the conditions of your bourgeois production and bourgeois property, just as your jurisprudence is but the will of your class made into a law for all, a will, whose essential character and direction are determined by the economical conditions of existence of your class.

"Does it require deep intuition to comprehend that man's ideas, views, and conceptions, in one word, man's consciousness, changes with every change in the conditions of his material existence, in his social relations and in his social life?

"What else does the history of ideas prove, than that intellectual production changes its character in proportion as material production is changed? The ruling ideas of each age have ever been the ideas of its ruling class.

"Law, morality, religion, are so many bourgeois prejudices behind which lurk in ambush just as many bourgeois interests."

These must be replaced with ideas, principles, economic theories which reflect the real situation and its changing structure. But it must be recognised that "the theoretical conclusions of the Communists are in no way based on ideas or principles that have been invented, or discovered, by this or that would-be universal reformer.

"They merely express, in general terms, actual relations springing from an existing class struggle, from a historical movement going on under our very eyes."

In *The German Ideology* Marx had enunciated the principle that "it is not the consciousness of men that determines their existence, but, on the contrary, their social existence determines their consciousness". This is not a statement either of determinism or of crass materialism. It states simply that since man lives in a given historical and social situation, his thinking too must be within that social framework, and the shape of his thought on political and economic matters will be derived from, and will correspond to, the shape of the society within which the thinking is done.

Social conditions, however, far from confining thought within the limited categories of the time, will compel men to frame questions and to confront the problems arising under these conditions, and from this thinking will arise new ideas, new projects, so that thinking becomes a powerful and indispensable force in the shaping of economic conditions. Marx's point is not that thought is impotent in the shaping of man's destiny, but that it is neither arbitrary nor capricious in its working only when it concentrates on the concrete situation, seeking an answer to questions set by the conditions of contemporary society. It then becomes effective, as thought never can be if it merely contemplates abstract ideals and principles in the fashion of idealist philosophers.

As Marx puts it, "The mode of production in material life determines the general character of the social, political and spiritual processes of life."[1] Marx thus distinguishes between the actual transformation of one economic system into another and "the legal, political, religious, aesthetic or philosophic—in short, ideological forms in which men become conscious of this conflict and fight it out".[2] It is thus clear that Marx does not for a moment say that the only ideological forces in the social struggle are motives of self-interest. The terms in which men fight out the class war may be idealistic or religious. Every ruling class regards the moral precepts which safeguard its interests as absolute. Men will always attribute universal values to their particular class ends, persuading themselves and others that it is the good of society as a whole for which they are concerned. They identify the social order which they have created with the principle of order itself and regard the threat of a competing order as synonymous with the peril of chaos.

So long as the social relations do not change, the psychology of society does not change either. People get accustomed to the prevailing beliefs, concepts, modes of thought and means of satisfying their aesthetic requirements. But when the development of the productive force reaches the point of requiring a substantial change in the economic structure of society, and in consequence in the reciprocal relations of the social classes, the psychology of these classes will also change.

When the social system is a form of development of the productive forces, this, so to speak, is the best time of its life, just because in the heyday of the system it was so suited to these forces that it stimulated their advance. It grows strong, develops and reaches its height. Everyone regards it as natural, obvious, right, even as sacred. But when the productive forces demand a new social form, decline sets in, old age

[1] Preface to *Critique of Political Economy*. [2] *ibid.*

comes on. People begin to notice that not everything about this system is as splendid as once they thought. They begin to struggle against it; now it seems unnatural, not sacred, but evil, and finally they destroy it.[1]

This profound psychological change is manifested in the appearance of new political ideas, new philosophical concepts, new religious or anti-religious beliefs, and new trends in art.

Ideas may therefore serve the purpose of maintaining a system of class exploitation and resisting its supersession. But at the same time society will give rise to ideas of an opposite character, representing the interests of a rising class working for progress. The social conflict will thus be expressed in a battle of ideas, which may take the form of religious controversy, as in the time of the Reformation, or of war over constitutional principles versus monarchical principles.

No resistance to power is possible while the sanctioning lies which justify that power are accepted as valid. While that first and chief line of defence is unbroken there can be no revolt. Before any injustice or oppression can be resisted, the lie upon which it is founded must be unmasked, must be clearly recognised for what it is.

Acting as the theoreticians of the working class, communists identify themselves with the existing working-class movement and do not form a sect of their own. Nor is it their role merely to present socialism as a more just and humane form of society, but to demonstrate that it is the next step in the historical development of the human race. It is not to be advocated as though it were the natural and necessary state of human life in all times and in all places. On the contrary, it appears on the agenda of history only after the development of capitalism. It is the consequence of the dissolution of that form of society.

The theoretical basis of socialism must be on the one hand a theory of history and on the other a diagnosis of the maladies of the existing social order and a prognosis of their inevitable outcome. As a theory of history, Marxism not only shows the succession of social forms, but the relation of each form to a particular stage in the development of technology and therefore to a particular stage of economic organisation. In effecting the transition from one system to its successor, class struggle plays its necessary role because the advanced system represents the interests of a new class arising in new patterns of social and economic organisation brought into existence by the developing form

[1] Plekhanov, *The Materialist Conception of History*.

of production. Its conflict with the classes representing the once efficient but now obsolete economic system leads after victory to the reconstruction of society on a new model. Hence, Marx describes "the history of all hitherto existing society" as "the history of class struggle".

The present stage is, however, different from all preceding levels in two particulars. In the first place the proletariat cannot emancipate themselves without emancipating society as a whole, since only common ownership solves the economic problems confronting them. Secondly, in this transition we pass from blind advance to conscious progress. The coming of socialism demands the clear understanding of the situation and of its requirements, it demands political consciousness, intelligence, will and organisation.

THE SIGNIFICANCE OF THE "MANIFESTO" TODAY

The importance of the *Manifesto* lies in the value of its analysis of the process of social development, especially its emphasis on class struggle in that development. Beyond that it evaluates the role of class forces, the importance of their ideologies, their rise and fall, their opportunities and destiny.

Written over a hundred years ago by a man of thirty, deeply involved in the political struggles of the German nation, it expresses his anticipation as to their outcome, which was not fulfilled. He believed, in 1848, that Germany was on the eve of a bourgeois revolution that would be immediately followed by a proletarian revolution. Social development has proceeded less quickly than Marx anticipated. The revolution did not arrive until thirty-five years after his death—but it did come. In this anticipation, therefore, he was mistaken, as he speedily came to recognise after the defeats of 1849. His estimate of the close relation under certain conditions of the bourgeois and socialist revolutions is an important question of tactics and was deeply considered and reconsidered by Marx throughout his life. It is, however, independent of the basic theories of the *Manifesto*.

His evaluation of class forces, his proposals for immediate programmes of reform and similar questions are also dependent on the situation as Marx found it in 1848 and in his own lifetime, and it received after his death the inevitable recasting and reformulation demanded by the development of the labour movement, of capitalism and of the international situation. If Marxism were the inflexible dogma it is sometimes thought to be, this would not be the case; but neither would Marxism be the political force it is today.

These estimations and policies must necessarily be made again in every generation, just as in war, strategy and tactics have constantly to be adapted to the developing military situation, even though the overall plan and objectives remain.

Like all far-reaching theories, Marxism sees its subject matter from a new angle, it picks up the other end of the stick. It starts enquiry off along a new path, but it is not a finished system. Consider Galileo, Darwin, Dalton, Lavoisier—much of their work is outdated: they made serious errors, but they revolutionised human thinking, and ever since their day we see the world differently, we think in new terms. In every case, too, these pioneers of science break a deadlock in human thought, so that it leaps forward—and the very fact that it receives this impetus makes it inevitable that the position reached by them will be superseded.

Marx thought capitalism nearer its end than it actually was: nor was the working class sufficiently organised at that time for the task allotted to it. Marx himself pointed out later how narrow had been the field occupied by the working-class movement of 1848; though he had believed at the time that the German revolution would pass on to the struggle for socialism because the proletariat was more developed than in the French Revolution of 1789. In this he was mistaken.

In the Preface to the German edition of 1872 Marx points out that "the practical application of the principles will depend, as the *Manifesto* itself states, everywhere and at all times, on the historical conditions for the time being existing". But he remarks confidently that "however much the state of things may have altered during the last twenty-five years, the general principles laid down in this Manifesto are, on the whole, as current today as ever".

Any suggestion that Marx predicted this or that, either in the sense that a prophet or an astrologer foretells events, or in the sense that a physicist or an astronomer makes a prediction based on mathematical calculations, is beside the point. As we shall see later, granted the unconscious operation of the process of capitalism, which capitalism itself claims to operate automatically, certain consequences will follow, though Marx always stated that their operation could be modified by trade union and political pressure; but Marx never extended the realm of mechanical necessity to include the organisation, courage and will of the working class, and even in the *Manifesto* he speaks of a struggle which can end "either in a revolutionary reconstruction of society, or in the common ruin of the contending classes".

Accurate prediction in the astronomical sense or as the physicist employs it is out of the question, because the field is completely different from that of physics or astronomy. The social sciences not only contain too many independent variables to allow for this kind of accuracy, but the observer is not endeavouring to foretell the effect of the forces independent of himself whose development and interaction he is estimating; he is himself preparing to intervene and to persuade others to intervene, and his decision to do so cannot therefore depend on what he expects to happen independently of that intervention. It is the same in medicine. Prognosis does not merely envisage the course of the disease, assuming that nothing will be done about it. What happens depends on treatment, on the sensible behaviour of the patient, on environmental and climatic conditions as time goes on.

But this does not mean that in medicine and the social sciences scientific understanding is impossible and useless. Intelligent foresight and scientific understanding make reasonable action possible and success probable. But cast-iron tactics are fatal. Plans must be modified on the basis of experience as we venture forward. Theory itself is profoundly modified by practice in every branch of science, none more so than in the social sciences. Marxism is thus a theory which is continually being recast, even though its basic principles remain the driving force behind it.

What then can be said about the relevancy of the *Manifesto* a hundred years and more since its publication?

Schumpeter[1] has described it as "one of the greatest individual achievements of sociology to this day". It remains the most successful attempt hitherto to account for the historic process by the means at the command of empirical science.

Marx fuses economic history and economics. He was the first economist to see and to teach systematically how economic theory may be turned into historic analysis and how the historical narrative may be turned into rational history.

He shows how the forms of production determine the social structure and, through the social structure, all manifestations of civilisation and the whole march of cultural and political history.

His theory of classes, by linking his economic interpretation of history with the concepts of the profit economy, unites the fate of

[1] Joseph A. Schumpeter, *Capitalism, Socialism and Democracy*.

class phenomena with the fate of capitalism, so that socialism is seen to be the only form of a modern classless society.

Marx also sees the modes of production as having a logic of their own; that is to say, they change according to the necessities inherent in them to produce their successors.

He further sees the close relation of all forms of human thought and social organisation to the basic economic pattern. The forms and conditions of production are the fundamental determinants of social structures which in turn produce attitudes, actions and civilisations. It is our location within the productive process which determines our outlook. We think and choose from standpoints, views and propensities which so far from being independent are moulded by the objective data of the environment.

Finally, Marx goes beyond the task of finding answers to historical and economic questions. He teaches humanity the inner meaning of its struggles. Politics ceases to be mere politics, dependent on either propaganda or the disinterested consideration of alternative sets of purely political principles. Politics is itself determined by the structure and movement of the economic process. Marx finds his interpretation in terms of class struggle, of exploitation; of day-to-day changes in capitalism, so that those who understand no longer feel out of it in the great affairs of life—all at once they see through the puppet figures of politics and industry, who never know what it is all about. Marxism thus brings new light and a new meaning to life to those who understand its interpretation of the modern world.

10

THE YEAR OF REVOLUTIONS

In the year 1848 there were revolutions or threatened revolutions in every country in Europe. Together with his ally, the Emperor Nicholas of Russia, the Austrian Chancellor Metternich, the leading figure in European reaction since the Congress of Vienna, and the real enemy of all that was new and progressive throughout the first half of the century—was congratulating himself that the uprisings of 1820 and 1830 had been effectively dealt with and that order and authority were everywhere in the saddle. But social and political unrest was seething below ground and the economic crisis of 1847 released these revolutionary forces. It was a year of barricades and class struggle. Everywhere the people rose against the absolute sovereigns.

In Germany, Austria and Italy the movement against absolutism was especially active. The universities were seats of vigorous propaganda. Innumerable protesting movements of every kind—nationalist, liberal and socialist—were creating a revolutionary situation.

Discontent with the rule of the citizen king, Louis Philippe, had been growing in France. A vigorous Republican, lower-middle-class opposition to a government of vested interests came into being. The corruption of high dignitaries, the wide diffusion of socialist ideas, and finally the commercial crisis of 1847, all helped to bring the monarchy into discredit. When, in February 1848, a powerful agitation for franchise reform developed into a revolution, Louis Philippe fled from France. The purpose of the revolution was to complete the bourgeois transformation of the country, to replace the monarchy by the republic and to extend political power to wider sections of the bourgeoisie. In effect it gave a powerful impulse to the bourgeois transformation of Europe. What was remarkable about the February revolution in Paris was the decisive role of the workers. Although the workers did not know how to exploit the victory, they did demand fundamental changes in the conditions of labour; and in face of grave unemployment they called for the proclamation of the right to work. Louis Blanc, a utopian socialist, was included in the provisional government and given the task of establishing national workshops. Within two months 66,000 men were receiving funds and more unemployed were continuously pouring into the city. Lamartine, poet, orator and historian, a republican but not a socialist, was at the head of the government.

These events fanned the fire of revolution smouldering in Vienna into a blaze—a blaze fed by national feelings, economic distress and the clamours of the peasant communities for the end of feudal tyranny.

In the patchwork of nationalities which formed the ramshackle empire of Austria, the spirit of nationalism was particularly strong. The Empire was an extraordinary amalgam of different nations, all despotically governed, under the overall supremacy of the Emperor.

The government relied for support upon two classes; on the one hand, the feudal landlords; on the other, the more important industrialists and bankers. The former could not but support a power that was their only protection against their downtrodden serfs. The large capitalists depended on the government for the vast share they had in the public funds. In addition, Metternich had the Army and bureaucracy at his disposal. Beyond the frontiers of Austria itself his policy was to play off each nationality against its rivals, but to keep each separate dependent nation subordinate to its own rulers, so that the failure of one of them should not imperil the most artificial of them all, Austria itself. Two issues confronted the government; the semi-feudal condition of the peasantry and the demand for independence of the Hungarians, Slavs, Poles and Czechs. All these people loathed each other and Metternich. He himself described their misery: the gaunt peasants working in the fields in nothing but their shirts, the naked, starving children. Not only were the peasantry ready for revolt but industry was expanding and was also coming into collision with the old feudal institutions.

The uprising began in Vienna where students and radical bourgeoisie led the street fighting, strongly supported by workers from the industrial outskirts of the city. Europe was astounded when in March 1848 Metternich himself, the symbol of repression, was driven into exile. On March 1st the Emperor Franz Joseph II issued an edict promising a National Guard, a parliament and freedom of the press.

"It is the fate of all revolutions," said Marx, "that this union of different classes, which in some degree is always the necessary condition of any revolution, cannot subsist long. No sooner is the victory gained than the victors become divided among themselves into different camps." This was very soon to happen in Vienna. The bourgeoisie and petty tradesmen were at first supreme, since they constituted the members of the National Guard. But the workers had some arms, and the students, about 4,000 strong, constituted a well-armed and disciplined Academic Legion—the real nucleus of the revolution, The upper bourgeoisie, once their own demands were attained, had no desire for the revolution to go any farther. However, when they moved in the direction of compromise more fighting broke out, as was the case on May 15th and again on May 26th. At last the Emperor fled to Innsbruck and the revolution was considerably strengthened.

The peasants who had supported the revolution up to this point gave it no further support, for their own liberation from feudal shackles was granted. They were the real gainers of the revolution and their substantial advantages were never lost.

As this wave of national feeling spread, the Empire was threatened with dissolution. Nationalism meant not integration as it did in Germany, but disintegration—the demand for separation and independence by the various nationalities which constituted the Empire. Hungary declared its independence and organised a republic under Kossuth. Bohemia was in revolt, and General Windischgratz proceeded to Prague to deal with it. To the south the flames of revolt reached Italy and Papal Rome.

Germany presented quite a different problem. She was not at that time united, but was a loose federation of 296 territorial and ecclesiastical principalities and fifty-one free cities. She had no constitution, no national army, no central government, and no political liberty. Prussia, the largest and most powerful of the German states, was ruled by Frederick William IV. There was therefore a powerful movement for unification, which at the same time demanded constitutional government. Following the February revolution in Paris, events moved quickly all over Germany. The upper bourgeoisie (the rising class of industrialists and financiers), supported by the lower bourgeoisie of small shopkeepers and the workers, rose against the absolute rule of their kings and princes. Thrones tottered in the small states as well as in the central areas: autocratic governments in Baden, Bavaria, Württemberg, Brunswick, Saxony, Thuringia, Hanover were all overthrown.

When the news of the Austrian events reached Berlin, the capital of Prussia, the situation there was already tense. The king had dismissed the parliament which had refused him a loan and demanded a constitution. It was a time of much unemployment and poverty. Huge open-air meetings were held, in which the claims of the middle classes were joined to workers' demands for social reform. After the news of the downfall of Metternich, the King appeared to give way, sent away the troops and paraded around the city in the colours of the revolution, making liberal speeches. He even granted the constitutional reforms he had previously refused.

But when the Prussian bourgeoisie "saw at the head of the government in Paris men whom they considered as the most dangerous enemies of property, order, religion, family and of the other Penates of the modern bourgeois, they at once experienced a considerable cooling down of their own revolutionary ardour. They knew that the moment must be seized, and that without the aid of the working masses they would be defeated; and yet their courage failed them."[1] After the first concessions they were prepared to consider the revolution as completed.

Not so the workers, who broke into violent protests. A great demonstration outside the palace was broken up by the military. Fighting raged for many hours and nearly 200 people were killed and many more wounded. The King was shaken. Parliament was recalled and a Constitutional Assembly convened, which was instructed to draw up a constitution in agreement with the Crown. The revolutionary action of the masses had thrust the Prussian bourgeoisie into power. "The working class, which it had been the tendency of the bourgeoisie to keep in the background, had been pushed forward, had fought and conquered, and all at once were conscious of their strength."[2]

Marx, after his expulsion from Brussels, had been cordially invited to Paris by the revolutionary government, which contained such socialist members as Louis Blanc and Flocon.

As soon as he arrived in Paris, Marx at once set about reorganising the Communist League for action. Leading members from London and Brussels arrived, including Bauer, Moll and Schapper. Paris was full of Germans and there was a wildcat scheme for organising a revolutionary contingent and marching into Germany, which Marx strongly opposed. Instead, he organised the return to Germany of as many revolutionaries as possible, travelling singly. As a result, the majority of the members of the Communist League succeeded in getting back, and wherever they turned up they made their influence felt in no uncertain manner.

[1] Engels, *Revolution and Counter-revolution*. [2] *ibid.*

In Germany the democratic forces, now in power in many states, demanded a constitutional government for the whole of Germany. The first step was the election of a Constituent Assembly, which met at Frankfurt in May 1848 to form a government and a constitution. Early in 1849 the crown of a new German Empire was offered by the Assembly to Frederick William of Prussia. It was, however, refused.

Marx and Engels saw that the time had come for them to return to Germany and play their parts in these revolutionary struggles. They proceeded, with their communist friends, to the Rhineland, the most industrialised and progressive part of Germany. The Rhineland coke ovens had just been installed, the first railways constructed, the customs barriers had been removed and already the workers and the new bourgeoisie were sweeping aside the old ruling class. The workers, in fact, were the most active section, and put forward their own demands. It was here that the liberals had started the *Rheinische Zeitung* which Marx had edited from October 1842 to March 1843. Now he again determined to make Cologne, where a powerful democratic movement had come into being, the centre of his activity. On June 1st, 1848, the *Neue Rheinische Zeitung* first appeared as "The Organ of Democracy".

Marx found two quite different organisations in Cologne. There was the District Committee of Democratic Societies, which was very broadly based and had the support of the liberal bourgeoisie; but there was also a vigorous working-class organisation called The Working-men's Union of Cologne, which had been organised by a physician called Gotschalk, an enthusiastic revolutionary, and by Willich, an ex-officer. This body had brought off something like a popular insurrection in Cologne, and consisted of some 7,000 members.

Marx and Engels threw their whole weight behind the Democratic Committee, because their considered view, based on long consideration of the problem, was that this was not and could not be a socialist revolution. The next advance in Germany must be the defeat of political autocracy and the formation of a constitution, and this could only mean the advance of the bourgeoisie to power. Marx therefore deliberately restrained the socialists from pressing their advanced views and rallied them behind the more moderate liberals. "It was not," said Marx in the first number of the *Neue Rheinische Zeitung*, "a question of fulfilling this or that political idea or of holding this or that opinion, but of grasping the general trend of development." What matters is "the immediately possible practical steps".

But he hoped that success would at once give them the opportunity —having defeated the common enemy, the monarchy and its supporters—of pushing straight on towards socialism in a further struggle with the bourgeoisie. While fighting for these immediate aims they would, of course, have their own aims and their own organisation ready to engage in the inevitable struggle with the bourgeoisie after defeating the common enemy. This victory, he believed, would give them a new form of the state in which the basic "contradictions of society could collide in open struggle and thus attain a solution".[1]

It was clear, however, that in Berlin the Prussian bourgeoisie would not break with the monarchy, and they refused to take the lead in the struggle for an all-German constitution. But in the south, the States took the initiative in convoking the Constituent Assembly in Frankfurt. All the leading liberals of Germany were there and endless discussions proceeded on the drawing up of a constitution. Between March 1848 and April 1849 these debates continued, while Austria was reorganising her armies and the forces of reaction were gathering for a final settlement with the constitutionalists.

Marx and Engels sharply and continuously criticised the activities of the Assembly. During all these months his editorship of the *Neue Rheinsche Zeitung* showed him to be a brilliant publicist and a skilful tactician. "Every one of his articles," declared Engels, "struck like a shell and burst."[2] But in spite of all his efforts, no decisive action came from Frankfurt. Even when troops began to move upon them they made not the slightest attempt to call to their aid an armed people.

Outside the Assembly there was a different spirit. The Democratic Party held demonstrations in favour of the Constitution and these became more turbulent and insistent in their demands. "The mass of the working people, led by the men of the most extreme party, were ready to take up arms in a cause which, if it was not their own, at least gave them a chance of somewhat approaching their aims by clearing Germany of its old monarchical encumbrances."[3] But the Democrats became alarmed at their own demonstrations and began to take desperate measures to suppress the very insurrectionary movement they were preparing.

[1] Engels, *loc. cit.*

[2] Lenin said that the paper was an "unsurpassed model of what an organ of the revolutionary proletariat ought to be".

[3] Engels, *loc. cit.*

In their subsequent review of these events and the formulation of the political lessons to be learned from them, Marx and Engels had much to say on "insurrection as an art". It was, they said, subject to certain rules: "Firstly, never play with insurrection unless you are prepared to face the consequences. Secondly, the insurrectionary career once entered upon, act with the greatest determination, and on the offensive. The defensive is the death of every armed rising, it is lost before it measures itself with its enemies. Surprise your antagonists while their forces are scattering, prepare new successes, however small, but daily; keep up the moral ascendancy which the first successful rising has given you.

"This the revolutionaries of 1849 signally failed to do. They went on talking, protesting, proclaiming, pronouncing, but never had the courage or the sense to act, while the hostile troops of the government drew nearer and nearer."[1]

The other critical centre of the German revolution was Berlin. In Berlin, parliament confronted a king who was clearly going to take the first opportunity of regaining the authority he had lost. Here the same deadly fear of victory that overcame the Frankfurt Assembly paralysed the parliament. The bourgeoisie was more alarmed by its proletarian allies than by the autocracy, and made its main aim to create a basis for its own dominance by compromising with the old feudal and police state. The *Neue Rheinische Zeitung* declared that such a policy could not be brought to a successful issue. "In this ambiguous and contradictory task it sees itself and its aim, the founding of bourgeois dominance, outwitted at every turn by the reaction in the absolute and feudal interests—and it will be the loser. The bourgeoisie can not establish its own dominance without winning the whole people as its temporary ally and without taking up a more or less democratic attitude."

Marx had up to this time been careful to lay the emphasis on the leadership and primary responsibility of the progressive bourgeoisie. He says little about the activities of the German workers and avoids socialist propaganda. But in April 1849, when the bourgeois wing of the progressive forces began to waver and collapse appeared imminent, Marx and his supporters resigned from the democratic Committee and turned to Gotschalk's Working-men's Union, with the intention of organising a congress to meet in June in Leipzig.

We have a vivid picture of Marx at this time given by a nineteen-

[1] *ibid.*

year-old student, Karl Schurz. "Marx was thirty years old at this time and already the acknowledged leader of a socialist school of thought. The thick-set man with his broad forehead and dark flashing eyes, his jet-black hair and full beard, immediately attracted general attention, He had the reputation of being a very considerable scholar in his own field and, in fact, what he said was weighty, logical and clear." A few years later an Army officer said of him that he was "the first and only one amongst us to whom I would ascribe the quality of leadership, the capacity to master a big situation without losing himself in insignificant details".

An American correspondent of the *New York Tribune*, who was in Cologne together with its publisher, Charles Dana, also met Marx at this time. "His features," he says, "indicated great energy and behind his moderation and reserve one could detect the passionate fire of a daring spirit." That was a correct estimate of his cool but decisive leadership of the Cologne democracy.

Meanwhile, outside Germany reaction was triumphing. The Austrian monarchy, having recovered from its first shock and gained a breathing space by compromising with the liberal bourgeoisie, began to exploit national differences to strengthen its own position. The popular rising in Prague was suppressed when Windischgratz bombarded the city on June 16th. And now the Slav national groups, industrially and politically backward, began to desert the revolution and move over to the reaction. Vienna, the centre of revolutionary radicalism, lost support everywhere. Even the peasantry, having achieved their aims, returned to their villages, leaving Vienna in the lurch.

The Hungarian revolt was led by the brilliant young Kossuth, who in his speech in the diet at Pressburg on March 2nd declared war on the Austrian tyranny. "From the charnel house of the Vienna cabinet a pestilential air breathes upon us, which dulls our nerves and paralyses the flight of our spirit." Hungary was liberated, to become the centre of freedom for all races under the Austrian crown. Unfortunately, an astute move by General Jellacic drew Croatia, the Slav enclave in Hungary itself, back to Austrian influence on the pretext of supporting its own independence, and on September 16th he invaded Hungary.

In Vienna for several months the radical bourgeoisie, the students, who played an important role, the workers and the National Guard were continually in the streets, forcing the pace and pressing their demands. But the court returned and strife broke out between the government and the workers. Aid was withdrawn from the unemployed. The workers demonstrated and the bourgeois National Guard massacred them. Thus the unity and strength of the revolutionary force were broken. Outside the city, the concessions granted to the peasants and the defection of the Slavs in Croatia and Bohemia left Vienna with no support but the radical Germans. Everywhere, the Slavs were moving over to the support of the Austrian monarchy and against the revolution. Windischgratz, the conqueror of Prague commanded the army that gathered outside Vienna and became the hero of the Slavs. Jellacic and his Croats came in from Hungary to join him, but Kossuth was ready to support Vienna.

Marx himself hurried to Vienna, where he remained from August 20th to September 7th, endeavouring to rouse the masses for a last effort. Vienna had, however, no organised industrial proletariat and he was unsuccessful. Windischgratz advanced on the city and reached it before the Hungarian army could arrive.

The Viennese, considering their utterly inadequate means of defence, considering their utter absence of military skill and organisation in the ranks, offered a most heroic resistance. But force prevailed. Barricade after barricade was swept away by the Imperial artillery in the long wide avenues which form the main streets of the suburbs. By the end of October all resistance was overcome and the flag of the counter-revolution flew from the steeple of St. Stephen's Cathedral.

There followed brutalities and executions by military law, unheard-of cruelties and infamies committed by the Slav troops let loose upon Vienna. Revolutionary Germany failed to come to her aid in the hour of trial. But Imperial Austria was now to prove a deadly enemy to democratic Germany herself.

Engels felt bitterly about the Slav betrayal. "If they should try again under similar pretexts to ally themselves to the counter-revolutionary force, the duty of Germany is clear. No country in a state of revolution and involved in external war can tolerate a Vendée in its very heart."

The most serious setback of all was the counter-revolution in Paris led by Cavaignac, because it was here and here only that the proletariat was in a position to fight for genuinely revolutionary aims. The "Red Republic" was denounced in the electoral campaign leading up to the National Assembly, and the reaction won. On June 21st, the Government dissolved the national workshops, which had never been intended to do more than discredit those who were pressing for socialist measures, and the workers of Paris replied with a call to arms. For four days from June 23rd to 26th they fought on the barricades. It was the first time that the proletariat fought all the other classes of bourgeois society, and they fought so bravely that Thiers suggested that Paris be temporarily abandoned. Finally, the army and the National Guard succeeded in suppressing the insurrection with frightful slaughter and the way was prepared for the *coup d'état* of Louis Napoleon in 1851.[1]

In June the defeat of Paris immediately gave reaction the chance to raise its head in Prussia, in Austria and in Russia. The Tsar offered money and military to suppress the revolution—Austria accepted the big battalions, Prussia the money. Marx, remembering how armed intervention had strengthened the revolutionary forces in France after 1789 and brought them ultimate victory, at once took the line in the *Neue Rheinische Zeitung* that war with Russia was the only means of saving the revolution in Western Europe. Nothing less would awaken the revolutionary passions of the German people. Moreover, Tsarism was the only power which maintained Austrian absolutism—the second great obstacle to revolutionary advance. The *Neue Rheinische Zeitung* had come out from the beginning on the side of every nation in revolt against Austria and Russia—the Poles, the Hungarians, the Italians. The two great enemies of the people in these struggles were the counter-revolutionary Russians and the Austrian Emperor.

In Berlin things went from bad to worse: the parliament found itself strengthening the "state power" against "the forces of anarchy", so that the old Prussian military, police and bureaucratic state rose to its feet again. Feeble verbal protests and votes against each successive menacing move were ineffectual. The counter-revolutionary press declared quite truly, but to the dismay of the bourgeoisie, that the liberal victory depended entirely upon the Berlin masses. The only possible course for them was to repudiate their allies and surrender. This they did, and Frederick William was shortly reinstated to full power in Berlin.

Everywhere, the forces of reaction were rallying to overthrow the revolution. The ferocity of the Prussian Government swept like a storm across the country. Neither the German nor the Austrian parliament had secured control of the armed forces. There were no troops available to support them in the last struggle against the reaction. The government's armies swooped down through the Rhineland.

[1] For the February revolution and the June Days in Paris see Chapter 12, "Marx as Historian".

The Rhineland, with the beginnings of an industrial proletariat, a higher level of political understanding than anywhere else and the energetic presence of Marx, Engels, Schapper, Moll, Willich and many others, presented the biggest anxiety to the forces of reaction, and it was flooded with troops. The democratic forces, which still included all sections from the upper bourgeoisie to the workers, were organised in numerous committees and associations throughout the country, and had brought into existence fighting forces prepared to defend the considerable political victories of the early months. But the Frankfurt Assembly never found the courage to take decisive steps to consolidate these gains or even to defend them by ceasing their endless debates and leading the revolutionary forces in the country. They failed to realize that a revolutionary assembly is lost if it stays on the defensive. They never dreamed of summoning the army of Baden and the Palatinate to their defence. Resistance was well organised in Cologne, where a large public meeting addressed by Engels passed a resolution which called upon the National Assembly not to yield even to bayonets if an attempt were made to dissolve it.[1] Another resolution was despatched to Frankfurt promising that the Rhineland would fight heart and soul for Germany against Russia; Engels appeared in Elberfeld, the district in which his own family owned factories, where barricades had been thrown up by the democratic forces and the prison was stormed. Here Engels heard that the rising in Dresden was holding its own and there had been fighting at the barricades in Breslau. In Baden the Grand Duke had fled and a democratic army was in command. In the Palatinate the revolutionary forces were in complete control. But wherever he went, Engels found little seriousness and no organisation. The democratic government in Baden were even unaware of the presence of twenty-seven Prussian infantry battalions near Saarbrucken.

In the fighting which followed, Engels, who displayed a talent for soldiering, played an important part as A.D.C. to August von Willich, who commanded the army of Baden and the Palatinate. In a letter to Jenny Marx he says that the whistle of bullets is nothing to talk about and the courage required for hand-to-hand fighting was the most ordinary quality in the world.

[1] Engels even went so far as to support the attempt of Prussia to recover the German-speaking province of Schleswig-Holstein from Denmark, an attempt which was thwarted by the combined pressure of Russia and Britain. Prussia, England and Russia, he declared, had most to fear from the German revolution and German unity. War against the three great powers of the counter-revolution, he believed, was the indispensable condition of victory for the democratic cause.

It was all in vain. On July 12th, Willich's troops were driven across the frontier into Switzerland.

Meanwhile, trouble was gathering in Cologne. Martial law was declared and the *Neue Rheinische Zeitung* temporarily suppressed (September 27th). It appeared again on October 12th, but the editorial board had broken up and it was in desperate financial straits. Marx had received a small legacy from his father; every penny went in salvaging the paper. The reaction had still not finally triumphed, but as its power grew Marx's position became more difficult, as he had no Prussian citizenship and was in danger of being expelled from Germany.

Back in Cologne, Marx was faced with the fact that the Prussian Government had dismissed the Assembly in Berlin and imposed a new constitution. In a last blow for democratic rights the Assembly declared that all taxes now imposed by the government were illegal. Marx vehemently supported their decision. The *Neue Rheinische Zeitung* declared that the moment had arrived to oppose the counter-revolution with a second revolution, and it called upon the masses to oppose the violence of the authorities with every possible form of counter-violence and to refuse to pay taxes which the government had no constitutional right to demand.

On November 18th, the Democratic District Committee in Cologne issued an appeal signed by Marx, Schapper and Schneider demanding that any attempt made by the authorities to collect taxes by force should be resisted by every possible means and if necessary by force. In Berlin, the Assembly, although it had declared that the taxes were illegal, had not the courage to act, and on December 5th it was dissolved by the government of Frederick William.

In Cologne the betrayal paralysed the Democratic Committee and gave the reactionaries new strength. Marx and his associates were charged before a jury on February 8th with having incited the people to armed resistance. Marx defended them with a long and powerful speech. He argued that the Assembly could not be judged by the laws of a defunct feudalism, since it is not society which is based on law as such, but laws which arise to serve the needs of society. Bourgeois society, therefore, it not subordinate to any law but its own. Marx concluded his speech by declaring that only the first act in the drama had been played out; the conclusion would be either the victory of the counter-revolution or a new victorious revolution after the final defeat of reaction.

The result was surprising. The accused were at once acquitted, and the foreman of the jury thanked Marx in his own name and on behalf of them all for an unusually instructive and entirely convincing exposition of the constitutional position.

The situation of both Marx and the *Neue Rheinsche Zeitung* was now hopeless, but the imminence of its suppression was accompanied by a steady rise in its circulation. Marx had no legal standing in the country, because he had given up his citizenship and the authorities had refused to give it back to him. The only thing that held them back from expelling him was the fear of the Democratic Committee. The tide was running against them now, and on May 11th the government felt itself strong enough to order the expulsion of Marx. This sealed the fate of the newspaper. In May the final issue appeared, printed in red, and including a defiant farewell article by Marx and an eloquent poem by Freiligarth. Twenty thousand copies were disposed of. Many copies were framed by their possessors. The editor announced that his last word would "always and everywhere be the emancipation of the working class".[1]

Marx sold all his possessions and sacrificed the last of his resources to settle the paper's debts, keeping only the family silver (his wife's), which he was subsequently compelled to pawn in Frankfurt for his own necessities. His adventures were not over: he was arrested by Hessian troops and taken to Darmstadt; but finally he was released and made his way to Paris.

In Paris the early democratic successes had been swept away in the June massacres, and a reactionary government found Marx an unwelcome guest. The counter-revolution had triumphed here too.

On July 19th the Prefect of Police ordered Marx to move to the marshy region of the Morbihan in Brittany, unhealthy and fever-racked. Marx determined to leave France. There was now only one country which he was free to enter. Somehow his friends got enough money together for the fare, and he left for London, followed a few weeks later by his family. Engels joined him in November. This was the end of Marx's wanderings. He remained in London to the end of his life.

[1] A copy of the last issue is in the archives of the Marx Memorial Library, Clerkenwell Green, London.

II

EXILE IN LONDON

When Marx and Engels arrived in London in the summer of 1849 they still believed that the revolution had not been finally defeated and that it would not be long before the lost ground would be recovered and victory achieved. The first thing for the exiles to do, then, was to start their paper again and get it into Germany. By this means they would keep the flame alight, link up their scattered forces and above all give them direction and leadership. But only four numbers of the *Neue Rheinische Revue* appeared, and then publication ceased.

While he was still full of hope Marx, in March 1850, presented a programme for the new revolutionary phase in his *First Address of the Central Committee of the Communist League to its Members in Germany*. Here he distinguished three classes, each with its own programme: the bourgeois liberals, the petty-bourgeois democrats and the proletarian communists. Throughout the coming struggle the workers should maintain the independence of their organistion and programme, but they should support first the liberals until the first objectives were won, then the Democrats, at each stage stepping up their demands, and finally they should aim at victory for the proletariat.

But events developed otherwise than Marx had anticipated, and he began to see clearly not only that no political revolution was independent of current economic conditions, but that the world expansion of capitalism had entirely altered the situation. The possibilities for a socialist revolution were indeed remote.

The *Neue Rheinische Revue* published in the first three numbers (1850) a series of reviews of the month drawn up by Marx and Engels jointly, dealing chiefly with the course of economic events.[1] Here they referred to the discovery of the Californian gold mines as a fact of "even greater importance than the February revolution", and one which would have even greater and more far-reaching results than the

[1] Mehring, *Aus dem Literarischen Nachlass von Marx, Engels und Lassalle*, Vol. III.

discovery of America. "Californian gold is pouring in streams over America and over the Asiatic coasts of the Pacific", sweeping the peoples of the East into the orbit of world trade. They saw the extreme likelihood of the rapid development of American capitalism reducing the countries of Europe to industrial, commercial and political dependency just as London and Liverpool had earlier displaced Genoa and Venice. Only a socialist revolution could so liberate and develop new forces of production as to maintain the superiority of European industry.

At the same time he even anticipated the possibility of revolution in the East, following the impact of capitalism on the farther Pacific coast, so that Western reaction might find confronting it, on the Great Wall of China, the inscription "Republic of China, Liberty, Equality, Fraternity". Many years later Engels was to say, "The conquest of China by capitalism will at the same time furnish the impetus for the overthrow of capitalism in Europe and America."[1]

Already by 1858 Marx was clear that this immense expansion of capitalism beyond the bounds of Europe rendered the chances of early revolution "in this little corner" remote, for "in a far greater territory the movement of bourgeois society is still on the ascendant".[2]

Later, Engels made it clear that in 1848 they had not realised that the state of economic development on the Continent was not ripe for the transformation of capitalism into socialist production. It still had a great capacity for expansion.[3]

Summing up the situation in Germany in 1850 Marx saw that while the crisis in 1847 had made the revolution of 1848 possible, now trade was definitely improving and in consequence the situation was unfavourable for a further revolutionary upsurge. By November of that year he reached the conclusion that any attempt to start a new uprising was doomed to failure. "In view of the general prosperity which now prevails and permits the productive forces of bourgeois society to develop as rapidly as is at all possible within the framework of bourgeois society, there can be no question of any real revolution. Such a revolution is possible only in a period when two factors collide: when the modern productive forces collide with the bourgeois mode of production. . . . A new revolution will be made possible only as the result of a new crisis, but it is just as certain as the coming of the crisis itself."[4]

[1] Engels to Sorge, November 10th, 1894.
[2] Marx to Engels, October 8th, 1850.
[3] Engels: Preface to *Marx's Class Struggle in France*.
[4] *Neue Rheinische Revue*, November 1850.

But his German colleagues Willich and Schapper, who saw the situation only in political terms, and still placed all their hope in the will and determination of the progressive forces, were convinced that revolutionary ardour could again be awakened. In 1850 an open split occurred, with Willich and Schapper in the minority and Marx and Engels in the majority. From this moment the Communist League was finished, and Marx and Engels regretfully concluded that any connection between them and these doctrinaire revolutionaries was impossible.

Marx's final words to his old comrades were completely realistic: "The minority replaces critical observation with dogmatism, a materialist attitude with an idealist one. It regards its own words as the driving force of the revolution instead of the real facts of the situation. Whilst we tell the workers that they must go through fifteen, twenty, perhaps fifty years of war and civil war, not only in order to alter existing conditions, but even to make themselves fit to take over political power, you tell them, on the contrary, that they must seize political power at once or abandon all hope."

In November 1850 the last number of the *Neue Rheinische Revue* appeared. It contained a long and important article by Engels on "The Peasant War in Germany of 1525". In it he said, "We shall find that the classes and factions which played the traitor in 1848 and 1849 did the same in 1525, at a lower stage of their development." Speaking of the tragic fate of Thomas Munzer, he said: "The worst thing which can happen to a leader of an extremist party is that he should be compelled to take over the government at a time when the political movement is not sufficiently developed either to maintain in power the class which he represents or to carry through those measures which the situation demands. He is then in an insoluble dilemma. For he is compelled to stand, not for his own class or party, but for the class to whose domination the political movement is at the moment suited. The man in this unhappy situation is utterly lost."

Marx was convinced that what was now needed was firstly a thorough examination of the rapid changes in the balance of forces during the revolution. He and Engels alone among them all saw clearly that it was the strategy and tactics of revolution that needed thorough examination. The events of 1848 constituted a trial run, a dress rehearsal, and had endless lessons to teach them.

When Marx was asked to write regularly for the *New York Tribune*, his first series of articles was a review of the events of 1848, entitled

Germany, Revolution and Counter Revolution. As Marx's knowledge of English was inadequate, Engels wrote them, but they represented Marx's considered judgment on the tactics of 1848 and the lessons to be learnt from it. But it goes far beyond his estimate of the play of political forces in Germany and raises the whole question of the strategy of the transition from capitalism to socialism. It was a task continued in his essays on *The Class Struggles in France* and occupied his mind throughout his life.

Marx had always seen that the revolution in Germany would be in the first phase a democratic one against feudal absolutism. In it the bourgeoisie would take the lead supported by the petty bourgeoisie of small craftsmen, shopkeepers and so forth, the workers and the peasantry. In this stage the aims of the workers would have to be subordinated to those of the united democratic forces, though they would formulate their own advanced programme.

But in fact the democratic coalition broke up. First the bourgeoisie, startled by the early successes of the workers in Paris uprising in 1848, and by the strong demands of their own Left, grasped what concessions they could for themselves and then virtually sided with the discredited and all-but-defeated feudal government. "Before this danger all former differences disappeared. Against the victorious working man, although he had not yet uttered any specific demands for himself, the friends and foes of many years united, and the alliance between the bourgeoisie and the supporters of the overturned system was concluded upon the very barricades of Berlin."[1]

In the Frankfurt Assembly the Democratic wing consisted of the petty bourgeoisie and the workers. The latter did not put their demands in the foreground. "In fact, as long as the ground was not cleared for the independent action of the workers, as long as direct and universal suffrage was not yet established what else could the proletarian party do. . . . but struggle in common with the petty shopkeepers for the attainment of these rights, which would allow them to fight afterwards their own battle?"[2]

But when the great body of conservative members in Frankfurt withdrew, alarmed at the prospect of liberal advance, and thus left the Assembly with a democratic majority, what happened? The Democrats in words and resolutions expressed the determination to go forward with the framing of a constitution. But Prussia, Austria and Bavaria took this as a declaration of war and prepared to take military

[1] Engels, *Revolution and Counter-revolution*, IV. 5. [2] *ibid.*

action against the Assembly. The people were ready to resist, a revolutionary wave swept over Germany, and when Prussia took the first move the country was in a blaze. Half Germany had taken arms in the defence of the National Assembly in Frankfurt. Yet the Assembly vacillated, was alarmed at the determination of some of its supporters, would infinitely have preferred to be allowed to go on debating. "In short, they went on talking, protesting, proclaiming, pronouncing, but never had the courage or the sense to act, while the hostile troops of the Government drew nearer and nearer."

This is what Marx called "parliamentary cretinism", "a disorder which penetrates its unfortunate victims with the solemn conviction that the whole world, its history and failure, are governed and determined by a majority of votes in that particular representative body which has the honour to count them among its members".[1] So that when the Assembly was threatened with dissolution by the violent intervention of the reaction, they collapsed ignominiously. "On the day of danger it was nowhere, and it never felt more comfortable than the day after decisive defeat, when, everything being lost, it had at least the consolation to know that somehow or other the matter was settled."[2]

When a great portion of Germany was in open insurrection, the real fighting body of the insurgents consisted of the working classes of the towns, who entered upon the struggle to remove some at least of the obstacles to their own emancipation. But the Democrats, although they represented the leading class in the insurrection, panicked when power fell into their hands. The inevitable consequence was overwhelming defeat by the military forces of the reaction.

Having reached these conclusions, and being now convinced that there was no possibility of an immediate revolution in Germany, Marx and Engels found themselves isolated from most of their former comrades-in-arms. They were aware of the occupational disease of revolutionary exiles and were quite resolved not to succumb to it themselves. Everywhere among the *émigrés* they found intrigue, suspicion, quarrelling and recrimination. Many of them, Engels remarked, "fell into dissolute habits" and lived futile and disorganised lives.

Marx had only contempt for the arrogance and self-importance of the revolutionary phrase-mongering of many of the exiles. In February 1851 he wrote to Engels, "I very much like the public isolation in which we two find ourselves. It is quite in accordance with our atti-

[1] Engels, *Revolution and Counter-revolution*, XV. [2] *ibid.*

tude and our principles." "From now on", Engels replied "we are responsible to ourselves alone. . . . The violent events of a revolution leave a disturbing heritage in the minds of those who take part in it and in particular in the minds of those who are hounded into exile away from their homes. This mental disturbance affects even capable men and makes them irresponsible. The result is that they indulge in conspiracies and romantic revolution which compromise both them and the cause they have at heart. . . . Storms always raise a certain amount of dirt, and a revolutionary period does not smell of attar of roses. It is clear that occasionally one is bespattered with all sorts of muck."

But there was one more scene to be played out before the curtain fell on the German Revolution of 1848. The German section of the Communist League met with disaster. One of the members of the League who was visiting them on behalf of Marx was arrested and the names of his comrades were found. An imposing trial was staged. Evidence was fabricated. Marx, working night and day in England, effected a complete exposure of the government forgeries. The Public Prosecutor was compelled to withdraw the faked evidence, but seven men were found guilty of high treason and sentenced to imprisonment of from three to six years. They included Friedrich Lessner, a close friend of Marx, whose invaluable memoirs of the events of 1847 and 1848 give a vivid picture of these events by one who played an active part in them. Marx's two rooms became a sort of office. Helpers were writing, running messages, collecting money, while Marx prepared the material. This had to be sent to Germany by devious ways, since all letters were opened by the police. During these hectic days the family was ill. They had no money to pay the doctor. "For about eight to ten days", Marx wrote to Engels, "we have all been living on bread and potatoes, and it is doubtful whether we shall be able to get even that. I have not even had the money to buy newspapers."

Jenny Marx gives an account of these events in a letter to an American friend begging her to excuse her confusion, "but I have also had some part in all this, and I have copied and copied until my fingers ached. And all the time my three lively children are singing and whistling, occasionally earning a severe rebuke from their father. What a life!"

Lessner came to London in 1856. His reminiscences give a moving picture of Marx among his friends. Unlike many others, he never found

Marx proud or arrogant. "He was always keen to hear the opinion of the most ordinary workers in the working-class movements. Thus he often came to me in the afternoon, took me with him on his walk, and spoke to me about all sorts of things. In general he was splendid company and exerted a powerful attraction on all who came into contact with him."

Marx did not welcome people who came to see him out of mere curiosity—to them he was unapproachable. Utterly unconcerned with popularity, he despised those who sought it. He loathed cant and what he called phrasemongering. The very depth of his moral sincerity drove him to describe the well-intentioned preaching of ideals as "so much worthless earnestness". There were few prominent radicals whom he had failed to castigate for these reasons at some time or other.

He was vehement and eager, fierce and intolerant in controversy, but without rancour. He was indeed a man cast in heroic mould, who could arouse passionate devotion or violent hatred.

With increasing years his dislike of the society in which he lived became more and more acute, and his personal contact with those who accepted it and approved it more and more difficult. Yet a normally polite and tolerant person could hardly have accomplished the task which it was his destiny to carry through—a task which required the fortitude to resist or to break off all those ties which might unsettle his purpose and determination or compromise him in the eyes of his disciples.

He has often been regarded as hard and inflexible. In part this was his defence against the blows which fate rained upon him; but it also reflected his iron determination not to allow the cause he believed in to be called in question by either sentimentality or muddle-headedness. His judgment on his enemies, and often enough on his friends, developed a searing trenchancy which wounded even those who were not unduly sensitive; but when those who crossed his path turned out to be men of integrity, he could be warm-hearted and generous to a degree. Particularly was this the case when banished socialists from the Continent sought him out.

But he was entirely free from vanity—nor did he ever strike an attitude; he was always himself. This, many people found disturbing; but he was incapable of wearing a mask. He spoke his mind completely and without any reserve and his face was always the mirror of his heart.

He was prepared to sweep aside in a moment any proposition however dear to him as soon as he was convinced of its incorrectness. He often made mistakes, but he never resisted the recognition of error when the events themselves compelled it. Mehring said that until the end of his days his insatiable desire for knowledge never left him, whilst his merciless self-criticism would never allow him to leave a subject until he had mastered it. "Marx could find no limit and no end to his self-criticism."

When Marx arrived in Cologne in 1847 his family consisted of the first daughter, Jenny, who was born in May 1844 and his second daughter, Laura, who was born in September 1845. A son, Edgar, was born in 1847. Since its Paris days the family had been accompanied by Helene Demuth, who had come to them from the Westphalen family as a young girl and remained with them through all their troubles, a loyal and devoted servant and friend.

Marx found a second home in England, and was never interfered with as men like him were by those continental governments which hunted down their enemies with every measure of police oppression. This was to a large extent due to the isolation of England. Refugees were tolerated, but received no sympathy, except in the case of liberals like Mazzini or picturesque figures like Garibaldi.

During the first years of his exile in London his endless labours went on against a background of utter destitution, during which his three younger children died of want.

The boy Edgar who had been born in Brussels in 1847, a gifted child, had been sickly from birth. He died in 1855.

In November 1849, his fourth child, Heinrich, was born at Chelsea, where the family had taken lodgings at 4 Anderson Street. They were rather brutally evicted in the spring of 1850 and after a short stay in the German Hotel, Leicester Square, they moved to Dean Street, Soho—first to No. 64 and then to No. 28, where they occupied rooms until 1855.[1] Marx in desperation got his friend Weydemeyer in Frankfurt to sell the family silver which he had left in pawn there, except for a small case of spoons belonging to little Jenny. His wife wrote to Weydemeyer in 1850, "The thing that hits me hardest of all and makes my heart bleed is that my husband is worried by so many petty troubles. He could be assisted with so little, but he who has always so readily helped others is left helpless himself." In March 1851 his third

[1] The house is still standing, unaltered (1963).

daughter Franziska was born. There was not a penny in the house, but Marx stuck doggedly to his work. Louis Napoleon had just secured power by a *coup d'état* and Marx penned a brilliant analysis to show "how the class struggle in France created conditions and circumstances which made it possible for a mediocre and grotesque individual to play the role of a hero".[1]

Now he fell ill and could not even leave the house because his clothes were in pawn, or buy meat because no shopkeeper would allow them credit. At Easter 1852, the little girl Franziska died; Heinrich had died in 1850. His wife Jenny says in her diary, "Her small lifeless body rested in our little back room whilst we all went together into the front room and when night came we made up our beds on the floor. The three surviving children lay with us and we cried for the poor little angel who now rested cold and lifeless in the next room."

Now a gleam of hope appeared. It was at this time that Dana, the publisher of the *New York Tribune*, who had met Marx in Cologne during the revolution had been greatly impressed by him, asked Marx to become a regular contributor to his journal. Marx was paid £1 per article. For nearly ten years he continued to pen these weekly despatches, covering the widest field of international affairs; and even today they remain of absorbing interest. It is difficult to imagine how Marx would have survived, or how he could have continued his work at this time, without the generous and devoted help of Engels. Engels wrote a good many of the articles for the *New York Tribune*. But much more was needed, and in November 1850 he departed for Manchester to take up a position in his father's cotton firm of Ermen and Engels, so that out of his salary he could help to maintain Marx and his family.

It was now that, in penury, hunger and deep family distress, Marx sat from nine in the morning to seven in the evening in the British Museum. His revolutionary friends derided him. Marx replied: "Naturally, the democratic simpletons whose inspiration comes from above, have no need to do anything of that sort. Why should the innocents bother their heads about economics and history? Everything is so simple! they say in their confused heads, perhaps, for they are really great simpletons."

The major part of Marx's theoretical work lay before him. Yet he was again and again to turn aside from his studies to organise the International, and to play an energetic part in its work, to engage in fierce polemics with his critics, to write innumerable articles for the

[1] Marx, *The Eighteenth Brumaire of Louis Bonaparte.*

New York Tribune on European affairs, on the Far East, on India, on the Crimean War and on the American Civil War.

But however practical he could be, and whatever organisational responsibilities he assumed, he always returned to the fundamental task of his life, the elaboration of his basic theory of social development, his philosophy of history. "Before the proletariat fights out its battles on the barricades," he declared, "it announces the coming of its rule with a series of intellectual victories." It was these victories he now set out to win.

However deeply absorbed in these exhaustive studies or involved in controversy and political organisation, Marx was, in his more intimate relationships, a warm and generous friend and a devoted husband and father. On reading his letters to his daughters one wonders where the stern man found such a spring of tenderness and sensitiveness. When they were young, almost the only thing which could draw him away from his study was the delight of an hour's play with his children. When they were older, "relations between Marx and his daughters were most intimate and unconstrained. The girls treated their father more as a brother or a friend. Marx scorned the exterior attributes of paternal authority. In serious matters he was his children's adviser, otherwise, according as his time allowed, their playmate."[1]

Wilhelm Liebknecht describes the Sunday walks to Hampstead Heath. The girls, he says, were excellent walkers, nimble and tireless. It took them an hour and a half to get there from Soho, and they generally set off at about eleven o'clock. Liebknecht used to lead the way with the two girls, entertaining them with stories and picking wild flowers. When they arrived, the hamper would be opened and after a picnic meal the children raced and played while those older members of the party who did not prefer a nap got out the Sunday papers and talked politics. There were also exciting donkey rides, Liebknecht tells us.

The walk home was always a merry one. Generally, someone struck up a song, probably a folk-song from old Germany or a Negro song from America. Literature and art were often the topics of conversation, and here Marx displayed his astonishing memory. He used to recite long passages from *The Divine Comedy*, which he knew by heart, and scenes from Shakespeare. His wife, whose knowledge of Shakespeare was almost as good as his, often took up these recitals instead of Marx himself.

[1] Friedrich Lessner, *Before 1848 and After* (*Reminiscences of an old Communist*).

From their early youth Marx's daughters took a most heartfelt interest in the working-class movement of the time, which was always the main topic of Marx's family. The youngest, Eleanor, born in 1855, became her father's secretary and the companion of his declining years. She conducted her father's correspondence and had in her hands the threads of the International. She was interested in literature, and made the first English translation of *Madame Bovary* and also translated some of Ibsen's plays.

We have a picture of Marx's family as it was in 1861 in a letter which Jenny Marx wrote to Frau Weydemeyer, an old friend from Germany. The seventeen-year-old Jenny, who was born in 1844, was called after her mother. She was like her father, "with her rich, dark glossy hair, brilliant soft eyes and her dusky complexion". The fifteen-year-old Laura, who was born in 1845, was more like her mother, "with wavy, curly chestnut hair and green eyes flashing fire. Both girls have a really beautiful complexion and at the same time are really so little vain that in secret I am often surprised." But the idolised darling of the whole house was Eleanor. "The child was born when our poor little Edgar died, and all the love and tenderness we bore him was then transferred to his little sister, and the older girls looked after her and nursed her with almost motherly care. It would be difficult to find a more lovable child, as pretty as a picture and sweet tempered."

When the outbreak of the American Civil War cut off Marx's only source of income, the education of the growing girls became a serious problem. Jenny and Laura were acutely conscious of the troubles and privations of their parents. Their mother was taken ill with smallpox and the children were looked after in the home of Wilhelm Liebknecht. By now they had left school and were studying French and Italian, and taking lessons in drawing and singing. Both girls were musical. Jenny shared her father's love for classical music and for Shakespeare.

The interests of Marx extended far beyond his sociological studies. It was Hegel who had shown him that nothing could be understood in isolation. Engels said of the wide range of his reading: "For a man who examined everything to discover its historical origin and the condition of its development, naturally every single question gave rise to a series of questions. Ancient history, agriculture, Russian and American land-holding relationships, geology, were all in turn studied." He read all German and neo-Latin languages with ease and then learnt Old Slav, Russian and Serbian.

His intense concentration on economic and social history never separated him from the literature he loved so well and which was his great consolation throughout his life. He read Aeschylus in the original at least once a year. "It gave him childlike pleasure", says Liebknecht, "if he could show me some difficult passage from Aristotle or Aeschylus which I could not immediately construe." He considered Aeschylus and Shakespeare as the great dramatic geniuses of humanity.

Marx's knowledge of German literature was extensive. He had known Heine well in his Paris days and had memorised much of his and Goethe's work. As far as French literature was concerned, he liked Diderot, as one might expect, but he had little use for the French romanticists and was particularly critical of Chateaubriand whom he accused of "tuppence-coloured sentimentality and Byzantine exaggeration". Balzac, however, he especially admired, and he longed to write a critical estimate of *La Comédie Humaine*.

Marx was a great novel reader, raking particular delight in Fielding's *Tom Jones*, Charles Lever, Dumas and Walter Scott. He could read Spanish, but had no practice in speaking it. He even set about teaching it to his son-in-law, Lafargue. His favourite among the Spaniards was Calderon and he knew *Don Quixote* well. In it he saw the epic of an outdated chivalry whose virtues were ridiculed and scoffed at in the emerging bourgeois world.

Basic to his whole philosophy was the conviction that man only begins to rise to the measure of his full manhood when the radical division of society into owners and wage-earners gives way to the co-operative commonwealth. That was why he chose as the motto of emancipated humanity the words which Virgil addresses to Dante in the *Purgatorio*:

> Free of thine own arbitrament to choose,
> Thy will upright and whole, to distrust its call
> Were henceforth error. Wherefore do I crown thee
> Lord of thyself.[1]

[1] Dante, *Purgatorio*, Canto XXVII.

12

MARX AS HISTORIAN

In his presidential address to the American Historical Association in 1933, Charles Beard declared that he saw the historian as compelled to choose among three possibilities; history as senseless; history as a cyclical, mystical drama; or history as actuality. He proceeded to disclaim any idea that there could be a science of history embracing either its totality or any large phase of past events. More than one British historian has also reached the conclusion that the idea that history as a science has perished.

This is a considerable departure from Hegel, who conceived the task to be to find a scientific explanation of the entire historico-social process in its totality, that is to say welding into a unity all aspects and manifestations of the activity of social man as the attributes of the Universal Spirit. It has often been supposed that Marx adopted such a philosophy of history and held that historical tendencies or trends "can be immediately derived from universal laws alone".[1]

Unfortunately for any such conception of the views of Marx, this is precisely what he denied. History follows a course of its own from which we may infer certain laws of process and development, but it does not suffer us to interpret it in terms of abstract laws or thoughts revealed to speculative metaphysics.

Society is something autonomous, a complex of relations and conditions, not however moving irresistibly to some predetermined goal. Man makes his own history, but not in order to march along any fixed line of progress, or because he must obey the laws of some abstract evolution of the Idea. He does so in the endeavour to satisfy his basic needs, and it is for the social scientist to discover how the successive methods of satisfying these needs in the course of history have influenced man's systems of production and spiritual activities.

All this assumes the continuous development of technique and with it society in its successive forms, incessantly revolutionising its tools and with them not only the pattern of society but the form of the

[1] K. R. Popper, *The Poverty of Historicism.*

state and its legal support. Historical science, then, proceeds to investigate this foundation of society, its origin, its changes and its transformations. There is no historical event that does not in the last analysis owe its origin to social economics.

Marx never for a moment stated or implied either that this would happen automatically or that the only motive was the conscious self-interest of individuals. Every such technological, economic and organisational change follows a definite state of consciousness, and the motive may be nationalism, or religion, or the rights of man, or liberty. But the motive by itself would be insufficient in the absence of a basic class necessity derived from social conditions.

The Marxist analysis of social change makes no attempt to deny the importance and effectiveness of the ideological and political forms in which the conflicts of history clothe themselves, or to belittle the significance of the convictions and ideals, and of the passionate devotion to monarchy, Church, or Christian conscience, which have constituted their specific character.

Nor is historical change either automatic or fatalistically determined by economic necessity. Even when men were not aware of the ultimate consequences of their actions, what they did they did on the basis of their understanding and by their conscious and deliberate intention. The transition to socialism which Marx envisaged carries this consciousness one stage further to a clear prevision of a socialist goal; now clear understanding, intelligent resolute decision, are the final historical factors which convert the possibility of advance into a reality.

And when all is said and done it must not be supposed that Marx is rendering unnecessary the concrete study of events because they are all explained in advance by his economic interpretation of history. Replying to one of his critics in 1877 he says: "He feels himself obliged to metamorphose my historical sketch of the Genesis of Capitalism in Western Europe into an historico-philosophic theory of the *Marche General* imposed by fate upon every people, whatever the historic circumstances in which it finds itself."[1] Any such attempt by superficial writers, said Engels, "to get their own scanty historical knowledge fitted together into a neat system as quickly as possible",[2] is not a Marxist procedure. He advises his correspondent to "study this theory further, from its original sources and not at second hand."[3]

[1] Marx to the Editor of *Notes on the Fatherland*.
[2] Engels to Conrad Schmidt, August 1890.
[3] Engels to J. Bloch, September 1890.

This is indeed the case. Marxism makes no claim to the truth of *a priori* theories. It is not the intellectual vision of a design for a new world, but a method of research to be tested by its relevance to the facts of modern history. It is the systematic completion of experience or nothing. Therefore, it can only be understood when it becomes the instrument for the interpretation of the events passing before us.

THE CLASS STRUGGLES IN FRANCE

Marx applies his new method of analysis first of all to the dramatic events in France between the July Revolution of 1848 and the Paris Commune of 1871. He inaugurated this venture with a product of mature genius, *The Class Struggles in France* (1849-50) which appeared in the *Neue Rheinische Zeitung* in 1850. When it was reissued after the death of Marx it contained an Introduction by Engels, reviewing critically and constructively the interpretation of these political struggles given at the time, in the light of forty-five years of further historical development and political experience. It was followed in 1852 by *The Eighteenth Brumaire*, dealing with the *coup d'état* of December 1851: and finally, in 1871, by *The Civil War in France*, which analysed the episode of the Paris Commune. In these works Marx is at his most vivid and most trenchant in the closeness and exactitude of his political observation. We are made to feel the excitement of his revelation of the currents running below the surface of French politics in an account of events which is compressed, clearly articulated, witty and illuminated by the fire of his tragic invective.

In February 1848 the reign of the bourgeois monarch Louis Philippe (the King with the umbrella) supported by a financial aristocracy of bankers, speculators and merchants came to an ignominious end. The new government had powerful support from the working-class and socialist movement, but the forces which obtained the mastery were those sections of the bourgeoisie which had played no part in the previous government. Marx's exposition of the events that followed the revolution was designed to make clear that at this stage it was impossible for the workers to take the lead, capitalism had to develop further. Nevertheless, for the first time they had appeared on the stage of history as an independent force. It was precisely this fact, and the threat to capitalism which it implied, that drove the whole of the bourgeoisie, including the small businessmen and craftsmen, into the single camp of the enemies of the "Red Republic". The result was the massacre of June 1848. Over 3,000 workers died and 15,000 more were transported without trial.

For Marx the experiences of 1848 are of importance because they show clearly, for the first time, the tactics of the bourgeoisie in a democratic revolution in which the workers appear as an advanced and independent force. At the same time it shows the part played by the small masters and businessmen, the petty bourgeoisie, who frequently find themselves in opposition to the bourgeoisie proper, when the workers, instead of merely aiding them, came forward with their own independent demands. When this happens the petty bourgeoisie goes over to the camp of the counter-revolution.

This terse and biting study of an episode in French history sets forth in a series of concrete examples the Marxist understanding of class struggle and politics. Marx points out that behind the political slogans and manœuvres were the class issues which were the determining factors in these events.

Whatever the ideas and ideals, the principles and watchwords, under which the various groups and parties fought, and in which they no doubt believed, Marx endeavoured to show that it was from the first to the last a matter of competing class interests. The ideas and principles were not themselves the final causes, however strongly they were believed in. They were in fact believed in because they were the symbols and watch-words of much deeper class interests. Upon the different forms of property, upon the social conditions of existence, as foundation, there is built a superstructure of diversified and characteristic sentiments, illusions, habits of thought, and outlooks on life in general. The class as a whole creates and shapes them out of its material foundation, and out of the corresponding social relationships. The individual in whom they arise through tradition and education believes them to be the true determinants, the real origin, of his activities.

The ideals of 1789 and of 1848, the appeals to the classical traditions of republicanism, powerful motives though they had been, now fall away to reveal the real forces behind the revolution. Revolutions, says Marx, tend to romanticise themselves. The French Revolution dressed up in the traditional costume of Republican Rome, borrowed ancient names, revived old war cries. And now the revolution of 1848 borrows the trappings of 1789. But this can never last. The inner purpose of 1789 reveals itself as the liberation of the bourgeoisie to establish modern bourgeois society. The Jacobins rout feudalism, Napoleon establishes the conditions which make it possible for free competition and the nation's industrial power to develop. And when the new social powers have come into being, the illusions fade; the real leaders are not Brutus, the Gracchi—but the men in the counting-house. "Absorbed in money-making and in the peaceful warfare of competition it (the revolution) forgot that the shade of ancient Rome had sat beside its cradle. . . . In like manner, more than a century earlier, and in another phase of development, Cromwell and the English people had borrowed the phraseology, the emotions, and the illusions of the Old Testament as trappings for their own bourgeois revolution. As soon as they had reached the goal, as soon as the bourgeois transformation of English society had been effective, Locke supplanted Habakkuk."[1]

Many of the gains of 1789 were lost, and decline from the form of a republic to a dictatorship of the bourgeoisie proceeded rapidly. The mask of social aims is thrown off—these are indeed quite utopian within the framework of capitalism. The propertied classes can now win their way to power. The Republic which emerges is not the revolutionary weapon of the workers, but the political consolidation of bourgeois society—a state using all its power to foster the interests of the rich and keep the workers in helpless subjection. Of course the bourgeoisie were convinced that their interests were those of society itself, including those of the workers. The workers had yet to learn that this was not so. The workers had really fought for a bourgeois monarch in 1830 and a bourgeois republic in 1848. To secure their help there had to be the profession of social aims, but there would be no realisation of these. The workers had mistakenly identified their own interests with those of the bourgeoisie.

It was nevertheless an advantage that many groups were stripped of their illusions, that the result was not an Assembly representing an abstraction, "the people", but *real* people—that is to say, different classes with different interests, the predominant interest being that of the bourgeoisie now ruling in its own interests in the name of the people.

Marx still hoped that the time was not far distant when the development of capitalism and the gathering strength of the workers' movement would bring France to "the point of revolutionary departure". But he was now convinced that nothing was likely to happen until the outbreak of a new economic crisis, and he looked forward to a long struggle between the various antagonistic elements concealed within

[1] Marx, *The Eighteenth Brumaire*.

"the people". When Engels wrote his Introduction to *The Class Struggle in France* in 1895, he went even further. It seemed to him that even then the state of economic development was not by a long way ripe for the proletarian revolution.

"THE EIGHTEENTH BRUMAIRE OF LOUIS BONAPARTE"

"Never, after we have read *The Eighteenth Brumaire*", says Edmund Wilson, "can the language, the conventions, the combinations, the pretensions, of parliamentary bodies, if we have any illusions about them, seem the same to us again. They lose their consistency and colour—evaporate before our eyes. The old spirit of competition for office, the old game of political debate, look foolish and obsolete; for now we can see for the first time through the shadow-play to the conflict of appetites and needs which, partly unknown to the actors themselves, throw these silhouettes on the screen."[1]

After the defeat of the workers, the Republican Party appeared to be firmly established in power. The events which followed were totally unexpected. The Republicans were isolated and out-manœuvred and eventually completely defeated by Louis Bonaparte, the nephew of Napoleon, who had returned from exile, and by virtue of astute electioneering assisted by "vagabonds, disbanded soldiers, discharged prisoners, fugitives from the galleys, sharpers, jugglers, professional beggars, pickpockets, conjurers, gamesters, pimps, brothel-keepers, porters, men of letters, organ grinders, rag-pickers, knife-grinders and tinkers"[2], and taking full advantage of the Bonapartist tradition, easily outwitted his opponents and seized power in the *coup d'état* of 1851. On this event Marx in his opening paragraphs makes this caustic comment: "Hegel says somewhere that, upon the stage of universal history, all great events and personalities reappear in one fashion or another. He forgot to add that, on the first occasion, they appear as tragedy; the second, as farce".[3]

Marx was well aware of Louis Napoleon's cunning, and traces his every move with exactitude. But he has unmeasured contempt for the man and is clearly aware that every step forward is only preparing his ultimate downfall and that of France.

Louis Bonaparte had secured the support of the peasants, "the class that represents barbarism within civilisation", the army (who worshipped Napoleon and were for war and glory), and a considerable

[1] Edmund Wilson, *To the Finland Station.*
[2] Marx, *The Eighteenth Brumaire.* [3] *ibid.*

section of the proletariat who sought to defeat Cavaignac and the Republicans by voting for Bonaparte. The petty bourgeoisie, who were in great financial straits, were voting against their wealthy creditors when they supported him. The big bourgeoisie regarded him as likely to oppose the Republicans and maintain the interest of the Party of Order. The Jacobin Democrats still opposed him.

But the Democrats were completely demoralised. They even walked out of parliament. But they did nothing. "No other party," said Marx, "takes so exaggerated a view of its powers, no other is more easily deceived as to the realities of the situation." They wanted to resist, but wished to see the battle fought out in the clouds over their heads. They were never defeated without assuring everybody that, whoever was to blame, they were guiltless.

"The revolutionary threats of the petty bourgeois and their democratic representatives are nothing more than attempts to frighten the enemy. When they have found their way into a blind alley, when they have compromised themselves so thoroughly that they have no resource but an attempt to carry out their threats, the attempt is made half-heartedly. They sedulously shun the means that might ensure success, and seek excuses for submission. The crashing overture which has announced the opening of the campaign, subsides to a dispirited growling when the time comes for the guns to be fired; the actors cease to take themselves seriously; the action collapses like a pricked air-balloon."[1]

Thus the so-called Democrats, who had been trying to unite the socialist working class with the republican petty bourgeoisie, were routed as the result of their inability to rise above the intellectual limitation of the petty-bourgeoisie and grasp the class interests actually involved.

The Machiavellian President daily grew more skilful, manœuvring between the rival parties and classes. He sedulously courted the masses, using every kind of demagogic trick. He posed as "the father of the workers and won the hearts of the peasants". At his side were his accomplices, men ready for anything, whose only hopes were bound up with his future, and the infamous Society of December the Tenth, a partisan fighting force of gangsters who travelled about the country with him on his campaigns. He flattered the clergy and the Army and promised the prosperous bourgeoisie "order in the streets". His aim was to secure absolute authority, in appearance at any rate, from the people and to

[1] Marx, *The Eighteenth Brumaire.*

dominate all parties. The final moves in the game need not be described. Everything that the parliament of the bourgeoisie had done to destroy its democratic enemies was now turned against it by Louis Bonaparte, who posed as their enemy in the eyes of the masses even while he protected their material power. He took power from the capitalists to protect them from the workers, and at the same time to protect the workers from the capitalists. On December 2nd, 1851, he seized power; violating the constitution, imprisoning many leading citizens and politicians, and shooting some 1,200 innocent citizens; and yet he made it appear that he was not a tyrant but a deliverer. As against a Chamber that had disfranchised three million electors and pursued a policy of total social reaction, the President appeared well justified. The people had the government it preferred and the bourgeoisie the government it deserved.

Marx draws his conclusions in the final chapter of *The Eighteenth Brumaire*: "The French bourgeoisie rose in revolt against the rule of the working proletariat: with the result that it has brought the slum proletariat into power; the loafers and tatterdemalions, headed by the chief of the Society of December the Tenth. The bourgeoisie kept France breathless with alarm by talking about the menace of Red Anarchy; on December 4th, Bonaparte gave it a taste of the future it had prophesied when he had the most respectable burghers of the Boulevard Montmartre and the Boulevard des Italiens shot, while they sat at their windows, by the soldiers of the army of order, who had been made half drunk to keep up their enthusiasm. The bourgeoisie glorified the sword; now it is to be ruled by the sword. It destroyed the revolutionary press; now its own press has been destroyed. It subjected public meetings to police supervision, now its own drawing-rooms are under police supervision. It disbanded the democratic National Guard; now its own National Guard has been disbanded. It had cowed the workers by declaring a state of siege; now it is itself cowed by the same weapon. It had substituted courts martial for trial by jury; now its own juries are replaced by courts martial. It had put elementary education under the thumb of the priests; now it is to experience clerical dominion in its turn. It had transported the workers without trial; now the bourgeois are transported without trial. It had suppressed every kind of social stir by the use of all the powers of the State; now every social stir initiated by the bourgeoisie is suppressed by all the powers of the State. In its passion for its money-bags, it had rebelled against its own statesmen and men of letters; now its statesmen and men of letters have been swept out of the way, and its money-bags are rifled when its mouth has been gagged and its pen broken."

A year later Bonaparte was elected Emperor and took the name of Napoleon III. Industry flourished and so did corruption in every office; and the Army, though splendid in appearance, was ill supplied and its organisation chaotic.

Nemesis was not to be escaped. When Napoleon was foolish enough to allow himself to declare war on Germany in 1870, Bismarck was ready for him. The first shot was fired on August 2nd. On August 4th and 6th the French were utterly defeated. At Sedan on September 2nd Napoleon and the French Army surrendered. He was deposed, came to England, and there spent the rest of his days.

After the declaration of war (July 23rd) the General Council of the International published an address drawn up by Marx. It was a scathing indictment of Napoleon, whose Second Empire, he declared, would end as it had begun, as a parody.

On September 4th a Republic was declared in Paris, but the war continued. On September 9th the General Council issued its second address on the war. This was also written by Marx. His fears as to the aims of Prussian policy were justified, the war had become a German war of conquest. Forseeing the possibility of the French working class taking the opportunity afforded by the disappearance of Louis Napoleon and the formation of a republic to launch the revolution, he hastened to caution them not to do so, but to utilise their democratic liberties for the purpose of developing their organisational strength.

Paris was besieged and the government made terms. But the people of Paris, indignant at the almost total surrender to German demands, closed the gates and prepared for another siege.

Realising that not only had the government, which retreated to Versailles, surrendered everything to Bismarck, but that their own liberties were threatened, the people of Paris revolted, enraged and disgusted by the treachery, corruption and exploitation of their rulers, and set up the Paris Commune.

It was the first occasion in history on which the working class had seized power, and the prototype of the proletarian dictatorship which would one day undertake the transition from capitalist to socialist society. The Communards were represented by the entire press of Europe to be a band of criminal lunatics, guilty of every crime, social incendiaries pledged to destroy all religion and all morality.

The Commune came into existence on March 26th and survived

until the end of May, when the defences were broken down and thousands of workers butchered; but they were not defeated before, in their hatred for the very name of Napoleon, they had hurled to the ground the great column in the Place Vendôme cast from the cannon of the elder Napoleon's victories. They thus all unwittingly fufilled the prophecy of Karl Marx, written even before Louis Bonaparte had made himself Emperor, with which he closed *The Eighteenth Brumaire*:

"Harassed by the conflicting demands of his situation, forced like a conjurer to rivet public attention upon himself as substitute for the first Napoleon, compelled every day to carry out a miniature *coup d'état*, Bonaparte throws the whole bourgeois economy into confusion, lays sacrilegious hands on everything which the revolution of 1848 had regarded as sacred, makes some tolerant of revolution and others eager for revolution, and generates anarchy in the name of order. Through his deeds, the State machine is robbed of all sublimity. The cult of the Holy Coat of Treves is transferred to Paris, where it becomes the cult of the Napoleonic imperial mantle. But if the imperial mantle should, in the end, fall upon the shoulders of Louis Bonaparte, the iron statue of Napoleon will crash from the top of the Vendome column!"

Although Marx had tried to persuade the workers of Paris not to venture on revolution, the moment they did so he gave them unstinted support. He writes to Kugelmann: "What resilient vigour, what historic initiative and what self-sacrifice these Parisians are showing! After six months of starvation and ruin brought about more by internal treachery than by the open enemy, they rise in revolt as though there had never been a war between France and Germany. . . . History can show no similar example of such magnificence!"[1]

It was, however, much more than an heroic episode in the struggle for working-class emancipation. They had, firstly, "seized the governmental power"; but of equal importance was the fact that they knew that "the working class cannot simply lay hold of the ready-made state machinery and wield it for its own purposes". It must destroy the bureaucratic military machine and not simply place it in other hands.[2] Therefore, they not only "understood that it is their imperious duty and their absolute right to render themselves master of their own

[1] Marx to Kugelmann, April 12th, 1871.

[2] It is interesting to note that in 1871 Marx excluded England from this requirement. Here a people's revolution at that time appeared possible without the preliminary condition of the destruction of the state machine.

destinies by seizing upon the governmental power and taking into their own hands the governmental power". They dissolved the Army and the police and handed their duties over to the people themselves. They made all public officials subject to election or deposition at any time, and constituted the new representative assembly as a working, not a parliamentary body, executive and legislative at the same time; all such administrative work to be done at workmen's wages.

Yet they were defeated, and the reasons for this defeat were analysed by Marx in his *Address of the General Council of the International* of May 30th, 1871, signed by nineteen members, nine corresponding secretaries for the different countries represented and the five members of the Secretariat.

The trouble was that the Parisians were much too decent about it all—not sufficiently ruthless and decisive. Once a revolution is started one must keep the initiative and go right on with it. Paris halted—and was defeated.

The Central Committee surrendered its power too soon to make way for the Commune. Strong, determined, central direction is necessary in revolution.

They should have marched at once on Versailles and crushed Thiers and his government.

They should have seized the Bank of France. This would have been worth 10,000 hostages. "It would have meant that the whole of the French bourgeoisie would have brought pressure on the Versailles Government in favour of peace with the Commune."[1]

But was it, after all, no more than defeat?

Far from it: in the first place, "the struggle of the working class against the capitalist class and its state has entered upon a new phase with the struggle in Paris. Whatever the immediate result may be, a new point of departure of world-historic importance has been gained." The *historical initiative* of the people at this juncture was what so impressed and excited Marx. "This was the first revolution in which the working class was openly acknowledged as the only class capable of social initiative."[2]

In the second place, in spite of its excessive decency, it did seize power and apply compulsory measures to its opponent, it did *reconstruct* the governing apparatus to make it the instrument of popular rule. It would "have shamefully betrayed its trust by affecting to keep

[1] Engels, Introduction to the *Civil War in France*.
[2] Marx, *Address of the General Council*, May 30th, 1871.

up all the decencies and appearances of liberalism in a time of profound peace".

Thirdly it envisaged and began to put into operation radical measures of social reconstruction. It decreed free and universal education. It was prepared to uproot the economic foundation upon which rests class privilege, class exploitation, in other words "to abolish that class property which makes the labour of the many the wealth of the few".

When his friend Kugelmann expressed doubts as to the whole affair and seemed to regard the uprising as a piece of impracticable irresponsible romanticism, Marx replied that "world history would indeed be very easy to make, if the struggle were only taken up on condition of infallibly favourable chances. It would, on the other hand be of a very mystical nature if 'accident' played no part—including the accident of those who at first stand at the head of the movement."[1]

Again, Marx was perfectly well aware that the men who made the Commune were not perfect, had very mixed and muddled ideas and had no ready-made utopia to impose by decree. He knew that even if the venture had survived it would have had to work out its own development and application "through long struggles, through a series of historic processes, transforming circumstances and men. They have no ideals to realise, but to set free the elements of the new society within which old collapsing bourgeois society itself is pregnant. In the full consciousness of their historic mission, and with the heroic resolve to act up to it, the working class can afford to smile at the coarse invective and the didactic patronage of well-wishing bourgeois doctrinaires, pouring forth their ignorant platitudes and sectarian crotchets in the oracular tone of scientific infallibility."[2]

Marx concludes his address with these words: "Working-man's Paris, with its Commune, will be for ever celebrated as the glorious harbinger of a new society. Its martyrs are enshrined in the great heart of the working class. Its exterminators history has already nailed to that eternal pillory from which all the prayers of their priests will not avail to redeem them."

[1] Marx to Kugelmann, April 17th, 1871.
[2] Marx, *Address of the General Council*, May 30th, 1871.

13

MARX IN THE SIXTIES

THE Marxes were desperately anxious to get out of their tiny rooms in Soho, and when the income from the *Tribune* was coming in steadily and things were looking brighter they began to contemplate a move. They managed to borrow a friend's flat in Camberwell for a few weeks in 1855, but had to return once again to Dean Street. But that summer Jenny Marx's mother died and left her a small legacy, and at the same time one of her Scottish relatives died and also left her a small sum. A change was now at last possible, and they bought a little furniture and moved into what Jenny called "agreeable bourgeois cosiness" in Grafton Terrace, Kentish Town. The rent was £36 a year.

The year 1855 had witnessed the death of Marx's little son Edgar on Good Friday, a talented boy of eight and a great favourite with the family. Marx wrote at the time, "I am terribly upset. My heart is heavy and my head is in a whirl, but of course I have to keep up a brave front. The house seems empty and deserted since the boy died. He was its life and soul. It is impossible to describe how much we miss him all the time." Wilhelm Liebknecht, who lived near them in a tiny room in Soho, and was a constant visitor, says, "I cannot forget the scene—the mother weeping in silence bending over her dead child, Lenchen standing by and sobbing, and Marx, a prey to terrible agitation, answering violently and almost wrathfully any attempt to console him, the two girls weeping silently."

Their sorrow was relieved by the birth of Eleanor, their third surviving daughter, a little later in the year. She was to become his constant companion and the capable assistant of his later years. Lenchen was the family name for Helene Demuth, the German girl who came to them shortly after their marriage and remained with them to the end. She was a second mother to the children, and a kind of dictator in the house. She loved Marx and his wife, and served them faithfully; but she was totally unafraid of Marx's bad temper and knew all his whims and weaknesses. Jenny Marx, accustomed from early childhood to the comfort of a wealthy home, found life in London terribly difficult, and sometimes fell into despair and bitter complaint, Marx always excused and justified her, declaring that she had incomparably more to suffer than he himself.

It must have been in the darkest days in Dean Street that Marx took the last of the Westphalen silver, the spoons he had saved from the rest in 1848 for Jenny, and bearing the arms of the Argylls, to the pawn shop and was immediately asked to explain how he came to have the property of the Duke of Argyll in his possession.

When he finished his *Critique of Political Economy* he had no money to pay for the postage and the registration fee for sending it to his Berlin publishers. "I don't suppose anyone has ever written about money and suffered such a lack of it himself," he said when he wrote to Engels requesting enough money to send off the manuscript.

Marx himself, though as a young man he had a magnificent physique, began to suffer as a result of the privations he was going through and his own endless labours. He was a colossal worker. He worked all day and most of the night—sometimes for the whole night. At the end of the fifties he began to suffer from a liver complaint. He was ordered to give up his night work and to take more exercise. For a time he did so, and he and Liebknecht took long walks over the hills and heath of Hampstead. But Marx complained bitterly that incapacity to work was a death sentence on any human being not merely an animal. When he was too ill to work he read voraciously. He wrote to Engels to tell him that he had just read Carpenter's *Physiology*, Kolliker's *Histology*, Spurzheim's *Anatomy of the Brain and the Nervous System* and Schwann and Schleiden's *Cell Theory*.

These were the worst years of his life. He was fighting against adversity and sometimes it seemed a losing battle. On one occasion he had to stay at home because he had neither coat nor shoes to go out in; sometimes he could not afford writing-paper or newspapers. He lived in utter insecurity. Sometimes he revolted against the endless drudgery of his newspaper articles. "Grinding bones and making soup out of them like the paupers in the workhouse. That is how much the political work for such a paper amounts to." Everyone who knew him felt that his intellect and working capacity were being terribly restricted and broken by petty cares and worries. But though he had to go on writing his articles he never forgot the words he had written as a young editor in Cologne: "a writer must certainly earn money in order to exist, but he should not exist and write in order to earn money." It was in 1861 that he wrote, "I must follow my goal through thick and thin and I shall not permit bourgeois society to turn me into a money-making machine."

Not only could Marx not have gone on with his work without the financial assistance of Engels, but without it he would never have secured at last the very modest level of decency which came to him when he got out of Soho. The family remained at Grafton Terrace for some seven years and then in 1864 moved to 1 Maitland Park Road, Kentish Town,[1] and from there in March 1875 to 41 Maitland Park Road, where they lived until the death of Marx seven years later.

Engels was competently handling the family business in Manchester and was a respected member of the Stock Exchange. He was a convivial person as well as a good man of business, and being an excellent horseman often rode to hounds. When he left his office he went away to a quiet suburb where he enjoyed until her death in 1863 a life of quiet and happy domesticity with an Irish working girl named Mary Burns—a circumstance which did not entirely please the Marxes. She was very dear to him. "I cannot tell you how I feel," he wrote to Marx at the time of her death; "the poor girl loved me with her whole heart." But Marx was then preoccupied with his own troubles and he deeply wounded his friend by an unsympathetic reply in which he poured out the story of his own difficulties at great length. We know of no other occasion upon which the two friends were estranged. Engels wrote, after waiting a week, a bitter letter to Marx. Marx in his reply assured Engels that he deeply regretted the tone of his former letter, but he had written in the most desperate straits, for the landlord had put the bailiffs in and there was no coal or food in the house. There was one more letter from Engels which closed the matter. "No one can live so long with a woman," he said, "without being terribly moved by her death. I feel that with her I buried the last of my youth. I tell you, your letter stuck in my head for a whole week. I couldn't forget it. Never mind, your last letter made it quits; and I am glad that when I lost Mary I did not also lose my oldest and best friend."

Later, Mary's sister Lizzie went to live with him, and he always described her as his wife. An Irish girl, like Mary, she was passionately concerned with the oppression of her people, and their house was a place of refuge for Irish rebels. Engels himself became deeply sympathetic to the cause of Irish freedom. Lizzie died in 1878. Engels said of her: "She came of real Irish proletarian stock, and the passionate feeling for her class, which was instinctive in her, was worth more to me than

[1] Originally No. 1, Modena Villas, Kentish Town.

all the blue-stockinged elegance of 'educated' and 'sensitive' *bourgeois* girls could have been."

Yet Engels himself wanted to study and to write, he was a man of exceptional talent with an immensely wide range of knowledge. All these ambitions he had to put aside until he had made enough money both to make Marx secure for life and to get out of business himself at last.

The interests of both men were far-reaching. They were writing on India, on Palmerston's foreign policy and the Eastern Question, on the Irish troubles, on the Civil War in the United States. They took within their range the whole scope of European affairs in those tumultuous years. They hailed the Crimean War (1855) because the three powers which had been the mainstay of counter-revolution had fallen out. Russian Tsarism was the prop of European reaction and they declared that its defeat proved how a state based on serfdom was incapable of fighting more developed countries.[1] But England and France came in for as much denunciation as Russia. Marx mercilessly exposed the attempts of Palmerston and Napoleon III to represent the war as a crusade for civilisation and progress against Asiatic barbarism.

In 1859 Napoleon III and Cavour, the Piedmontese statesman, engineered a war to liberate Italy from Austrian domination. It was to be the first step to the unification of all Italy. Napoleon thus posed as a champion of freedom, though he had just destroyed democracy in France. The conflict greatly disturbed Germany. If Austria fell might not that leave Germany unprotected? Marx saw no threat to Germany and thought it would be an excellent thing if the Austrians were driven out of Italy—but not by Napoleon III. Could this not be accomplished by Italy herself?

Then another dissident voice from the socialist ranks was heard—that of Ferdinand Lassalle. He saw Austria as the great rival of Prussia. He earnestly desired her total defeat by Napoleon whom he defended as the champion of liberalism, progress and civilisation. He even began to speak in friendly terms of Tsarist Russia, the potential ally of Prussia.

In the event, Napoleon suddenly made peace with Austria, helped himself to Savoy and left the Italians in the lurch. This hardly surprised Marx; but the attitude of Lassalle did—Lassalle, the socialist leader of the German workers who owed much to Marx. What did his extraordinary support for the Prussian Government mean? Was he trying to curry favour?

[1] Russia was forced to emancipate her serfs in 1861.

Bismarck was the power behind the throne in Prussia. Determined to make Prussia all-powerful and to unite all Germany under her, he knew he could only do this by defeating Austria; and that would require the friendship or at any rate the neutrality of Russia and France. It was Bismarck's policy that Lassalle, who was regarded as a follower of Marx, seemed to be supporting. The war came, France remained neutral. Austria was defeated and German unification was within Bismarck's grasp.

Who was Lassalle? He was a brilliant young Jewish lawyer, who had studied Hegel, written a scholarly study of Heraclitus and a legal work on the *System of Acquired Rights*. In 1848 he attached himself to Marx and Engels and those who represented the extreme democratic side of the revolution. Lassalle alternated between high life and working-class politics. He had a strange relationship with a certain member of the aristocracy, the Countess Hetzfeldt, who was estranged from her husband and denied certain rights in her property. Lassalle took up her cause and brought the case before no fewer than thirty-six legal tribunals, and eventually secured a favourable decision. He had money, he was a brilliant orator and extremely ambitious.

In 1858 there had begun a general rise of the opposition and radical movement in all Western European countries. The demand for German unification was raised again, but was it to be a wide-ranging union including Austria, or the grouping of the adjacent German states round Prussia? The working-class movement was also stirring, and Lassalle played an important part in getting it moving and getting it organised—a fact that Marx fully recognised.

Lassalle produced his *Workingmen's Programme*, which contained some of the fundamental ideas of the *Manifesto*, though he was very careful never to acknowledge the source of these ideas for fear of arousing prejudice. It was the first open declaration in Germany of the necessity of organising the working class into an independent political organisation sharply marked off from all, even the most democratic, bourgeois parties. He diverged radically from Marx, however, in insisting that "the iron law of wages" prevented any real possibility of raising wages under capitalism. It followed that he had little use for trade unions—again in opposition to Marx—but strongly advocated the organisation of producers' co-operatives, and even went so far as to seek financial aid from the government for them. He also attached more importance than Marx to universal suffrage, which with him was almost a miracle-working panacea. Nevertheless, he won over the workers' organisations that were coming into being and founded the Universal German Workingman's Association in Leipzig in 1863, addressed mass meetings everywhere and went on a triumphal tour through Germany, feeling, as he said, that it was like the founding of a new religion. Everywhere he went he declared that they were now entering on a new era in history, of which the working class were the makers and representatives. He told the liberals in Germany, still struggling for constitutional rights, that constitutional questions were not legal questions, they would never get a constitution by filling a sheet of paper with words, but only by changing the relationship of power.

But while posing as the spokesman of the poor, Lassalle was a man of decidedly fashionable and luxurious habits. When he visited Marx he incensed the whole family by his behaviour while they were straining their resources to dress the girls decently for his visit and make the poor household a little presentable. He found Marx in great straits and lent him money, but on strangely uncomradely terms which wounded Marx deeply. Marx found Lassalle to be as brilliant as ever but vain, insanely over-confident, and posing as "a revolutionary Cardinal Richelieu". Marx saw through him, fixed upon him a terrible eye which shrivelled his pretensions; and Lassalle retreated to Germany. He went back full of new Machiavellian schemes. He hated the liberal progressives and conceived a policy of outflanking them and furthering the interests of the workers by joining forces with Bismarck, who also hated the liberals, but for very different reasons. Now it became clear why he had backed Prussian ambitions and policies. He actually believed that Bismarck would accept him and the workers' movement as an ally and treat him virtually as an equal partner. He would buy concessions from Bismarck in return for working-class support, and would secure measures for state-controlled economy, which was a step towards socialism, loans for his co-operatives, even perhaps the franchise.

How far Lassalle had in fact gone in this direction has subsequently been revealed. He actually negotiated on these lines with Bismarck, who had a considerable regard for his talents and was certainly prepared to make use of him, as Lassalle intended to make use of Bismarck.

All these plans came to nothing. In 1864 he was killed in a foolish duel. Marx was furious at the wave of adulation that rose throughout the working-class movement at his death. "He was a very uncertain friend and for the future a certain enemy"; but he was "the most important fellow in Germany. In spite of everything, he was the enemy of our enemies. Even aside from his abilities, I personally loved him. The unfortunate thing is that we concealed it from one another as if we were going to live for ever."

KARL VOGT

In 1860 Marx became deeply involved for a whole year in a furious polemic with Dr. Karl Vogt. During this year, to the distress of many of his friends, all his other work was put aside and he wrote a large book of 192 closely printed pages exposing and denouncing this man.

Dr. Karl Vogt was an able zoologist and geologist who had been one of the leaders of the Left wing in the Frankfurt Assembly. After the collapse of the revolution he withdrew to Geneva where he died in 1895. He had a European reputation and was well known as an aggressive exponent of a particularly crude form of materialism. "Thought," he said "stands in the same relation to the brain as bile does to the liver."[1] This was the view from which even Ludwig Buchner, the leading materialist of those times, strongly dissented. Thought, argued Buchner, is not a form of matter, but a function of matter. Marx and Engels also repudiated this crude philistine way of thinking, and Marx argues against it in his *Theses on Feuerbach*. In the political field Vogt had a considerable influence among the international revolutionary *émigrés* who forgathered at his home in Geneva for discussions and for planning their activities.

Vogt, like Lassalle, came out strongly for Napoleon III's intervention in Italy. Information reached London that he was receiving money from Napoleon. Liebknecht passed this information to a German paper and Vogt sued for libel and lost. He countered with a scurrilous attack on Marx, in which he even accused him of living in luxury at the expense of the workers. His pamphlet caused a sensation and Marx felt under the necessity of replying to it and at the same time pressing home his suspicion that Vogt was in the pay of Napoleon.

It is without doubt one of the most brilliant and even entertaining of Marx's works.[2] He pursued the unfortunate doctor up hill and down dale, exposing his tricks and artifices until not a vestige of his case remained and his whole propaganda line was clearly seen to be an echo

[1] A similar statement had been made by the French physiologist Cabanis in 1799. Cabanis had espoused with enthusiasm the cause of the revolution in 1789.

[2] This work has never been translated into English.

of Napoleon's policies. The invective is sublime and the book becomes a pyrotechnic display of considerable virtuosity. When Marx was accused of wasting his time, he replied that it is never waste of time to expose the false in their own ranks, so far more dangerous enemies than open enemies. But was Marx correct in maintaining that Vogt was bribed? The answer came some years later after the overthrow of Napoleon III. The Government of National Defence found in the archives of the Tuileries a receipt signed by Vogt in August 1859 for 40,000 francs from the secret funds of the Emperor. Naturally the only person who was not surprised by this disclosure was Karl Marx.

Jenny Marx wore herself out in helping her husband in this crisis. She copied the whole enormous manuscript for the printer, since no one but her could read Marx's handwriting. Then she collapsed and was found to be suffering from smallpox. Liebknecht looked after the children, Lenchen (Helen Demuth) looked after the sick woman and Marx. Immediately afterwards (March 1861) Marx himself developed an acute condition of the liver and was completely incapacitated. When he recovered he determined to make a desperate bid to secure financial help. He went to Holland to see his uncle. The visit was not unsuccessful. Marx went on to Berlin and was received with great friendliness by Lassalle; but he disliked the whole atmosphere there. From Berlin he went to Cologne to visit old friends and to see his old mother, whose end was drawing near. He was back in London at the beginning of May.

It was at this time that the outbreak of the Civil War in America (1861-65) brought to an end his articles to the *New York Tribune*. He and Engels followed the war closely, Engels as much from a military as from a political angle. They wrote a series of thirty-five articles on the war for the Vienna *Presse* and the correspondence between Marx and Engels during this period is of absorbing interest.[1] It was amazing how Marx never allowed his growing poverty to affect his objectivity and the trenchancy of his political comments. But he was now in such straits that he tried to find work in a clerical capacity with one of the railway companies, but he never succeeded because no one could read his handwriting.

In 1864 Engels became a partner in the firm of Ermen and Engels, and his financial position considerably improved. It marked the beginning of the end of the distress and poverty of the Marx family. It was towards the close of 1863, after they had received the legacy

[1] See Chapter 20, "Marx and America".

from Marx's mother, that they moved to Maitland Park Road where they remained until the death of Marx in 1883.

At the same time, the development of the international situation prepared the way for the return of Marx to the field of political organisation. On September 28th, 1864, the International Working Men's Association was formed at a meeting in St. Martin's Hall, London. Marx was placed on the committee and for the next seven years it became the task to which he devoted all his powers.

14

THE INTERNATIONAL

A GREAT movement cannot be confined within national barriers. The idea of socialism and the common interests of the working class increasingly bound together the revolutionary elements of the countries of Europe. Experience drove home their common antagonism to capitalism. In the competitive struggles of rapidly developing industrialism the cheap labour of one nation could be thrown into the scale to lower the standard of living of another. Capitalists were engaged in shielding themselves from competition by tariffs, why should not the workers, too, seek to regulate their international interests?

Efforts towards the international organisation of labour were initiated chiefly by men who, banished from their own country by reactionary governments, emigrated to other lands, particularly to Paris and London, and meeting abroad those of like mind and like fate with themselves, naturally planned the overthrow of their common oppressors. But the defeat of the 1848 revolution was followed by a prolonged period of stagnation in the political life of Western Europe. Marx understood well enough how the working-class groups, by failing to take the initiative from the bourgeois parties, had failed to make any serious impression on the course of events during the revolutionary upheaval. Almost ten years elapsed before the revolutionary movements began to recover from their defeat.

Economic developments proceeded vigorously until the crisis of 1857. In the eighteen-fifties there began a period of unprecedented industrial advance. Capitalism began to extend from Britain and France into the more backward countries and break through and destroy pre-capitalist forms of production, thus bringing ruin to the peasantry and to the urban petty bourgeoisie and creating a propertyless working class and the conditions for capitalist industry.

In England, the trade union movement was taking the place of the Chartists; and there was a rapid development of co-operative societies and mutual benefit associations, which drew the workers away from political life. There was one last burst of revolutionary feeling during the Crimean War, owing to the activity of Ernest Jones (1819-65), a splendid orator and a brilliant journalist, who had built up with the assistance of Marx the best socialist organ of those times. The *People's Paper* published Marx's masterly articles directed at the policies of Palmerston and Gladstone, and they attracted wide attention. But the movement was all the time being weakened by a wave of emigration from England to America and Australia. In the course of a few years, two million workers left the country and the working-class movement was drained of the reserves from which it drew its strength.

The men who kept socialism alive, however, were mostly in London, whither they had fled from Germany in 1849 and from France after 1851. There were refugees of all kinds in London, but Marx and Engels refused to play any part in *émigré* politics, which tended to lapse into petty squabbles and futile intrigues.

By 1852 the Fraternal Democrats were forced finally to disband and Harney dropped out of active politics. Ernest Jones rallied some of the old stalwarts around him and became chairman of a new body called the International Committee, on which sat representatives of the refugee groups in London. This organisation issued manifestoes and called commemorative meetings, but the tendency was to repeat the old slogans of 1848 and fall back on empty rhetoric. But something was to come from this attempt to keep the spirit of 1848 alive.

In France there had been an immense industrial expansion in the epoch of Napoleon III, but economic crisis caused the discontent which the war of 1859 with Austria was designed to sidetrack. The labour movement began to revive and with this came the awakening of the old socialist groups—the followers of Proudhon, pursuing a peaceful policy of free credit for co-operative associations, no strikes and no politics; and the revolutionary disciples of Blanqui, who had resumed their propaganda among the workers as well as among the intelligentsia and the student youth. Among these were Paul Lafargue, a medical student, and Charles Longuet, both of whom subsequently became Marx's sons-in-law.

Events had also been moving in Germany. Up to the sixties, workers' organisations were mainly educational societies, under which form many of the more revolutionary workers carried on their work. But the rapid development of industry brought with it an advance in the labour movement which became more and more politically independent. In 1862 the workers of Saxony asked Lassalle to indicate the immediate tasks of the working class, and in 1863 the Union of

German Workers was formed in Leipzig under his leadership; but any attempts at closer links with workers' organisations outside Germany were rendered difficult if not impossible by Prussian law.

The revolutionary movement was practically confined to Western Europe, but in Russia the development of industry and railways had begun; the disasters of the Crimean War clearly indicated the necessity for economic advance and reform. The burning question of the day was the abolition of serfdom, and it was a time of much underground revolutionary ferment by such organisations as the Land and Freedom Society. Russian revolutionaries of all kinds, liberals, anarchists and socialists, were to be found in Western Europe, especially in Paris and London, and many of them such as Bakunin and Annenkov were well known to Marx.

In Poland, revolutionary feeling of a purely nationalist and political kind was strong and burst forth in repeated attempts to overthrow Russian domination. What the Western internationalists called "the Muscovite invasion of Europe" was bitterly resisted in the Polish insurrections of 1830 and 1863. To this event the workers responded with passionate sympathy. In England and in France they organised agitation in support of the insurrection. A British National League for the Independence of Poland was set up in London, and support for the Polish revolutionaries came from all sorts of working-class and radical gatherings. In London there was a strong group of democratic Polish *émigrés*, and in both France and the United States Poles who had taken part in the uprisings of 1830 and 1863 were to be found playing an active part in all radical political movements.

On July 28th, 1863, a great public meeting to express sympathy with the Polish insurgents was held in London at which there were present English trade unionists and representatives of the French workers. It was at this meeting that the first step towards the foundation of an international association embracing English and continental workers was taken.

Internationalism was no less potent a factor in the economic sphere of the labour movement. In England very many retained as a legacy from the Chartist period strong sympathies for progressive movements abroad. During the American Civil War they demonstrated their sympathies for the Northern States, in the time of the Polish insurrection of 1830 and 1863 they were heart and soul with the revolutionaries; the movement for freedom and unity in Italy too could rely on the friendly support of British labour, and when Garibaldi came to London, he was given a royal welcome.

But there had come into existence another movement which was led by those already deeply interested in international affairs. This was the campaign for universal suffrage which became the Reform League and caused the government to introduce and carry the Second Reform Bill. The same men who organised public meetings in favour of the anti-slavery Northern States, who formed the Fraternal Delegates, who demonstrated on behalf of the Poles, were also leaders of the Reform League—George Odger, a shoemaker, President of the recently formed London Trades Council; W. Randall Cremer, one of the founders of The Amalgamated Society of Carpenters and Joiners; Robert Applegarth, General Secretary of the same union. These men were the leaders of the trade union movement in London.

It was at the meeting in support of Poland that the trade unionists brought forward the suggestion for a discussion on the necessity of joint action to resist the driving down of wages by the competition of cheap foreign labour. It was decided to appeal to the French workers in this sense, and after the meeting an address was drawn up and despatched to Paris. In September 1864 a delegation came to England with the answer of the French workers. On the 28th of the same month there was held that historic meeting in London which led to the foundation of the International. It was summoned by Odger and Cremer, who invited representatives of all working-class societies in London to attend either as speakers or participants. The meeting was held in the St. Martin's Hall, Long Acre, and was packed.

A French delegation arrived headed by Tolain, who had been a workers' candidate in recent elections. Major Luigi Wolff, Garibaldi's adjutant, represented the Italians, and Professor Edward Spencer Beesly, the historian, presided. Marx was among the invited guests on the platform and it was he who quickly assumed the leadership of the new organisation.

Odger read an address to the French delegation, Tolain replied, and Marx's friend Eccarius spoke on behalf of the Germans. Johann Georg Eccarius, who came from Thuringia in Germany, had been among the supporters of Marx in the Communist League split of 1850. He had contributed an article to the *Neue Rheinische Revue* at that time which greatly pleased Marx. Eccarius was a working tailor and he realised that the replacement of handicrafts by large-scale industry was a great step forward and created the conditions for a proletarian revolution. Marx saw this as an immense advance on the usual emotional denunciation of the evils of industrialism. It also showed him that his own teaching was not without success. Eccarius was to play an important role in the International and was to become its Vice-President.

A committee was elected at the meeting, which included British trade unionists like Odger and Cremer, bourgeois radicals, Owenites like Weston, Chartists, French and Italian representatives, and Eccarius and Marx as representatives of the German workers. There were forty members present at the first meeting of the Committee. They were a very mixed collection, representing greatly divergent points of view. Not only were there Chartists and trade unionists, Owenites and French revolutionists, but an influential group of Italian patriots, headed by Mazzini. Then there were the Poles, the Germans, including Marx and Eccarius, and a number of philanthropically disposed middle-class persons. The Committee had no instructions. There was no programme, no constitution, not even a name. Only on the insistence of Eccarius was it decided to call the new society the International Working Men's Association, a name which unequivocally defined the distinctive character of the organisation. As soon as the name was decided upon the Committee proceeded to consider the question of a programme and statutes. A sub-committee (including Marx) was appointed to draft a declaration of principles and provisional rules. Two documents were submitted, one by Major Wolff representing the views of Mazzini, and another of John Weston, a carpenter, and subsequently a manufacturer, who later was to plunge the General Council into an economic discussion of the first importance. It was, says Marx, "a programme of indescribable breadth and full of the most extreme confusion".[1] Both documents were remitted for abridgment and revision. Marx had not been present at the meetings up to this point. Eccarius wrote an urgent letter to him criticising both documents and strongly urging Marx to take a hand. "Weston", he wrote, "is an old Owenist, who seems to know no other basis for labour movements than the hackneyed phrase, Truth and Justice."

A new version rewritten by Lubez, a French representative, was submitted, Marx being present, and was approved and once more remitted to the sub-committee to be put into final form. Three of them met at Marx's house on October 20th. After a long discussion on the rules, Marx was left to work over the material. He scrapped it entirely

[1] Marx to Engels, November 4th, 1864.

and wrote instead *An Address to the Working Classes*, followed by a short preamble and ten rules, instead of the original forty. At the meeting of the general committee the whole thing was enthusiastically agreed to.

Marx had succeeded in a very difficult task. The Address was designed to secure acceptance by all sections of the new Association and its leading elements of what was basically the Communist point of view. It had to take into account a very different situation from 1848, the year of revolution. Now the political consciousness of the masses was at a low level. Marx formulated the demands upon which the maximum unity could be secured and maintained.

He begins in a thoroughly concrete way by pointing out that in spite of immense economic advances poverty was as deep and widespread as ever it had been. "On the present false basis, every fresh development of the productive powers of labour must tend to deepen social contrasts and point social antagonisms."

Nevertheless, there had been two considerable advances: first, the ten-hour day had been established, rebutting the contention of capitalist economists that such improvements in workers' conditions would ruin industry; second, there had been a great extension of producers' co-operatives, proving that production can be carried on without a class of masters employing wage labour. Not that the indefinite extension of such a system is possible, because the lords of land and capital will use their political power to break the final emancipation of labour. Therefore, before production can be subjected to the control and direction of society as a whole, the workers must conquer political power, and not in one country only, but with the fraternal concurrence of all.

But, the *Address* continues, if emancipation of the working class demands the conquest of political power and their fraternal unity across all national boundaries, "how are they to fulfil their great mission with a foreign policy in pursuit of criminal designs, playing upon national prejudices and squandering in piratical wars the people's blood and treasure?" Clearly it is the duty of the working classes "to master themselves the mysteries of international politics; to watch the diplomatic acts of their respective governments; to counteract them, if necessary, by all means in their power; when unable to prevent, to combine in simultaneous denunciation, and to vindicate the simple laws of morals and justice, which ought to govern the relations of private individuals, as the rules paramount of the intercourse of nations.

"The fight for such a foreign policy forms part of the general struggle for the emancipation of the working classes.

"Proletarians of all countries, unite!"[1]

Thus Marx, exercising amazing tact and skill, in effect arrived again at the basic conclusion of *The Communist Manifesto*. Under certain circumstances he could be brusque and intolerant, but when the occasion or the person required it, no one could show such forbearance and infinite patience.

The *Provisional Rules* were equally important. They begin with the basic affirmation "that the emancipation of the working classes must be conquered by the working classes themselves"; and continue by stating that the economic subjection of the worker to the capitalist owner of the means of production is at the bottom of servitude in all its forms, and must be ended. This requires solidarity between the different sections of labour in each country and the fraternal unity of the working classes of all nations.

The International made steady progress both at home and abroad. Marx proposed individual membership and things went ahead, and 50,000 copies of the Inaugural Address were distributed. By the end of 1865 it could claim that several thousands of members had been enrolled in France, Germany, Switzerland and Belgium. Later things began to move in Italy, where Mazzini revealed himself as a bitter enemy, and also in Spain, where Lafargue worked for a year and conducted the struggle against the anarchism of Bakunin. Germany presented a serious problem because of the bitter opposition of the Lassalleans, and the Prussian law prohibiting workers' organisations joining societies in other countries.

At one of its earliest meetings the General Council drew up an Address to Abraham Lincoln, congratulating the American people on their having elected him as President and vigorously affirming that no true freedom for white labour could ever have been achieved until slavery had been abolished. The slave-holders' rebellion had been a crusade of property against labour. Only a few months later they were called upon to send a second address to President Johnson on the occasion of Lincoln's assassination, "a man neither to be browbeaten by adversity, nor intoxicated by success, inflexibly pressing on to his great goal, never compromising to blind haste, slowly maturing his

[1] Written by Karl Marx, October 21st-27th, 1864, and adopted by the General Council at its meeting of November 1st, 1864.

steps, never retracing them, carried away by no surge of popular favour, disheartened by no slackening of the popular pulse".[1]

Two important questions of foreign policy confronted the General Council in its early years: the problem of Poland and the Austro-Prussian War of 1866. There were always the parochially minded who saw no point in involving the working-class movement in support of Polish independence. After all, they argued, it could only benefit the nobility, not the Polish peasantry; and as for establishing a bulwark against Russia, Russia was no worse than any other reactionary power. Marx replied that the workers supported this cause, though middle-class writers and publicists ignored it, because without a democratic Poland Germany would become the bastion of the Holy Alliance. Russian domination of Poland was left unchecked "because both aristocrats and bourgeois look upon the dark Asiatic power in the background as a last resource against the advancing tide of working-class ascendancy".[2]

In the discussions, the idea that political questions of this sort should be ignored, since only social questions concerned them, was rejected —"Where was despotism to stop if the voice of humanity was not raised against it?" The International, therefore, continued to maintain its original position, "that an integral and independent Poland is an indispensable condition of democratic Europe, and that so long as this condition is unfulfilled, revolutionary triumphs on the Continent are short-lived preludes to prolonged periods of counter-revolutionary ascendancy".[3]

When Prussia declared war on Austria in 1866 there were long discussions on the General Council in crowded meetings. It was eventually resolved that the International considered the war to be between governments, and advised the workers to remain neutral and build up their own strength for their ultimate emancipation.[4]

Marx and Engels, who believed that Austria would prove victorious, were gravely mistaken as to the outcome of the war.[5] They had obviously lost touch with the situation in Germany, and overestimated the strength of the Austrian Army. They even imagined that after the defeat of Prussia the *Landwehr* (the Reserve) would revolt. In the

[1] Both addresses were written by Marx.
[2] Marx, *Instruction for the Delegates to the Geneva Congress*. 1866.
[3] Resolution submitted on behalf of the International to the Polish Meeting on March 1st, 1865.
[4] General Council Resolution. July 17th, 1866.
[5] Marx subordinated himself to Engels' judgment in all military questions.

event the Prussians won an overwhelming victory at Sadowa after only eight hours' fighting. This was an unpleasant pill for them to swallow, but they frankly admitted their misjudgment. Marx and Engels might make mistakes, and they often did so, but they never resisted the recognition of error when the events themselves compelled it.

The International received growing support from trade unions all over England, but especially in London.[1] In a most practical way it intervened in labour disputes, supporting the locked-out Manchester tailors and defending the wire-workers against endeavours to break their struggle by importing labour from the Continent.

It is interesting to note that in the early period the International was quite fairly treated in the press. But when the part which it played in strikes, and the decisions of the Congresses, revealed its intention, it suddenly became a "band of incendiaries", "men to whom nothing was sacred", who "aimed at anarchy and the annihilation of civilisation". The whole question of trade union policy, organisational and economic, greatly exercised the General Council and was to form a major issue at the first Congress of the International to be held at Geneva in 1866.

In August 1865 the General Council took up the question of forming a newspaper company to "advocate the interests of the working class and defend the cause of labour", existing newspapers being "the property of capitalists, established for their own use". In September, *The Workman's Advocate* became the official organ of the International.

An important economic question was vigorously debated during the spring and summer of 1865. John Weston, who repeatedly demanded more attention for questions of fundamental theory, raised the issue of whether wages could be increased under capitalism by trade union action. The debate was continued from meeting to meeting and eventually Marx intervened on June 20th, concluding his contribution to the discussion a week later. This lengthy reply to Weston is the well-known essay by Marx entitled *Value, Price and Profit*, which was published only in 1898 by his daughter Eleanor. This is one of the smaller classics of Marxist economic theory. Marx showed that Weston was, in effect, advocating passivity and submission to capitalist

[1] In the first two years membership and support came from the Bricklayers, Bootmakers, Tailors, Book-binders, Cabinet-makers, Compositors, Coachmakers, Cordwainers, Coopers and other unions.

exploitation. This was a criticism not only of Weston but of the French followers of Proudhon, who took a negative attitude to trade unions. Marx held that the trade unions could counteract the tendency of wages to be driven down and that they could also be successful in shortening and regulating the hours of labour.

The first important event that the International had to plan for was the London Conference of 1865 at which Marx proposed that they should thrash out the major issues of policy before the first congress which was to be held at Geneva in the following year. At this Conference, Marx strongly and successfully resisted the French suggestion that they should wage an unflinching war upon religion. Other subjects discussed were the length of the working day, co-operatives, and the work of trade unions and, of course, the Polish question. Reports on the growing movement for franchise reform in England, for which the International took credit, were received, and reports also came in from France and Belgium.

The financial position of the General Council caused some anxiety. The total income for the first year had been £33.

The private sessions in the morning were followed by public meetings in the evening, and the Conference concluded with a social gathering or soirée in the St. Martin's Hall with musical items by the Italian Workers' branch, songs by the German Chorus, speeches and a programme of dances. "Wines, spirits, ales, stout, tea and coffee" were also provided. An *Address to the People of the United States of America* was carried by acclamation. It appeared in *The Workman's Advocate* for October 14th, 1865. It congratulated them on the end of the war and the preservation of the union and on the abolition of slavery, but went on to declare that "if you fail to give them citizen's rights, while you demand citizen's duties, there will yet remain a struggle for the future which may again stain your country with your people's blood".

INTERNATIONAL CONGRESS, 1866-68

The first Congress of the International was held on September 3rd-8th, 1866, in Geneva. The majority consisted of Proudhonists from France and Switzerland. Opposed to them were the English delegates who had come prepared with a memorandum covering every issue which would be raised.[1]

[1] *Documents of The First International*, Volume I, "Instructions for the Delegates of the General Council".

It was a critical occasion. Two groups of French delegates attended: the Proudhonists with a policy of no trade unions, no strikes, no political struggle, reform through producers' co-operatives and financial credits. The Proudhonists also demanded an all-out attack on religion. On the question of female labour their attitude was particularly reactionary. They opposed the participation of women in public life and production, and asserted that woman's place was the home. The other French section consisted of revolutionary Blanquists, mostly students with no credentials who were unceremoniously thrown out.

Most of the Proudhonist proposals were rejected by the Congress, and the proposals of Marx, mainly concerned with trade unions, were carried in the form of resolutions. The unions were treated as vital centres of working-class organisation, which the proletariat could use not only in daily economic struggle, but also as a means towards the abolition of the capitalist wage system. Therefore the unions must concern themselves with politics as well as industrial affairs, and function as the centre of the working-class struggle against capitalism. They must become the champions of the whole working class, and fight for and win the support of the unskilled and unorganised workers as well as the craftsmen.

The Congress declared its hostility to the imperialist designs of Russia and advocated the restoration of an independent Poland reconstituted on democratic principles.

The Congress aroused interest and support everywhere. The Sheffield Conference of English trade unionists (1866) passed a resolution expressing "unqualified appreciation of the efforts of the International to unite the workers of all countries by the common bonds of fraternity".

The influence of the International increased rapidly during the next two years. At the Lausanne Congress, September 2nd-8th, 1867, a considerable advance was achieved. For the first time its policies looked in the direction of socialism; but the Proudhonists were still strong and secured the passing of a resolution in favour of a "national credit system". One of the most important resolutions declared that the winning of political power was the first and most urgent task of the working class.

From the time of this Congress the influence of the International was felt more and more strongly in industrial struggles, and it played an important part in several major strikes, especially by its resistance to the importation of foreign workers as strike breakers.

The Brussels Congress, held from September 5th to 30th, 1868, saw the victory for a socialist policy. A resolution was passed demanding the collective ownership of transportation, communication and land. "Quarries, coal-mines and other mines, as well as railways, will, in a rational society, belong to society collectively as represented by the State." This marks the defeat of the Proudhonists, and thereafter their influence declined. Correspondingly the influence of Marx increased. The first volume of *Capital* had been published—the final stages of its preparation account for the absence of Marx from both Lausanne and Brussels. At the suggestion of the German delegation a resolution was passed which urged the workers of the different countries to study *Capital*, and declared that to Marx belonged the honour of being "the first economist who subjected capital to a scientific analysis and who reduced it to its basic elements".

The International was now attracting attention in the European Press. *The Times* devoted four leading articles to the Brussels Congress, and concluded: "It is not a mere improvement that is contemplated, but nothing less than a regeneration, and that not of one nation only, but of mankind. This is certainly the most extensive aim ever contemplated by any institution, with the exception perhaps, of the Christian Church."

The International was, however, not as strong in fact as it appeared to those who feared it. Its prestige was based rather on the potentialites of the cause it championed than on a realistic assessment of its present power. If Brussels marked the successful termination of the struggle with the followers of Proudhon, now another danger appeared. Bakunin, the anarchist, had formed a society called The League of Peace and Freedom.[1] They asked to affiliate to the International. They were refused and told to dissolve and let their members join individually. Bakunin professed to have dissolved his society; but Marx was convinced that he had done nothing of the sort, but had left it intact and secretly organised for the purpose of capturing the International. Thus began the struggle with Bakunin which ended with his expulsion in 1872.

[1] Bakunin eventually left the League to form a new organisation called The International Social-Democratic Alliance.

BAKUNIN

Bakunin was a Russian artistocrat and artillery officer who resigned his commission, came to Paris in 1847, met Proudhon, many of whose views he adopted, and became a revolutionary. He played an active part in the German revolution of 1848, took part in the defence of Dresden, was captured and for eight years confined in various fortresses in Saxony, Austria and Russia. Then he was exiled to Siberia, but escaped and made his way back to Europe, via Japan and San Francisco. He came back burning with zeal to overthrow the whole of civilisation, declaring implacable war upon God and the state. He despised the working class and looked for revolutionary disciples only among the intelligentsia. He rejected every form of external authority, all legislation, even when it proceeded from universal suffrage. He contemplated a condition of human enlightenment in which the individual would be a law to himself and all public law and authority would be abolished to ensure perfect freedom. But first destroy, and then everything will take care of itself!

The originality of his ideas, his majestic stature, his picturesque and fiery eloquence, won him disciples everywhere, but particularly in Italy and Spain, where government was particularly irresponsible and despotic, and there was no organised working-class movement.

In the Council of the International, Bakunin brought forward one proposal—the abolition of inheritance. The Marxists replied that this was not the cause of the existing economic organisation of society but the effect. The aim should be to abolish the institution which gave the few the power to appropriate the fruits of labour of the many. The Basle Congress (1869) came to no clear decision and the question was shelved. The second London Conference met in 1871.

Marx regarded Bakunin at first with some affection and respect; but as his policies became clearer and his tactics more devious, Marx came to regard him as little more than an irresponsible scoundrel. Bakunin became involved with a still more sinister person, Nechayev, who persuaded large numbers of people that he was the executive leader of a powerful secret society. Returning to Russia he "executed" an unfortunate Russian student, Ivanov.[1] Together with Bakunin he produced *The Catechism of a Revolutionist* and went about announcing that he represented the International.

[1] Nechayev's programme of total destruction, and the murder of Ivanov, form one of the essential elements in Dostoevsky's novel, *The Possessed*.

The revolutionary, according to Nechayev, has only one idea: the revolution; and he has broken with all moral principles. Since the freedom and happiness of man can only be accomplished by an all-destructive revolution, he will himself foment all the evils which will goad the people to desperation. No constructive policy is required. "Our banner is simply destruction, terrible, complete, universal and ruthless. The future society will arise from the people themselves." Marx was horrified and furiously indignant.

At the Hague Congress of 1872 Bakunin was expelled.

There is a vivid account of Marx as he appeared at this last important Congress at The Hague in the *Reminiscences* of Theodor Cuno, who was the chairman. "Marx was sitting behind Engels. I recognised him immediately with his big, woolly head. His complexion was dark, his hair and beard were grey. He wore a black broadcloth suit, and when he wanted to look at anybody or anything intently he pressed a monocle into his right eye. When speaking, Marx was not very fluent; in fact he was not a practised orator, while Engels spoke in a conversational tone, often sarcastic and humorous."

Bakunin was greatly loved and admired for his selfless courage, and for his witness to the disinterested dedication of the human spirit against self-interest and timidity. There was something about his presence and his oratory that was elemental and incandescent. When he was expelled from the International there were men everywhere who sympathised with him and condemned Marx. It seemed to them that Marx was exerting a dictatorial, centralised control and that Bakunin was in the right to challenge this.

THE END OF THE FIRST INTERNATIONAL

These events undoubtedly weakened the International, but an even more serious blow resulted from Marx's support for the Paris Commune of 1871. The whole reactionary world mobilised its forces against the men of the International. Marx declared that "I have the honour of being the most slandered and the most threatened man in London. It is doing me good after twenty long and boring years of idyllic isolation like a frog in a swamp."

This and the socialist policy adopted at Brussels alarmed the more staid and cautious of the British trade union leaders. The trade unions had never really gone with the International as it became more and more socialist. Their aim was to improve working conditions on the basis of capitalist society and to obtain an extension of the franchise.

The International certainly played its valuable part in the fight for the Reform Bill; but after that the trade unions turned more to the Liberals. Odger and another member of the General Council withdrew. In 1871 Applegarth and several others refused to sign the General Council's address, *The Civil War in France*. Most of them came to regard strikes as a very primitive method of trade union activity. On the other hand, they were glad of the support of the International for the Nine Hours League and its successful attempts to prevent the recruiting of blackleg labour in Belgium and Denmark. Marx caustically observed that they remained aloof until they were in trouble, and then came to look for help.

Marx believed that there was still grave danger threatening the International from "idiots and adventurers" and got an unexpected resolution through, shifting the General Council to New York. It was an extremely unpopular move. Things were already falling to pieces and there was no recovery. There was one more poorly attended Congress at Geneva in 1873, and after that the International quietly expired in 1876.

The First International[1] exercised a great influence over the working-class movement. It spread wide the ideas of socialism as they were presented by Marx. It was the platform from which he spoke with such effect that Marxist socialism became the creed of millions of workers in the next fifty years. It was often asserted, especially by the Bakuninists, that Marx and Engels exercised authoritarian control over the organisation. But as Engels pointed out, whatever might be the view of middle-class theorists who have little experience of industry, joint action of any sort is impossible without some kind of authority. No factory or railway can be run without direction, that is without authority. "I should very much like to know whether the gallant Bakunin would entrust his large person to a railway carriage if that railway were administered according to principles by which nobody would be at his post if he did not please to submit to the authority of the regulations, far more authoritarian in any possible state of society than those of the Basle Congress!"[2]

The resolutions adopted by the General Council of the International,

[1] The Second International (1889-) was supported by the large and growing Social Democratic parties of Europe and reflected their policies. The Third (Communist) International was founded in 1919 and came to an end during the Second World War.

[2] Engels to Lafargue, December 30th, 1871.

to which Bakunin subsequently took violent exception, gave the General Council the right to suspend any section, pending the decision of the next Congress, when such section acted against the spirit of the International. But these resolutions did not emanate from the Council, but were brought forward by the Belgians and strongly supported by Bakunin himself! So far from the General Council exercising rigid control, the most contrary opinions were represented within the International, ranging from the rigid centralism of the Austrian workers to the anarchist federalism of the Spaniards. But the International could close its ranks in the face of a common enemy, as it did when it gave its full support to the Paris Commune, and as it was finally compelled to do when Bakunin endeavoured to organise a faction within the movement.

The International won the organised working-class movement for the idea that it must seek its own salvation by the seizure of political power and the ending of capitalist ownership. It thus gave a tremendous stimulus to the formation of independent workers' parties, which were inspired by the conviction that they were identifying themselves with the course of history and that they would ultimately triumph, whatever difficulties they encountered. Marx handled the affairs of the International with consummate sense and tact, converting the workers' movements from a collection of disunited and virtually utopian sects, or trade unions concerned only with day-to-day improvements of conditions, into a number of realistic and well-established parties with a scientific socialist theory at their disposal for guidance and support.

PART III

The first requisite for philosophising is a free and fearless mind.

Marx

We do not at all regard the theory of Marx as something complete and inviolable: we are convinced to the contrary, that it has laid the cornerstone of that science which socialists must further advance in all directions if they do not wish to lag behind life. We think that it is particularly necessary for socialists independently to analyse the theory of Marx, for this theory provides only general guiding propositions which must be applied differently in England from France, in France from Germany, in Germany from Russia according to the particular circumstances.

Lenin

15

MARX AS ECONOMIST

MARX's *Capital* is marked by an intrinsic and inseparable bond between strict scientific procedure and the revolutionary spirit. An encyclopaedic work, it reflects the extraordinary breadth of the scientific interests of its author. Lenin in his *Philosophical Notebooks* also draws attention to the dialectical framework of this book. Marx left us no textbook of the new Logic; "he did leave us the *logic* of *Capital*. . . . In *Capital* he applied to a single study logic, dialectic and the theory of knowledge of the Marxist system, taking from Hegel all that was valuable and advancing the valuable further."

It may with good reason be claimed that in this work a durable foundation was laid for the understanding of human society and the laws of its development. It is thus far more than a treatise on economics, it is an economic interpretation of history and an historical interpretation of economics.

"To us," says Marx, "so-called 'economic laws' are not eternal laws of nature but historic laws which arise and disappear; and the code of modern political economy, in so far as it has been drawn up with proper objectivity by the economist, is to us simply a summary of the laws and conditions under which alone modern bourgeois society can exist—in short the condition of its production and exchange expressed in an abstract and summary way. To us also, therefore, none of these laws, in so far as it expresses *purely bourgeois conditions* is older than modern bourgeois society."[1]

Yet for the bourgeois economist even the victory of Adam Smith over the mercantilists is regarded as a victory of correct over incorrect ideas, as the final discovery of ultimate economic truth, instead of the reflection in thought of changed economic facts; which is as much as to say that if Richard Cœur de Lion had only introduced free trade instead of getting mixed up in the Crusades we should have been spared 500 years of economic folly.

Marx is not primarily interested in economics as such, or in merely

[1] Marx to Lange, March 29th, 1865.

finding answers to technical questions, but in society as a whole. Nor did he believe that economics could be abstracted from society, and its fundamental principles stated as though the laws of social life were something permanent. He is concerned with the process of social change, fusing history and economic development, turning economic theory into historical analysis. This turns historical narrative into rational history and shows politics as determined by the structure of the economic process.

He is not, of course, trying to reduce everything to economic terms, but to show the relation between the economic and the non-economic aspects of social development, to show how men come to construct a pattern of social relationships in the business of earning a living, a pattern appropriate to the technological level, and above all to show the *movement* of society, how the redirective activity of man, in developing technique and reorganising the social structure to correspond to it, carries society forward from stage to stage.

It is particularly important to realise that by the "economic system" Marx always means the social relationships of production, how men are related in the necessarily co-operative task of satisfying their human needs, whether as lords and serfs, as independent craftsmen and farmers, as capitalists and wage-earners, or in joint ownership of the means of production.

Marx held that all historical and cultural changes were to be explained in terms of the organisation and development of each basic type of human economic relationship.

Marx was not attempting this enquiry into social development as an academic exercise; his object was to give society a consciousness of itself, to explain to it the reason for its conflicts and social struggles; it was not his ideas that he wished men to accept, he spoke only of the objective processes of history in which they were involved, so that those who understood need no longer feel helpless but might understand the possibilities and opportunities of their situation, what it required of them, with what perils it confronted them. The economics of Marx, then, is not the construction of a number of interacting laws, or the logic of a static system, but an analysis of the actual sequence of economic patterns, of the development of one into another as it goes on, under its own impetus, in historic time, producing at every instant that state which will itself determine the next one.

Marx arrived in Paris in 1843 completely ignorant both of economics and of socialism. As a student he had studied philosophy and jurisprudence. When government pressure made it useless for him to take up an academic career, he became the editor of the *Rheinische Zeitung* and made a name for himself as a radical journalist. When he arrived in Paris he immersed himself in the lively socialist movement, and began an exhaustive study of the English economists Adam Smith, Ricardo, McCulloch, James Mill, and of the Frenchman Jean Baptiste Say.[1] He was much enlightened by Engels' brilliant critique of the British economic system in the *Deutsche-Französischen Jahrbücher*.[2] Engels, only twenty-three at that time, drew attention to the contradictions and evils of the system, the recurring crises, the poverty of the workers, and accounted for them by "the unreasoning unfeeling mechanism of open competition", and not as many economists did, by the Malthusian theory of population, which he described as "a hideous blasphemy against nature and humanity". All these things are the consequences of private property in the means of production and of the wage system. Engels' conclusion was: "Produce consciously as men and not as atomised individuals without social consciousness, and you will have overcome all artificial and untenable contradictions."

It is sometimes supposed that Marx came out in opposition to orthodox capitalist economics, with a theory of his own—the labour theory of value. This is not so. The labour theory of value was the theory then generally accepted as put forward by Ricardo, the British economist. Marx was no heretic, but stood in the central tradition of political economy—the last, as well as the greatest of the classical economists.

Marx's treatment of Ricardo's labour theory of value shows that the capitalist's profit is the difference between the value of the worker's labour power, i.e. a day's wages, and the value of what he creates in that day, which to the employer appears to be his legitimate profit, but which Marx called surplus value.

Only Marx really understood where the capitalist's profit came from, the implications of Ricardo's theories never being realised by his own followers. Moreover, Marx saw in surplus value the secret of the exploitation of wage labour.[3]

WORK IN PROGRESS

Between 1843 and 1847 Marx filled twenty-four notebooks on economic questions—twice as much as is contained in the first volume

[1] Also Sismondi, Buret, Pecqueur and Skarbek.

[2] *Sketch for a Critique of Political Economy*.

[3] See *Wage Labour and Capital*, Marx's lectures to the German Worker's Educational Association in Brussels. See Chapter 8.

of *Capital*.[1] In these he summarised a large number of books on social conditions, trade, agriculture and theoretical economics.

The first important work on the economic question which he produced in the period of intense study following the defeat of the German revolution was *A Contribution to the Critique of Political Economy* (1859). This was intended to be the first part of a lengthy treatise to consist of three volumes. His work was interrupted by the *coup d'état* of Louis Bonaparte. And for months Marx was involved in political activity and the writing of articles and pamphlets.[2]

When he resumed his economic studies he prepared a series of special studies, not intended for publication. This is the 1857-58 draft of *Capital*, which runs to well over a thousand pages and has now appeared under the title *Grundrisse der Kritik der Politischen Oekonomie*.

The *Critique* was intended to deal with capital, but only got as far as the commodity and money; and both these topics were dealt with again in the first volume of *Capital*. Even Engels found it difficult. "The study of your abstract of the first part has kept me very busy. *It is a very abstract abstract indeed*."

Marx wrote in 1857 a Preface to the *Critique* which he omitted on publication.[3] This contains an interesting paragraph on art, in which Marx points out that "certain periods of highest development of art stand in no direct connection with the general development of society, nor with the material basis and the structure of its organisation". He goes on to show that certain forms of the imagination, such as mythology, reflect the inability of man to master the forces of nature and disappear when that is no longer the case. He confesses himself puzzled that the Greek epic should still constitute a source of aesthetic enjoyment, as it certainly did for him.

The Preface to the *Critique* contains the well-known summary of the Marxist theory of historical materialism, which was worked out at much greater length in *The German Ideology*.

The next part of the *Critique* was to contain the material which was eventually embodied in *Capital* itself, but which was intended originally to be the third chapter. In the autumn of 1859 he resumed his studies in the British Museum, re-read Engels' *Condition of the Working Class*

[1] In 1845 he began to prepare a two-volume work to be entitled *A Critique of Politics and National Economy* of which some parts have been preserved. But he abandoned this project in 1846 to write *The German Ideology*.

[2] His *Eighteenth Brumaire* appeared in 1852.

[3] It was not published until after his death, but is now included in all editions of the *Critique*.

and the works of Smith and Ricardo and made an exhaustive study of the Factory Reports between 1855 and 1859. Notebook after notebook was filled with this material, Marx working with exceptional speed and reducing his hours of sleep to a minimum. At this time he was accumulating material on the development of technique and prophesying to Liebknecht that steam power would be followed by electrical power, for he had seen the first model of a train powered by electricity.

Only those who lived and worked with him were fully aware of the thoroughness of his preparatory work. He was extremely conscientious and if even the slightest doubt arose as to a fact or figures he would hurry round to the British Museum Library to verify it. In order to write the twenty pages or so on English Factory legislation he went through a whole library of Blue Books containing reports of the Royal Commissions and the factory inspectors. Professor Beesly, who was closely associated with Marx in those days, says that no man knew them more thoroughly or made greater use of them.

From time to time the work demanded a careful reading of new material. "I had to wade through the new agricultural chemistry in Germany, especially Liebeg and Schonbein, who are more important in this matter (the discussion on ground rent) than all the economists put together, and also the enormous amount of material which the French have produced since I last occupied myself with this point. . . . The opening up of Japan was also important."

When he was dealing with the development of machinery (Chapter XV, Section 1) he tells us that he not only had to read through all his notebooks on technology again, but attended a practical course by Professor Willis at the Geological Institute in Jermyn Street, where Huxley also used to give his lectures, some of which Marx also attended.

The three volumes of *Capital* were planned as a whole. There are in fact several manuscripts of this overall project, and several long letters in which he outlines his scheme of work, which was to begin with the anatomy of bourgeois society, starting with its simplest cell, the commodity, and ending with the development of the world market, the nature of economic crisis, and the condition for the birth of a new socialist society. The first part would be an *historical* sketch of the development of economic categories, a *critique* of those categories which would be at once an account of the system and a critique of it given in the account itself. He had behind him in 1861 the set of monographs known as the *Grundrisse* and the various drafts of the first *Critique* with its Introduction. He took two more years to fill twenty-three notebooks with detailed material, including all the materials for the *Theories of Surplus Value*, and the last notebooks dealing exhaustively with the falling rate of profit.

He now reorganised the whole project for his great work, and in 1862 we have his outline scheme for what was now to be Volume I. In June 1863 Marx started to rework his material to correspond to his new plan.

Marx made no attempt in *Capital* to construct "an historical-philosophic theory of the general path imposed by fate upon every people, whatever the historic circumstances in which it finds itself . . . the universal passport of a general historico-philosophical theory, the supreme virtue of which consists in being super-historical."[1] On the contrary, he claims to do no more than provide an historical sketch of the genesis of capitalism. Marx never wrote a theoretical exposition of what has come to be known as Marxism. He saw that the important thing to do was to show the laws of social development in their concrete working out. In this way he would make it abundantly clear that he was not in the least imposing an *a priori* theory on the facts, applying laws arrived at abstractly to the movement of history. "There could be no question of building the laws of dialectics into nature, but of discovering them in it and evolving them from it. . . . Nature is the test of dialectics,"[2] and it is the accumulation of the empirical data which compels the recognition of certain processes at work in the world.

It was Hegel who made history the manifestation in time and space of certain developing ideas, "the self-development of the concept". Marx as we have seen reversed this Hegelian conception, seeing the basic principles not as determining social development from above, but as reflecting the actual interaction of man and the productive force which he creates. Here was the key to the understanding of social development, and it is the dialectics of his *Capital*. Hegel was right when he said that in making his world man made himself; and in remaking it, he remakes himself.

Hegel saw the future integration of the individual and the community, the overcoming of antagonism and contradiction, in a higher activity of the mind. Marx saw it in the actual transformation of the

[1] Marx to the Editor of *Otyecestvenniye Zapisky* (Notes on the Fatherland), 1877.
[2] Engels, *Anti-Dühring*.

mode of production. This is the dialectic of negativity, which drives every being and every form of society to go beyond its determinate mode of existence in order to realise its possibilities.[1]

In such a process of development the new reveals the truth of the old, it shows what it really was: both a preparatory stage and a limiting system, at a particular point in history, the true meaning of which is only known when it passes over, by negation, into its fulfilment.

Now for Marx this is the genesis and development of capitalism and its dialectical transformation into socialism.

When the form of organisation limits advance, that is the negative phase; when it is replaced by a better one allowing advance, the negation is itself negated and some of the essential features that belonged to the earlier phase are lifted up into the new form and used under the conditions of the new, so that the change not only overcomes but preserves, transforms and enhances the old.

The contradictions that develop within the capitalist system, as these are shown in *Capital*, are essential aspects of the unity which is capitalism, one aspect of the contradiction cannot exist without the other, both are inseparable from capitalism conceived as a new and progressive form of society in its beginnings and development, and as a necessary preparation for socialism. The development of the contradiction prepares its overcoming and resolution, and also brings into existence the new social groups, forms of organisation and forces that are going to overcome it. All this is what Marx calls the self-movement of society. Therefore the idea of some reformers, of whom Proudhon was an example, that one can leave the structure of capitalism intact and merely remove its "bad side", is absurd. The bad side forms a whole with the good side, the proletariat cannot exist without the bourgeoisie, the constructive and progressive role of capitalism is carried out by the very process which involves its evils and contradictions; and the continuance and development of these contradictions constitutes the movement and the force which carry it forward towards socialism.

[1] Marx never suggested that the dialectical process came suddenly to an end with the coming of socialism. But neither did he like Hegel derive the process of social development—whether that which culminates in socialism, or that which follows it—as the consequence of some dialectical law, determining history. In actual *fact* there are growing antagonisms which can and must be overcome by going forward to socialism. And in actual *fact*, quite other contradictions emerge within socialism, which are themselves overcome as socialism itself develops from one phase to another.

How far does Marx regard this process as driven forward by a blind necessity? It is not blind in as much as every step is carried out as an intelligent decision of men seeking to attain definite objectives and devising means to that end. It *is* blind in as much as the ultimate consequences are not seen and the whole historical process and its goal are not comprehended. But this is only true at the lower stages. Later, men become clearer as to what they are doing and as to the class interests involved; but complete clarity does not appear until the working class comprehends its own position, its own historic destiny and the necessity for social transformation.

The laws of capitalism work with iron necessity to create the insoluble contradictions of capitalism, to bring about the concentration of capital, the socialisation of labour, the emergence of an organised proletariat. But one cannot argue from the inexorable necessity that governs the development of capitalism to a similar necessity in the matter of transformation to socialism. When capitalism is rejected, social processes no longer stand under the rule of blind natural laws. There can be no blind necessity in tendencies that terminate in a free and self-conscious society. In the phases that precede revolution there is active, rational spontaneity; the revolution itself requires a self-conscious and organised working class that can seize upon and direct the conditions of social change towards the socialist goal. No natural necessity or automatic inevitability guarantees the transition from capitalism to socialism.

In two and a half years, from the middle of 1863 to the end of 1865, Marx wrote the rough draft of all three volumes of *Capital*. On January 1st, 1865, he began to prepare the fair copy and final draft for the first volume. Marx was now working thirteen hours a day, his labours interrupted by illness and want. So indecipherable was his handwriting that his wife had finally to copy the whole manuscript out for the printer. The last sheet was sent off on the night of August 16th, at 2 a.m.

Marx worked with extraordinary intensity. He was concerned not only with the content, but also with the form of his writing. "This work," he says, "is the result of fifteen years of research, i.e. the best period of my life. For the first time it gives scientific expression to a view on social relationships that is of great importance. Therefore I owe it to the party not to allow the thing to be vitiated by a heavy and wooden manner of writing." Therefore it was not finished without much painstaking revision and polishing to attain the utmost precision and clarity. How carefully he worked is shown in his letter to Engels in July 1865. "Whatever shortcomings they may have, the merit of my writings is that they are an artistic whole, and that can only be attained by my method of never having them printed until they lie before me as a *whole*."

They could not be prepared for publication, he says, by any one but himself—not even by Engels. "I begun the copying out and the polishing of the style *punctually* on the first of January [1866] and the thing proceeded very merrily, as I naturally enjoyed licking the infant clean after so many birthpangs." Marx was plagued at this time by carbuncles, and often could only stand or lie down. To finish the job he wrote to Engels, "I must at least be able to sit down". As he sent off the last sheets to the printer on the night of August 16, 1867, at 2 a.m., Marx wrote to Engels: "So *this volume is finished*. This has been possible thanks to you alone. Without your self-sacrifice for me I could never possibly have done the enormous work for the three volumes. I embrace you, full of thanks!"

It is often believed that *Capital* is an obscure and badly written book. It is not. Much depends on what subjects are being treated. The historical chapters, the moving and remorseless pages dealing with the expropriation of the peasants, the struggle between the worker and the machine, and the nature and the length of the working day, are brilliantly and powerfully written. As we read them we feel that we have been taken through the real structure of our civilisation and been shown the impact of competitive capitalism on both workers and masters. In the earlier chapters, which are the most difficult, he deals, logically enough, with his basic analysis of capitalism and his theory of commodities. Here he is elaborating systematically and comprehensively the new economic theory which had appeared in his lectures and in the *Critique*, and he is as clear as the profundity of his problems permits; and far from being dull and abstract it is this section which puts in moving and concrete form the fundamental views on alienation and the creation by man of economic forces and entities which destroy him. So far from repudiating the idea of alienation in its human meaning, Marx demonstrated that it cannot be divorced from the concrete and real life process of the individual. The whole important section on *The Fetichism of Commodities*[1] is an elaboration of the view first set forth in *The Jewish Question* and in the Paris Manuscripts of 1844. There he shows that in the products put up for sale on the market,

[1] *Capital*, Vol. I, Chapter 1, section 4.

in the apparently objective and purely financial determinants of the wage level, profitability, demand for labour, in the irresistible operation of economic law, which neither consumer, nor worker, nor capitalist can defy, we have what is in origin and basically a relation between men confronting us "in the fantastic form of a relation between things".[1]

"In order, therefore, to find an analogy, we must have recourse to the mist enveloped regions of the religious world. In that world the productions of the human brain appear as independent beings endowed with life, and entering into relations both with one another and the human race. So it is in the world of commodities with the products of men's hands. This I call the Fetichism which attaches itself to the products of labour, so soon as they are produced as commodities, and which is therefore inseparable from the production of commodities."[2]

This economic process is of course the working out of the philosophy of individualism, which seeks to set free the economic man to pursue his own private interests through the profitable use of his capital. "An economic system", as Ruskin said, "which considers men as activated by no other moral influences than those which affect rats or swine."[3] The dynamic pressure of the market then takes charge of things. It produces a money-driven, standardised type of man, interested only in quantities because he is interested only in means. The transformation of society into one big market, the control even of cultural literacy and scholarly activities and publication by commercial considerations, perverts human life and dehumanizes the man of modern society who is supposed to be by this means developing and fulfilling his personality. Individualism ruins individuality. As Marx puts it in a speech he delivered in 1856: "All our invention and progress seem to result in endowing material forces with intellectual life, and in stultifying human life into a material force."

Technology and the market do their work, in Hegel's phrase, "behind the backs" of the people engaged in them. People are the instruments of that "ruse of reason" which uses their freedom and conscious motives for the attainment of ends altogether invisible to them and outside their intentions and reach. People are given the illusion of activity in freedom and spontaneity, and are in reality har-

[1] '*fantastic*' in its literal meaning, as an illusion, a mental image, not as meaning eccentric or grotesque.

[2] *Capital*, Vol. I, p. 43. [3] Ruskin, *Unto this Last.*

nessed into a strictly preordained objective process whose anonymous majesty dwarfs them into insignificance and destroys their sense of responsibility. "For a man can be responsible only for things he controls",[1] and the economic forces liberated by capitalism are beyond his control.

At the heart of *Capital* is the representation of man being dehumanised and destroyed by a tyrannical force of acquisitiveness that has arisen and grown all powerful within him. It controls his movements, usurps his life energies, and, as a capitalist, obsesses him with a compulsive drive towards accumulation. Few works of literature or studies of the sick mind have portrayed with comparable insight the destructive and dehumanising character of the capitalist system.

This is seen in its effect on the worker with terrifying clarity in the increasing mechanisation of the labour process. The methods used "mutilate the worker into a fragment of a human being, degrade him to become a mere appurtenance of the machine, make his work such a torment that its essential meaning is destroyed; estrange him from the intellectual potentialities of the labour process in very proportion to the extent to which science is incorporated into it as an independent power".[2] As Lenin said, "In few scientific treatises will you find so much heart, so many burning and passionate polemical outbursts. It depicts capitalist society as a live thing, with the actual social manifestation of the antagonism of classes inherent in the relations of production."[3]

[1] Eduard Heimann, *Reason and Faith in Modern Society*.
[2] *Capital*, Vol. I, p. 661. [3] Lenin, *What the Friends of the People Are.*

16

CAPITAL

It has been said that Marx was one of those thinkers who spend their lives writing a single important book under a number of different titles. What is quite certain is that this single book was never intended to be a treatise on economics, or "political economy" as it was then called. It was, on the contrary, a critique of all economic systems, and his aim was neither to lay down the principles that every kind of economy must conform to, nor was he attempting to explain the working of the capitalist system as if there was a certain finality or absoluteness about its laws, which was the aim of the orthodox economist. On the contrary, Marx wrote *Capital* to show not how capitalism works but how forces immanent in it bring about its destruction and its supersession by socialism.

For Marx the history of economic thought does not show us a succession of attempts—some mistaken, others nearer the mark—to answer the same question, which concludes with what the writer believes to be the right answer. It is rather an enquiry into the particular questions which successive schools of political economy sought to answer. And these were quite different from period to period, depending in each case on the social and historical situation at the time. This is a matter of history and can only be settled by historical methods, since the problems stated and answered related to given conditions and to a particular stage in social development.

This was how Marx looked at things; and he also saw that the questions which arose at any particular time were always asked by particular groups appearing on the scene with some new contribution to make, brought into existence as a class and given their task and its problems by the development of the economy in which they came to be. In this way the mercantilists appear with the rise of foreign trade and pose the questions and make the demands required by it, and the physiocrats appear with the development of capitalist farming and frame their questions and answers in terms of the agricultural situation and its needs.

Marx discovered at the very outset of his career that men tend to project certain ideas derived from their actual condition beyond themselves and then to consider these as eternal principles ruling their lives, to which they are compelled to give allegiance. This indeed is how all transcendental and absolute ideas arise, particularly those of religion. Marx regards capitalist economics as a religious phenomenon —to use a philosophical phrase, as the hypostatisation of economic abstractions. He says that the political economists who treat capitalist institutions as the only natural ones "resemble the theologians, who also establish two kinds of religion. Every religion but their own is an invention of men, while their own religion is an emanation from God."

Therefore *Capital* has to be seen not as a treatise on economics, written to demonstrate the labour theory of value, the theory of increasing misery and the falling rate of profit, nor as a book of predictions, all of which must necessarily come about independently of human understanding, will and resolve. It is a dramatic history that is designed to involve its readers in the events it describes, so that they find themselves stepping on to the stage of history and participating in and bringing to an issue the working out of human destiny.

Marx laboured at his task for forty years. From the moment that he began to study economic questions in 1843 until his death in 1883 he was continuously engaged in this work. From an immense mass of material the finished volumes began to take shape, but only the first received its final form and was published in his lifetime.

Among this pile of preliminary work we find the manuscript of the third volume of *Capital* written in 1865 even before the first volume was published.[1] This is important because it has frequently been alleged that when the theory of value, expounded in the first volume, was seen to ignore the question of price fluctuation, he desperately tried to remedy matters by writing another volume.[2] But Marx knew perfectly well what he was doing—in the first volume he works out the basic principles without complications, and then proceeds to show how they explain the actual working of the capitalist system as we know it. Until the essential law of the unmodified system has been

[1] In the long letter to Engels written on August 2nd, 1862, Marx makes it perfectly clear that he had worked out the whole of his theory long before Vol. I of *Capital* was published. We have all the manuscripts of this year, which also contain the long section on rent which subsequently appeared in Vol. III.

[2] This is the well-known criticism of Böhm-Bawerk in *Karl Marx and the Close of His System* from which most subsequent economic criticism of *Capital* derives.

established we shall never be able to understand or predict the consequences of particular modifications. Thus in Carnot's "heat engine" which demonstrates the basic theory of energy-exchanges in the steam engine—and nowhere in the history of science is the close relation of technological progress and enlargement of theory more closely demonstrated—the theoretical balance is nowhere realised in practice; but it is nevertheless the key to practice. So with Marx, who in Volume I works out the money expression of value, and in Volume III the different conception of *price of production*, which is derived from values according to certain rules. Not only does this theory not contradict the theory of value, it is based directly upon it.[1]

It is understandable that economists concerned with the actual working of the present commercial system should dislike the emphasis which Marx lays on value. His system and theirs differ in fundamental scope and aim. Capitalist economics is a theory of exchange and of how profit is made and utilised for further investment; Marx is concerned with a theory of production. If the labour theory of value can be used to understand the movement of history and to make a revolution, the price theory can be used to understand the movement of stocks and shares and to make money. There is confusion, therefore, between a system characterised by the production of use-values as a means merely to the creation and accumulation of exchange-values (in the form of profit), and a system based on the direct and purposive creation of use-values for their own sake.

Once Marx has made plain by his theory of value how and for what purpose surplus value is obtained he is on the way to discover the "law of motion" of the whole capitalist system. Capitalism can and must work for the purpose of accumulating profit; hence the necessity for maintaining (or restoring) the conditions in which profit can be made. This is the prerequisite for the very existence of the system and to it everything else must be sacrificed.

Marx knew perfectly well that in a capitalist system commodities are not exchanged on the basis of their real value as measured in terms of labour-time. He expressly points out that the prices of commodities diverge more and more from their values. So much the worse for capitalism! For this divergence of prices from values is evidence of the ever-growing irrationality of the system. Marx is also able to show

[1] In the manuscript of 1857-58, the *Grundrisse* written ten years before the appearance of *Capital*, we find a full discussion on another question, the tendency of the rate of profit to fall which Marx is often said not to have adequately treated.

on the basis of his theory how the flagrant injustice and waste of the capitalist system have arisen, how as industrialisation became complete capitalism would necessarily move into a period of growing and insuperable difficulties. The labour theory of value enabled him to understand both how it was that the holding down of the workers' standard of life to a bare subsistence was *up to a certain point* the necessary condition of rapid industrialisation, and how it was that, after full industrialisation, this same pressure to minimise costs (wages) and maximise profit for further capitalisation turned into a barrier to the further expansion of production. This leads straight to the discovery of the central contradiction of capitalism which Marx reaches in Volume II and discusses at considerable length in Volume III.

The first volume was published in the beginning of September, 1867, in an edition of one thousand copies, by Meissner of Hamburg. It received several favourable reviews in the English press. The *Saturday Review* declared that Marx had the gift of lending even the driest economic question a certain fascination. Another reviewer said that Marx "in no way resembled the majority of German scholars who wrote their books in a language so dry and obscure that the heads of ordinary mortals are cracked by it".

Engels now undertook a whole campaign to publicise the first volume of *Capital* and wrote several anonymous reviews for the German papers. The historian Beesly was a friend of Marx; as a sub-editor of the *Fortnightly Review* he had promised to accept a review by Engels. But the editor, John Morley, sent it back with the remark that the subject was too abstruse for a journal of that character. All these notices of Engels were written to give the public some idea of the main pur-purpose of *Capital*, which was at last to furnish socialist aspirations with a scientific basis, "which neither Fourier nor Proudhon nor even Lassalle have been able to give them".

The French edition was completed in 1875 and published with alterations and additions by Marx. The first Russian edition came out in 1872. The English translation by Samuel Moore and Edward Aveling appeared in 1886, three years after the death of Marx.

Marx had prepared the material for the second and third volumes, and there was also a mass of material on *Theories of Surplus Value*, but his failing health prevented him from putting them into shape. After his death this was done by Engels, and Volume II, *The Process of Circulation of Capital*, appeared in 1886 and Volume III, *The Process of Capitalist Production as a Whole*, in 1894. *Theorien über den Mehrwert*

(Theories of Surplus Value) was published in Stuttgart 1905-10. This was to have formed the fourth volume of *Capital*.

Volume I (*A Critique of Political Economy*) begins by stating that the wealth of a capitalist society presents itself as an enormous accumulation of commodities for sale. The commodity is now examined in all its aspects and especially in its relations to other commodities in commercial exchange: the commodity under capitalism, including essentially labour power itself as a typical commodity; and the commodity in the form of surplus value realising its value in money (another commodity), creating a mass of profit for further investment and further profit.

This is the whole rationale and mechanism of capitalism.

Capital is not therefore concerned with the labour process as such but with labour as creating surplus value—the never-ending process of profit-making itself, which has no limit. In Marx's vivid words: "By transforming money into commodities which form the material elements of a new product or serve as factors in the labour process, and by incorporating living labour power with their dead substance the capitalist transforms value (past labour, dead labour) into capital, into self-expanding value, into a monster quick with life, which begins to 'work' as if love were breeding in its body." He goes on to show how this form of society rouses to life mighty productive forces of social labour and thus creates the material base for a new and higher form of society.

What then is the driving force and the essential mechanism of this new level of economic organisation? It is by no means merely the securing of profits by an exploiting class for its own pleasure. The surplus value which the capitalist obtains through the wage system is dedicated to the further expansion of capital investment.[1] Capitalism is a machine for converting surplus value into the means whereby more surplus value is obtained for the purpose of investing it in order to obtain still more and so on, *ad infinitum*.

"Accumulate! Accumulate! That is Moses and all the prophets! Industry furnishes the material which saving accumulates. Therefore you must save; you must reconvert the largest possible proportion of surplus value or surplus product into capital. Accumulation for accumulation's sake. This was the formula by which the classical

[1] Marx was prepared to assume that 80 per cent of surplus value was reinvested as new capital in the nineteenth century. *Capital*, I.611.

political economist gave expression to the historical mission of the bourgeois period."[1]

Marx was anxious to show that this method of obtaining surplus value and realising it was not mere cheating, was not, as many socialists were inclined to believe, the simple process of selling a commodity for more than you gave for it, or more than its real value as measured by the cost of production.

"The transformation of money into capital is to be explained on the basis of the laws immanent in the exchange of commodities, is to be explained in such a way that the starting-point is an exchange of equivalents (i.e. even if the price obtained is no more than the value of the commodity). Mr. Money-bags who is as yet only an embryo capitalist, must buy his commodities at their value, and must sell them at their value; and nevertheless at the end of the process he must draw more value out of circulation than he puts into it at starting."[2]

Marx achieves the highest artistic force and eloquence in the passages where he discloses the essence of capitalist exploitation. One cannot easily forget the picture illustrating the conversion of money into capital. The whole process of exploitation takes on a perfectly equitable appearance, and its very essence is the spirit of freedom of which the liberal is so proud. "There alone rule Freedom, Equality, Property, and Bentham are supreme. Freedom because both buyer and seller of a commodity, say of labour power, are constrained only by their own free will. They contract as free agents, and the agreement they come to is but the form in which they give legal expression to their common will. Equality, because each enters into relation with the other, as with a simple owner of commodities, and they exchange equivalent for equivalent. Property, because each disposes only of what is his own. And Bentham, because each looks only to himself. The only force that brings them together and puts them in relation with each other is the selfishness, the gain and the private interests of each. Each looks to himself only, and no one troubles himself about the rest, and just because they do so, do they all, in accordance with the pre-established harmony of things, or under the auspices of an all-shrewd providence, work together to their mutual advantage, for the common weal and in the interest of all."[3]

Capital thereafter is largely taken up with an extended exposition of how the capitalist maximises surplus value by intensifying the

[1] *Capital*, I.606. [2] *Capital*, I.144. [3] *Capital*, I.155.

exploitation of labour. There is first an inherent tendency to appropriate the whole twenty-four hours of theoretically possible labour-time, less the ever shorter period necessary to produce a bare subsistence. The thirst for surplus value is insatiable. Capital, vampire-like, only lives by sucking living labour, "it oversteps not only the moral, but even the merely physical maximum bounds of the working day. It usurps the time for growth, development and healthy maintenance of the body. It steals the time required for the consumption of fresh air and sunlight."[1]

Marx enforces and illustrates this characterisation of exploitation with a documented picture compiled from factory reports with their prosaic description of misery and filth, their remorseless enumeration of the abnormal conditions of nineteenth-century labour. After reading this volume the orthodox textbooks of economics never seem the same to us again: we can always see through their argument the realities of the economic processes they describe and explain in the abstract terms of their science.

Theory is always linked with actual fact, based on a documented picture of modern industrialism as it actually was. Those moving and remorseless chapters dealing with the expropriation of the peasants, the struggle between the worker and the machine, the length of the working day, are magnificently written. As we read them we feel that we have been taken through the real structure of our civilisation and been shown not only the degradation of the workers but also of the masters. Yet it maintains a strong feeling of objectivity and restraint which is the source of much of its authority and persuasiveness.

The increasing mechanisation of industry also has the effect of dehumanising the worker, mutilating him into a fragment of a human being, degrading him to become a mere appurtenance of the machine, divorcing him from the *intellectual* potentialities of the labour process. Thus the whole development of capitalism results in a condition in which "the worker does not use the instrument of labour, but the instrument of labour uses the worker".

This is the "despotism of capital". Within the factory the massed machines feed upon and slowly destroy their living appendages, who exist only to promote the expansion of capital and only so long as

[1] *Capital*, I.250. Marx was well aware of the counteracting forces to this tendency in trade union activity and legislation which, he stated, could considerably alleviate the condition of the workers.

they can find employment for this purpose. The unseen, dictatorial powers of the economic mechanism, "work out with an iron necessity towards an inevitable goal". Clearly this is Marx's portrait of hell!

Nor is this merely a picture of a single capitalist country; it is Marx's picture of the capitalist world as dominated by a process of production motivated by capitalism's boundless drive for self-expansion. The great incubus of accumulated capital does not function as a means for fulfilling human needs as, rationally, it obviously should; but dominates and oppresses the men who continuously increase it (and not their own welfare) by their labour. Marx again recalls Feuerbach. "Just as in the sphere of religion man is dominated by the creature of his own brain, so in the sphere of capitalist production, he is dominated by the creature of his own hand."[1] The productive powers of labour thus "appear as self-dependent powers of capital lording it over labour and standing in direct opposition to the labourer's own development."[2]

The first volume of *Capital*, far from being an elaborate exposition of economic abstractions, has the dimension and spirit of an epic account of the rise and development of a new, immensely impressive and yet appalling system out of feudalism with its more primitive but more human technique, putting "an end to all feudal, patriarchal, idyllic relations. It has pitilessly torn asunder the motley feudal ties that bound man to his 'natural superiors', and has left remaining no other nexus between man and man than naked self-interest, than callous 'cash payment'. It has drowned the most heavenly ecstasies of religious fervour, of chivalrous enthusiasm, of philistine sentimentalism, in the icy water of egotistical calculation."[3] Capitalism has swept all this away, "wrecking it and overspreading it; accelerating, reorganising, reassembling, in ever more ingenious complexity, ever more formidable proportions; breaking out of the old boundaries of nations; sending its commerce across oceans and continents to bring the people of distant cultures into its system, and as it lays hold on the destinies of races, reshaping their very personalities and their aspirations. And all this without their really grasping what has happened to them, and independently of their will".[4]

It is important to realise that Marx is not awarding praise or blame in his account of the development of capitalism. The evils of capitalism do not spring from the malevolence of capitalists. If this were so, a little more personal kindness might remove its harshness and injustice.

[1] *Capital*, I.634. [2] *Capital*, III.1027.
[3] *Communist Manifesto*. [4] Edmund Wilson, *To the Finland Station*.

In the Preface to the first volume Marx explains that individuals are dealt with only in so far as they are personifications of economic categories, embodiment of particular class relations and class interests. He points out that it is classical political economy itself that has shown us the irresistible mechanism of supply and demand, production costs and profitability, profit margins and foreign markets. "If to classical economy the proletarian is but a machine for the production of surplus value; on the other hand, the capitalist in his eyes is only a machine for the conversion of this surplus into additional capital."[1]

Yet this does not lessen his indignation at the resulting crucifixion of mankind upon this cross of gold. He describes the passion for gain as "at once the most violent, the basest and the most abominable of which the human breast is capable". He utterly exposes the selfishness and hypocrisy of those who try to convince mankind that the existing order is really man's highest achievement, that it is impossible to devise anything better. He had a peculiar psychological insight which sensed, as few have been able to, the capacity of men to remain oblivious or indifferent to the pains they inflict on others in the pursuit of economic self-interest. He reveals with tremendous force the self-satisfaction and obtuseness of those men of property who consider themselves the salt of the earth. He succeeds at one and the same time in showing the inevitability of capitalism and more, how indispensable it was for the progress of the race, that although it is an evil compared with socialism it was a huge advance over primitive backwardness, savagery, feudalism and patriarchalism; that the socialisation of production and centralisation of industry required for socialism could have been achieved in no other way than by capitalism. And all this is demonstrated in a work which is justly considered one of the most remarkable models of implacable objectivity in the investigation of social phenomena.

What passion breathes in the pages of *Capital*, dealing with the history of primitive accumulation, the expropriation of the peasants from the land, the merciless reckoning with the expropriated! Here the dry facts of the exploitation of the masses whose whole life was converted into a simple means for expanding the value of capital were transformed into lines that breathe indignation and wrath, sarcasm towards the oppressors and warm partisanship on behalf of the oppressed. How far is passion compatible with objectivity? It is impossible to bring any accusation of inaccuracy or falsification against Marx,

[1] *Capital*, I.606.

He is polemical not because he is tendentious in the sense of deliberately distorting the facts to make out his case, but because he accurately portrays all the contradictions that exist in life. His doctrine is passionate because it is true. He comes forward as representative of the class most vitally interested in the replacement of capitalism by socialism, the class that holds the future in its hands. But socialism up to the time of Marx had been no more than a utopian dream. In *Capital* he puts it on a firm scientific foundation and shows that it is the necessary and logical result of the whole course of development of civilisation. This meant a new conception of world history; chaos and arbitrariness give way to scientific theory. History is not the effect of fate, or accident, or heroes imposing their will on events. Its laws of development are now discerned. Until they were revealed, until man had learned to see, he was helpless in the clutch of circumstance. Laws of development, yes, but unlike the laws of nature they do not operate apart from the will and actions of people, but through the understanding and resolve, through the action of large groups of human beings, of classes. The peoples themselves make their own history, but with intelligent understanding of the conditions in which they find themselves, of the perils and demands of the situation which confronts them.

Thus Marx was able to see the capitalist economy in the perspective of historical development, as having a beginning and also as having an end. He designates the succession of systems "as so many epochs in the progress of the economic formation of society. The bourgeois relations of production are the last antagonistic form of the social process of production—antagonistic not in the sense of individual antagonism, but of one arising from conditions surrounding the life of individuals in society; at the same time the productive forces developing in the womb of bourgeois society create the material conditions for the solution of the antagonism. This social formation constitutes therefore the closing chapter of the prehistoric stage of human society."[1]

[1] Marx, Preface to *Critique of Political Economy*.

17

THE NATURE OF CAPITALIST CRISIS

THE second volume of *Capital* never had the careful revision and tightening of the argument, the sharpening and pruning of the sentences and paragraphs that give such drive and power to the first volume. It was prepared by Engels from the draft manuscript which Marx himself had not worked up with his accustomed care into its final form. It does not sparkle with quite the same intellectual brilliance. Yet it is indispensable to Marx's argument.

While nearer to the contemporary facts of capitalist economy and less deliberately abstract than the first volume, it is also more theoretical in its treatment. Volume I moves on a high level of abstraction in spite of its historical section and factual material on factory conditions. But Marx knew quite well that the theories formulated here required modification when applied to the actual operation of capitalism; and it is in Volumes II and III that this application, with the necessary modifications, is found. It is here that the *tendencies* arising from the nature of capitalism, as revealed in the first volume, are shown deflected by the counteractive forces of complex conditions. Yet as with Carnot's heat engine, and Galileo and Newton's laws of acceleration and motion, the operations of nature and the mechanical constructions of man are only rendered intelligible and made possible by abstract laws which neglect friction. In the same way, it is the basic principles enunciated in the first volume that explain the complex working of capitalism in real life.

In Volume I, Marx had shown how surplus value is obtained and how capital accumulates. What now has to be worked out in some detail is how in the world of trade and commerce commodities are realised in the form of hard cash. This would be impossible but for the credit system and the banks, which enable individual capitalists and business concerns continually to advance each other the credit they need and take up the available money, so that the uninterrupted progress of production and the sale of commodities are ensured both for the capitalist and for society as a whole.

What has further to be shown is how the commodities are thrown on to the market to compete with other commodities in the system of free competition, how in the confusion and anarchy of the market the manufacturer maintains his profit. What adjustments of wages and prices are required? How does the capitalist know what to produce and how much? What controls the amounts of labour and capital devoted over the whole system to each commodity in terms of the vagaries of individual demand?

Out of this seeming chaos a whole must result which will permit the capitalist to continue his business and at the same time satisfy the needs of society. In other words, the operations of capitalist economic law must keep in motion the circular movement of production, sale, profit and reallocation of resources for the next (and probably modified) circuit. The permanent circulation of production and consumption of society as a whole must be kept in movement within the confusion of innumerable deviating movements of individual capital.

All this is far more concrete than the matters dealt with in the first volume; nevertheless, it requires less concrete illustration, it is more theoretical. Marx's immensely important and lucid exposition anticipates much of later economic writing, to an extent insufficiently recognised by many economists.

Marx therefore proceeds to the investigation of precisely how the circular movement of investment, production, profit-making, accumulation of capital and reinvestment, whereby capital constantly changes from the money form into the commodity form and back again, proceeds. And this is being carried out by thousands of individual capitalists each concerned solely with his own interests and making his decisions as dictated by the laws of the market. How out of this anarchy do we arrive at the circulation of production and consumption in society as a whole?

Now, for the circular movement to continue without interruption, as is necessary if production, employment and the consuming power of the workers is to be maintained, it is absolutely necessary for each and every capitalist to sell the product of his enterprise. It is precisely here that contradictions arise because of the extremely complex conditions required for the circulation of the entire mass of commodities produced under capitalism.

Marx proceeds to show how the very process of capitalist *development* (i.e. profit-making for reinvestment and therefore for the general *expansion* of production) infringes upon these conditions and calls forth an interruption in the entire process of *re-production*,[1] and this must lead to periodic economic crisis.

In the second volume, therefore, Marx raises the question of economic crises. Capitalism is not, as was generally supposed, a stable system. On the contrary it is constantly throwing itself out of equilibrium "because the forces of production can never be utilised beyond the point at which surplus value can not only be produced but also realised in a society in which the great majority are poor".[2]

Marx does not, however, either in Volume II or in Volume III, in which the same problem is further discussed and the analysis of its complex nature carried farther, attempt to provide a final theory of capitalist economic crisis. He does not, because there can be no such complete theory. There are many kinds of crisis; many different and interacting causes, and many modifying influences. But whatever form crisis takes, it is the manifestation of the basic contradiction of capitalist society, and it is this contradiction that Marx lays bare. Of the various ways in which it works itself out, Marx discusses several, but others have since appeared and have been analysed in their turn. Even with regard to any particular crisis the interacting forces present a complicated picture in which every cause was once itself an effect and every effect becomes a cause, so that the reciprocal and interacting forces can be described from more than one point of view—as overproduction or underconsumption or disproportion, and so on. These explanations may be equally valid and their varied viewpoints illuminating. No one explanation need be selected as the true one. What *is* important is that they all reveal from their different angles, the same incompatible ends to which capitalism inevitably drives.

But Marx is able to make quite clear what is *not* the real cause of crisis: It is not simple underconsumption, the inability of the consumers to buy back the total product of consumers goods, as if the taking of excessive profit left the consumer without enough purchasing power to buy the commodities thrown on the market, and if employers

[1] The meaning of "reproduction" is important for the understanding of the problem as Marx presents it. In *simple* reproduction the profit is reinvested and the cycle of further utilisation of resources and sale of the products continues with the same quantity being produced each year. But under developing capitalism we get *extended* reproduction—that is to say, more and more commodities are produced and there is also growth in the number and scale of plants and factories. According to Marx the contradictions of capitalism become more severe in the process of extended reproduction.

[2] *Capital*, II.363.

were not so short-sighted as to keep wages down everything would be well.[1]

Marx points out that so far from this being the case, economic crisis follows a period of trade expansion which has led to the absorption of the unemployed, so that their competition for jobs no longer keeps wages down. Wages rise, profitability falls and crisis supervenes. If, therefore, it were to be said "that the working class receive too small a portion of their own product, and the evil would be remedied by giving them a larger share of it, or raising their wages, we should reply that crises are precisely always preceded by a period in which wages rise generally and the working class actually gets a larger share of the annual product".[2]

Marx concludes that although underconsumption is not in itself the real cause of crisis, that is not to say that it does not play a necessary role among other causes in bringing it about.

In the third volume of *Capital* Marx examines further aspects of the problem of economic crisis, which he relates not only to underconsumption, but also to the falling rate of profit, and the basic disequilibrium of an economy that always attempts to expand production without any reference to the consumption which alone can give it meaning.

But first of all he has to deal with an important source of difficulty in the capitalist economy—the falling rate of profit, and the tendency for the rate to fall. Firstly, how are the profits, after they have been turned into money, to be distributed? The employer, the merchant, the loan capitalist and the landowner, have all played their parts in the production and sale of commodities, and now each demands his share in the profit. Marx shows how each in fact receives a share in accordance with the size of his capital.

But the rate of profit does not necessarily rise with the development of capitalism; and Marx next sets out to show that there is in fact a

[1] In the nineteen-twenties there was vigorous propaganda by the Independent Labour Party, based on the assumption that a high-wages policy could cure unemployment. Similar theories were again advanced in the economic crisis of 1929.

[2] *Capital*, II.476. The crisis of 1931 verified this. The *Economist* for June 2nd, 1934, published a chart showing a rise in wages in France, Germany, Britain, Japan and the United States between 1929 and 1931, while prices were falling fast. This "was bound to diminish the amount of labour and other factors of production which could be employed at a profit, and to lead to an enormous increase in unemployment of men and machinery".

tendency for it to fall, and this can prove an important factor in the increasing disequilibrium of the capitalist system. An important section of Volume III is devoted to this question. Marx argues that this tendency appears when increased mechanisation leads to a smaller proportion of labour to machinery being employed.[1] When such a fall in the rate of profit occurs the process of further investment is arrested and crisis is precipitated; while, operating as a long-term tendency, it will constitute a progressively increasing drag on the process of expansion of capital.

Marx does not fail to point out that there are many counteracting tendencies to this factor in slowing down investment, such as the rise in labour productivity, cheapening of machinery and raw materials, and advantageous terms of foreign trade.

It has already been pointed out that in the first volume he is constructing a simplified model to make clear his basic theory of surplus value and how it originates, throwing into relief the basic influences which were shaping the configuration of the whole system, and incidentally showing that economic exploitation is not based on violence, robbery and cheating, but that everything that happens in capitalist society is the result of definite and regularly-operating laws and not of arbitrary forces or the decisions of evil-minded men.[2] In the second and third volumes Marx has moved from the basic level to the surface, to the world of bankers and shops, of the stock exchange and the market. Therefore having explained the nature of value and the relation to price or exchange value in the first volume, he is now perfectly willing to handle the problem of particular prices and to show the effect of a variety of conditions on his simplified model by the method of successive approximations.[3]

But it remains true that "the law of value dominates the movements of prices, since a reduction or increase of the labour time required for production causes the prices of production to fall or rise".

[1] In Marx's terms the ratio of constant to variable capital is raised, resulting in what he calls a higher composition of capital.

[2] *Capital*, III.286.

[3] As had already been pointed out it was supposed by Böhm-Bawerk (*Karl Marx and the Close of His System*) that when he came to Volume III Marx realised that his basic theory was incorrect and produced a new one which was totally incompatible with it. Unfortunately for this view, Marx had written most of Volume III before he wrote Volume I, and saw no such incompatibility. The theory as it is worked out in the later volume essentially depends upon that in Volume I. Böhm-Bawerk's contention that the theory of prices contradicts the theory of value is the very opposite of the truth.

It is necessary to be clear that *Capital* is not intended to be a descriptive and analytical study of the fixed structure of the capitalist economic system, but to show that structure as changing, as in flux, as a system having a determinate cycle of growth and decay. Marxism reveals the law of motion of capitalist society, the processes of its own self-movement. Social reality is not a fixed structure but a changing one, and change is effected by strains set up in the system by its own working at any stage. Marxism overcomes the fatal incapacity to see the present as a phase in historical development and subject to inevitable change and transformation.

It is in the light of this fact that everything in the three volumes of *Capital* must be understood. We are not considering an alternative system of explanation for the permanent economic facts and functions of an industrial society. We are treating all the items—profit, prices, money, exchange, the commodity, investments—as *factors of change*. Hence the crucial chapters will be those which show that the normal working of the system inevitably leads to disequilibrium and crisis.

Marx had already reached his first disclosure of this in Volume II, and now in Volume III it assumes a more and more important place in his analysis of capitalist development.[1] The classical economist had tended to identify the rule of economic law with the postulation of an underlying stability and harmony in the economic system. To this view Marx opposed the notion that capitalism was not a stable but an unstable system. It had been described by the economists as a self-regulating system—the variations in the price of capital, labour and commodities, under the pressure of supply and demand, keeping the whole system working efficiently. Marx now points out that the very forces which operate to maintain equilibrium generate counter-forces which periodically disrupt that equilibrium; that the measures which capitalism is forced to take when the first symptoms of disequilibrium appear are themselves "the forcible solutions of existing contradictions, violent eruptions which restore the disturbed equilibrium for a while". The crisis is thus not merely the expression of a breakdown of equilibrium, but itself the process by which the broken equilibrium asserts itself. The sequence of events and decisions, slowing down of investment and production, dismissals, reduction of wages, and falling prices, all operate to keep the system functioning. If they were not put into operation, the system would crash. The forces making for the stability of the system are the forces which disrupt it.

[1] *Capital*, III.292 f.

But Marx does not single out *one*, decisive cause of economic crisis—underconsumption, finance and credit, over-investment and so forth. Each crisis in turn may have its origin in something different, and all of them may well involve financial disruption *and* over-investment, *and* underconsumption. To ask for any such single solution would be to require a too mechanical and over-simplified answer. What is clear is that crises are an inevitable product of capitalist society, a product of the many-sided relation between the productive forces and the productive relation of capitalism.

"*The real barrier of capitalist production is capital itself*. It is the fact that capital and its self-expansion appear as the starting and closing point, as the motive and aim of production; that production is merely production for capital, and not vice versa, the means of production mere means for an ever-expanding system of the life process for the benefit of the society of producers. The barriers within which the preservation and self-expansion of the value of capital resting on the expropriation and pauperisation of the great mass of producers can alone move, these barriers come continually in collision with the methods of production, which capital must employ for its purposes, and which steer straight towards the unrestricted extension of production, towards production for its own self, towards an unconditional development of the productive forces of society. The means, this unconditional development of the productive forces of society, comes continually into conflict with the limited end, the self-expansion of the existing capital. Thus, while the capitalist mode of production is one of the historical means by which the material forces of production are developed and the world market required for them created, it is at the same time in continual conflict with this historical task and the conditions of social production corresponding to it."[1]

There is thus a contradiction between production considered as producing values (consumption goods) and as producing profit; ultimately capital goods are never produced and investment in capital goods does not take place except with a view to their ultimate utilisation in turning out consumption goods.

Capitalism attempts to expand production, since accumulated profits must be invested, without any reference to the consumption which alone can give it meaning. The two sides of the economy, which are mutually dependent, since production lacks any objective unless it issues in consumption, are, in the capitalist world, separated logically

[1] *Capital*, III.293.

as well as in time and space; on the one hand we have production and exploitation, on the other the ultimate realisation of surplus value in sales. But the latter is limited by the consuming power of society, whereas the former is only limited by available resources. Consuming power is not of course determined by need, but by available spending power, and since for every competitive business concern costs are an evil and must be as far as possible reduced, the consumption of the great mass of the population is kept at a minimum. The consuming power is further restricted, as Marx pointed out, by the tendency to accumulate, the urgent pressure to accumulate surplus value which is the driving force of the whole capitalist system.[1]

Therefore the forces of production can never be utilised beyond the point at which surplus value can not only be produced, but also realised in a society in which the great majority are poor. There is an inherent tendency for growth in consumption to fall behind the growth in the output of consumption goods. "The last cause of all real crisis always remains the poverty and restricted consumption of the masses as compared to the tendency of capitalist production to develop the productive forces in such a way that only the absolute power of consumption of the entire society would be their limit."[2]

It is clear that it is not within the competence of capitalism to plan its production in relation to its consumption, both maximising the former and at the same time distributing the requisite purchasing power for its appropriation by the consumers. For "capital and its self-expansion appear as the starting and closing point, as the motive and aim of production", which is not, and cannot be under capitalism, the satisfaction of consumption. "Production is merely production for *capital*, and not vice versa, the means of production are means for an ever-expanding system of the life-process for the benefit of the *society* of producers."[3]

Marx immediately points out, however, the immensely important role of capitalism as "the historical means by which the material forces of production are developed and the world market for them created". Yet at the same time it is in continual conflict with this historical task.

Two closely connected questions of some importance remain for discussion. Did Marx attempt to show the inevitability of the total breakdown of capitalism in some final crisis? This is not so, for Marx never forgot the importance of the counteracting tendencies which interfere both with the tendency to a falling rate of profit and the

[1] *Capital*, III.286. [2] *Capital*, III.560. [3] *ibid.*

decline of consumption power. Marx did not prophesy breakdown;[1] he was concerned to analyse actual trends, not to speculate on their hypothetical outcome.

Marx always took due note of such countervailing tendencies as the increasing productivity of labour (in relation to the falling rate of profit), the growth in organised labour's economic and political strength. Nor did the view that the whole working class would inevitably sink into pauperisation play any part in the Marxian argument. Marx seems to indicate that something like this would happen among the reserve army of the more or less permanently unemployed, but there is no evidence that he expected real wages to fall until the entire working class was at, or below subsistence level. The pressure on wages is, of course, real enough; but it represents an abstract tendency which asserts itself only in the absence of counteracting forces. Marx sees among such forces not only resistance to worsening conditions, but a growth in working-class solidarity, trade union and organisational strength, and political militancy, which by revolutionary action prevents final collapse by effecting the transformation to socialism.

The investigation of the causes of disequilibrium within capitalism as a dynamic system which generates its own compulsive drive to expansion and at the same time its own fetters on expanding production, has acquired a relevance to the modern world and its problems denied to other theories of the nature and problems of contemporary capitalism. Many economists see with apprehension the dependence of the American economy on a gigantic arms programme, and anticipate catastrophe extending far beyond America to Europe and the rest of the world, should the armaments race cease and the cold war be allayed. Obvious to most economists today is what has been called "creeping stagnation", a falling of the rate of increase of productivity to a level incompatible with a rising standard of living and the overcoming of the continuing evils of capitalist civilisation.

The immense importance of *Capital* is now recognised by many economists and social theorists who by no means accept Marx's general position. Schumpeter calls it "one of the greatest individual achievements of sociology to this day".[2] Professor W. Leontief of Harvard

[1] The question of inevitable breakdown has been exhaustively discussed by Kautsky, Bowden, Rosa Luxemburg, and in recent times by Sweezy (*Theory of Capitalist Development*).

[2] Schumpeter, *Socialism, Capitalism and Democracy*.

speaks of Marx's brilliant analysis of the long run tendencies of the capitalist system. "The record is indeed impressive: increasing concentration of wealth, rapid elimination of small and medium sized enterprises, progressive limitation of competition, incessant technological progress accompanied by an evergrowing importance of fixed capital, and last but not least the undiminishing amplitude of recurrent business cycles—an unsurpassed series of prognostications."[1]

[1] Proceedings of the 50th Annual Meeting of the American Economic Association.

18

MARX AND GERMAN SOCIAL DEMOCRACY

IN his lifetime Marx laboured unceasingly to establish organised socialist parties in Europe, and before his death he saw them appearing in Germany, France and Britain, while groups of his followers were active in Italy, Russia, Switzerland, Spain and the United States.

"All modern socialism," declared the *Encyclopaedia Britannica* in 1921, "even that of the schools which repudiate it, or at least profess no allegiance to Marx, has been profoundly influenced by him. . . . The organised socialist movement is in practically all cases definitely Marxist and bases its thinking and its propaganda throughout on Marxist terminology and Marxist ideas. But we find in the various parties the most varied interpretations of Marxist principles."

This was not due entirely to the influence of Marx's theoretical work, but to his guidance, during his whole lifetime, of the socialist movement; and his personal influence, by correspondence and rare visits abroad, on the development first of the International and later on the Marxist parties in Germany, France and elsewhere.

Marx was by no means a recluse, a scholar so deeply immersed in his books and his theories that he was hardly aware of the world of men and the complexities and demands of everyday politics. He had hardly entered the editorial office of the *Rheinische Zeitung* before he took up the cudgels on behalf of the Rhineland-Moselle peasants. Arriving in Paris, he is in the revolutionary atmosphere of active socialist discussion and rising political consciousness which in 1848 were to bring the proletariat on to the scene for the first time as a political force. In 1845 he visits England with Engels to become acquainted with the industrial and trade union advances there. In Brussels he is active in many political organisations; and exiled to England he organises the International with its strong backing of British trade unionists.

During the years he spent in London he was at first in close contact with the Chartists and through the International directed not only the labour movement abroad but to a remarkable extent the English labour movement too. He met a great number of active workers who came to see him from every part of the world; he delivered lectures; he argued fiercely; but, as the reminiscences written by those who knew him, and often disagreed with him, clearly show, his relations with them were warm and comradely. The members of the General Council of the International, who visited Marx in his dingy rooms, who witnessed his poverty, who always found him ready to put aside his studies to attend their committees, to play his part in every kind of activity on behalf of the working class, regarded him with profound respect.

GERMANY

His interest in the development of the German movement never flagged, and he maintained a close friendship with its leaders and more energetic members throughout his life. It was among them that we find his closest personal friends, like Ferdinand Wolff and Wilhelm Liebknecht.

When Marx first entered the political field in Germany in the 1840's there had not emerged any one class rising to a dominant position and capable of feeling itself as the representative of the whole of society, as had been the case in France. Owing to the extreme economic backwardness of Germany, the working class had to concentrate all its energies on the attainment of democracy in a bitter struggle against the combined forces of the monarchy, the landed aristocracy, the Army, and the leading sections of the middle class. When German labour finally entered the political arena, the struggle for social justice meant fighting against the existing undemocratic constitution, and against the accepted way of life of the rest of the nation. This was the main cause of that spirit of deep hostility against the existing state order which gave the movement the strength to withstand in proud defiance twelve years of Bismarckian oppression and persecution and to emerge after that period stronger and more self-confident than before.

The suppression of the 1848 revolution meant the destruction of the attempts at working-class association. Socialists were persecuted with crusading zeal. In Cologne the eleven members of the Communist League were brought to trial. The propaganda which had begun in 1836 ended in 1853 and was not revived for many years.

What did revive it was the intensification of working-class suffering which accompanied the rapid development of industrialisation, and the growing demands of the bourgeoisie for their own *laissez-faire* type of liberalism—*within* the autocratic state. The essential part of their fight for constitutional rights against the absolutist state was the demand for no state interference with industry in matters affecting the wages and conditions of the workers. It became clear that the liberals had no intention of fighting for any interests but those of the employers, and it became clear that the time had come when the workers would have to fight their own battles as an independent, disciplined and united class.

As we have already seen, the German proletarian and socialist movement, which began to gain momentum about 1840, was to a large extent the work of Ferdinand Lassalle, who in turn derived his understanding of the role of the working class and of the necessity for its independent organisation from Marx. But when Lassalle intrigued with Bismarck to defeat the liberal progressives, their common enemy, being promised by Bismarck state support for workers' co-operatives and an extension of the franchise, Marx realised that for all his energy and genius Lassalle was betraying the movement; and indeed when war with Austria was declared in 1866, the Lassallean socialists took the shamelessly chauvinistic line that might have been expected from the secret pact with Bismarck.

The Lassalleans were not to maintain their monopoly of the socialist movement. There arose in Saxony, following a powerful printers' strike organised by August Bebel, a new socialist society which maintained close relations with Marx and rejected the compromising policies of Lassalle. Wilhelm Liebknecht, a close friend of Marx, played a leading role in the formation of this party, which joined the International and at a Congress at Nuremberg in 1868 adopted a socialist programme.

The Nuremberg programme contained the following affirmations:

1. The emancipation of the working classes is the task of the working class themselves.
2. Political liberty is an essential condition for the economic liberation of the proletarians.
3. The social question is inseparable from the political.
4. The emancipation of the worker is not a local or national problem but a social problem which affects every country.

From that time the whole of the working-class and socialist movement in Germany revolved around the figures of Bebel and Liebknecht.

At the Congress in Eisenach in 1869 they founded the Social-Democratic Working Men's Party, and in the same year sent representatives to the Congress of the International at Basle.

Every step in this struggle was watched with anxiety by Marx, who gave Liebknecht constant guidance and encouragement in the extremely difficult tactical moves which were ultimately to lead to victory.

Then came the Franco-Prussian War of 1870. The Lassalleans voted the war credits in the general chorus of the bourgeois majority, but Liebknecht and Bebel abstained, published a declaration setting forth their reasons, and found themselves in prison. Marx approved their declaration, though both he and Engels perfectly well realised that the defeat of Louis Napoleon was as necessary as it was deserved.

After Sedan, however, both the socialist parties united in condemning Bismarck for the annexation of Alsace-Lorraine. Here was the opportunity for *rapprochement*. In the elections of 1874 the Eisenach Party (the Social-Democratic Working Men's Party) polled 170,000 votes and the Lassalleans (the General Association of German Workers) 180,000. They secured nine seats between them. The Chancellor was alarmed. There was a wave of police persecution resulting in the imprisonment of the socialist leaders. It became clear to both groups that they must form a united front against the Chancellor. In October 1874 negotiations began between Liebknecht, once more at liberty, and the Lassalle group. In the spring of the following year, 1875, the historic Congress of Gotha took place. The 9,121 members of the Eisenach Party were represented by 56 delegates and the 15,322 members of the Lassalle group by 73. Liebknecht drew up a draft programme and the leader of the Lassalle group, Hasenclever, presented the draft statutes, all of which were approved. Thus was born the German Social-Democratic Party.

What part did Marx play in these events?

The draft programme appeared in the organs of the two parties on March 7th. This was the first inkling that Marx and Engels had of this new basis for unity. Engels at once sent a long and extremely critical letter to Bebel (presumably via Liebknecht) which never reached him, and on May 6th Marx wrote to Bracke, a member of the Party Committee who had grave doubts about the programme, enclosing his critical notes, now known as the *Critique of the Gotha Programme*. Liebknecht, to whom they did not write directly, because he had not told Marx and Engels about this programme, admitted later that a majority might have been obtained at the unity congress for Marx's views, but they considered unity more important than a majority/minority decision. Marx on the contrary would have sought unity *for action*, leaving the theoretical questions for later discussion, and thus worked together with the Lassalleans on a basis which would have given them a chance to convince the Lassalleans of the soundness of their position: "... every step of real movement," he said "is more important than a dozen programmes." As Marx pointed out, the Lassalleans were in poor shape and had come to seek agreement because there was no other course for them. "If they had been told there would be no bargaining about principles, they would have had to be content with a programme of action." Liebknecht and his colleagues did not accept Marx's advice, and seriously compromised themselves by accepting a thoroughly confused programme which made concessions in all directions to the theories of Lassalle. Everything was sacrificed to the unity of the German working-class movement.

This *Critique of the Gotha Programme* is a vitally important contribution to socialist theory and its application to practical policies.[1]

The Gotha Programme declared that the road to socialism lay through state aid for producers co-operatives, which the state, and not the workers, would call into existence. As though a new society could be built by government loans just as easily as a new railway!

The state was held to be a neutral instrument of government which could be directed to socialist purposes. To this Marx objected that socialism demanded the conversion of the state from an organ controlling society to one completely controlled by it. Marx saw the state as an institution to be used by the workers to hold down the bourgeoisie by force after a political victory, which is what he meant by the dictatorship of the proletariat.

As far as the economic programme was concerned it affirmed Lassalle's theory of "the iron law of wages"—the view that the increase in population would always keep wages down to a bare subsistence. Marx had always opposed that view, holding that trade union pressure and other factors would successfully work against the tendency.

[1] It was first published with Marx's letter in the *Neue Zeit* in 1891 in a shortened form; but was not published after that until it was issued by the Marx-Engels Institute in Moscow in 1932. (Even in 1891 Bebel thought it ought not to be published.)

An apparently revolutionary demand was the programme's claim that the worker had the right to "the whole proceeds of labour". This, Marx pointed out, was economic nonsense, since a considerable part of the proceeds of labour are required for the further creation of capital growth, for reserves and insurance funds, for cost of administration, schools, public health, pensions and so forth.

When the programme turned to immediate political tactics, it set the Social-Democratic Party against all other sections and classes of society, which it described as "one reactionary mass". Marx on the contrary insisted on the importance of securing allies in other classes and groups. Later Lenin also criticised this "black and white" confrontation as irrelevant, as if two armies would confront one another, one saying "We are for socialism", and opposite them the other saying "We are for capitalism". This is political nonsense. "Those who wait for a 'pure' social revolution of this sort will never live to see it."

Finally, the programme ignored the necessity of *international* working-class unity in the struggle for socialism. Marx pointed out that the German workers had always given their loyal support to the international movement, "and now this principle was to be denied by them at the very moment when the workers everywhere abroad were emphasising it, in the same degree that governments are striving to suppress every attempt at its realisation in an organisation!"

What did this controversy reveal? That neither of the two socialist parties had a firm theoretical basis. The first derived its ideas from the writing of Lassalle, the second from *The Communist Manifesto*; but not even Liebknecht and Bebel really understood the views of Marx, or had any clear idea of *Capital*, which they seemed not to have read.

Marx's *Critique of the Gotha Programme* made no impression on the leaders of the new party. Even those who professed to be Marxist shared in the prevailing theoretical confusion. When, however, many of the leading figures began to turn to the pretentious arguments of Eugen Dühring, a Berlin professor, Engels decided that it was time to set down a clear statement of the principles of scientific socialism for which he and Marx stood.

Eugen Dühring was a German philosopher of Swedish extraction whose name is by no means unimportant in the history of German philosophy. Deeply interested in modern science, he was the most celebrated representative of the materialistic tendency in philosophy since Feuerbach, but he was also concerned with a critical examination of the relations between thought and reality, developed from the basic principles of Kant. He differed, however, from most German university teachers by working out a philosophy of society closely related to actual problems, and producing his own version of socialism, which rejected Marx's view that there was a definite law of social development. Dühring's sociology offered solid practical proposals for day-to-day use which exactly suited the mentality of those who attended his lectures, which were immensely popular. He quarrelled with the university authorities, lost his position, and became fiercely intolerant and suspicious, finding not "opponents" of his views but *enemies* everywhere, especially among professors, social-democrats and Jews.

He became more and more popular, winning sympathy by his blindness, confidence by his espousal of "socialist" aims, and some admiration for his vitriolic attacks on professors of philosophy.

The rapid growth of the party made it indifferent to the kind of discussion which it regarded as too abstract for practical socialists. All sorts of people were flocking into its ranks, and whoever showed goodwill and seemed seriously concerned with the social problem was sure of a welcome. A university professor who came out for socialism had no need to fear any very strict criticism of his intellectual stock-in-trade.

The German Social Democrats had few of them plunged into so difficult a book as Marx's *Capital. The Communist Manifesto* and Lassalle's *Workers' Programme* were really all they had read. There was no concise and clear presentation of the theories of Marx as they had developed since 1848. In consequence they flocked to Dühring's lectures and read his books. Bernstein sent a copy to Bebel who was at that time in prison. Bebel at once wrote an article which was full of admiration for the "new communist". Even Liebknecht thought well of him until Dühring's diatribes against Marx convinced him that he was a menace. Liebknecht asked Engels to reply to this criticism; but both Engels and Marx were inclined to ignore him and get on with their own work. Then another Social Democrat, Johann Most, extolled Dühring's philosophy in an article intended for *Vorwärts*, and Engels read it with indignation. He and Marx at once came to the conclusion that immediate and ruthless measures should be taken. Engels' criticism took the form of a series of articles in *Vorwärts* which began to appear in 1877. Strong objection was taken to them by many leading party members and the articles were only allowed to continue as a special supplement.

It is these articles which constitute the well-known presentation of scientific socialism known as *Anti-Dühring* (*Herr Eugen Dühring's Revolution in Science*). The book was immediately banned in Germany and its influence was not fully felt until the Introduction and three of the chapters were separately published in *Socialism, Utopian and Scientific* in 1880, which had an enormous sale in France, Germany (1883) and many other countries.[1] Engels says of it, "I am not aware that any other socialist work, not even our *Communist Manifesto* of 1848 or Marx's *Capital* has been so often translated" (this was of course in 1892). In this book, although it appeared to him at the time to be no more than an attempt to clear the minds of the German Social Democrats, Engels struck a decisive blow for the conversion of continental social-democracy to Marxism. It was really the first book to reveal the essence of Marxism to its leading figures, and it won thousands of workers for Marxism. In fact it was instrumental in creating for the first time a real school of Marxist thought on the Continent.

Socialism, Utopian and Scientific, which still remains the most lucid and comprehensive introduction to Marxism, began with an interesting account of the development of philosophy from the early materialists to the appearance of historical materialism, and proceeds to a discussion of the ideological role of religion in relation to successive class struggles and especially to the rise of the bourgeoisie and the influence of Protestantism.

The main theme is introduced by an account of the rise of socialist theories and ideals as set forth by the utopian socialists Saint-Simon, Fourier and Robert Owen. While recognising their greatness, Engels goes on to show how ineffectual utopian thinking can be. "If we have no better security for the revolution than the consciousness that capitalism is unjust and that justice must finally prevail, we should be in evil plight." But scientific socialism shows how it comes about that "the productive forces of modern capitalism as well as the system of distribution based upon it are in glaring contradiction to the mode of production itself", so that if a new system abolishing all exploitation and all class differences does not come into existence the whole of modern society will fail. Thus for utopianism Engels, using the

[1] The English edition was published in 1892 by Allen and Unwin as Volume 56 in their *Social Science Series*.

Hegelian interpretation of social and economic change, substitutes scientific socialism, showing that men do not change society by proclaiming the ideals of justice and equality but by virtue of the recognition of the economic conditions which make it an historic necessity.

The larger book, *Anti-Dühring*, while containing a good deal of polemical material of no more than historical interest, devotes several important chapters to the systematic exposition of Dialectical Materialism. Marx had intended to do this himself, but never found the time or the occasion to attempt the task. Engels defines the dialectic method of thinking as that which "comprehends things and their representations in their essential connection, concatenation, motion, origin, and ending. Such processes as those mentioned above (various natural occurrences) are, therefore, so many corroborations of its own method of procedure. Nature is the proof of dialectics. . . . An exact representation of the universe, of its evolution, of the development of mankind, and of the reflection of this evolution in the minds of men, can therefore only be obtained by the methods of dialectics, with its constant regard to the innumerable actions and reactions, of life and death, of progressive or retrogressive changes."

Anti-Dühring also contains important sections on Morality, Law, Equality, Freedom and Necessity. The last of these points out that "freedom does not consist in the dream of independence of natural laws, but in the knowledge of these laws, and in the possibility this gives of making them work towards definite ends". Thus Engels, with his own encyclopaedic knowledge and his incomparable mastery of the dialectical method, followed Dühring step by step, and not merely made short work of him, but (what was of far greater importance) produced a work of enduring value.[1]

In the General Election of January 1877 the socialists obtained 140,000 more votes than in 1874. Berlin and Dresden returned socialist deputies. Bismarck decided on suppression, and taking advantage of two attempts on the life of Wilhelm I by men with not the slightest contact with social democracy, a series of anti-socialist laws was passed. The Exclusion Bill declared that "the pathological ideas of socialism, the enemy of society and the state, cannot be stamped out by common law. Hence the urgency of the law of exclusion." The party was thus outlawed, its organ *Vorwärts* banned, together with the rest of the

[1] The tenth chapter of the section on economics was written by Marx, who also gave his approval to the whole work.

working-class press. The police dissolved all working-class organisations and mass imprisonment and banishment followed.

Engels believed that by these measures Bismarck would only benefit the party which he intended to crush, provided that it made no concessions to the government. The parliamentary group could not be touched by the new law, but it right away abandoned all resistance and looked for support to the liberal bourgeoisie. Bebel and Liebknecht, however, made no compromise. They were attacked both by the Right wing, and also by the extremists on the Left because they saw the folly of launching a revolutionary attack on the government without hope of victory—more exactly because this was what the government wanted as an excuse to obliterate socialism.

The movement in Germany went underground. Clandestine journals were passed from hand to hand. A group of socialist leaders including Bernstein, Schwamm and a wealthy young man called Höchberg, emigrated to Zürich to escape Bismarck's anti-socialist laws, and began negotiations with the leaders who remained in Germany to edit the party journal there, *Der Sozialdemokrat*.

It fell to Höchberg to lay down the policy of the journal;[1] but when this statement reached Marx the result was startling. Marx and Engels at once wrote to Bebel and Liebknecht in Leipzig in September 1879 protesting vehemently against the policy of the Zürich social democrats, which they regarded as a complete betrayal of socialism. Their letter is the classical Marxist reply to reformism.[2]

Of the three men concerned, Bernstein was regarded as the most brilliant of the younger Marxists. Höchberg was a well-to-do young man with little knowledge and no experience of political activity. Bernstein was to become the leader of the reformist movement after Marx's death. In Zürich they had published the *Yearbook for Socialist Science and Politics*, which contained the article by Höchberg, for which all three made themselves responsible. At that time German social democracy regarded Marx and Engels as their real leaders and as acknowledged authorities. It was therefore a serious matter when Engels declared it to be "absolutely impossible for us to co-operate with an organ in which Höchberg has anything whatever to say" Schwamm was an economist and in 1878 Höchberg's secretary. He was strongly under Dühring's influence.

[1] *A Review of the Socialist Movement* signed by Höchberg, Schwamm and Bernstein was really the work of Höchberg. It appeared in their *Jahrbuch für Sozial Wissenschaft und Sozial Politik*.

[2] Marx and Engels to Bebel, Liebknecht, Bracke and others, September 1879.

Marx sums up Höchberg's and Bernstein's case in his letter to Bebel and Liebknecht. "It is the representatives of the petty bourgeoisie who are here presenting themselves, full of anxiety that the proletariat, under the pressure of its revolutionary position, may 'go too far'. Instead of decided political opposition, general compromise; instead of the struggle against the government and the bourgeoisie, an attempt to win and to persuade; instead of defiant resistance to ill treatment from above, a humble submission and confession that the punishment was deserved. The overthrow of the capitalist system is unattainably remote and has absolutely no significance for practical present-day politics. The class struggle is hushed up, diluted.

"The Social Democratic Party is not to be a workers' party. . . . It should above all conduct energetic propaganda among the bourgeoisie; instead of laying stress on far-reaching aims which frighten the bourgeoisie and are not, after all, attainable in our generation, it should rather devote its whole strength and energy to those small patching-up reforms which by providing the old order of society with new props may perhaps transform the ultimate catastrophe into a gradual, piecemeal, and so far as possible, peaceful process of dissolution."

Marx is scathing about all this. Again and again similar views had appeared, especially as the "True Socialism" refuted in the *Manifesto*, which, since it rejected the class struggle, had reduced socialism to empty phrases about "humanity" and "justice". It was the work of people who "under the pretence of indefatigable activity not only do nothing themselves but also try to prevent anything at all happening except chatter; who want to confine history within their narrow petty-bourgeois horizon and over whose heads history invariably proceeds to the order of the day".

Who were these Höchbergs and Bernsteins who flirted with communism and then moved over to the camp of revisionism and reformism? Marx was well acquainted with them and had taken their measure. The compromise of the German Party with the Lassalleans had opened the door to "a whole gang of half-mature students and super-wise doctors who want to give socialism a 'higher ideal', replacing its realism by the modern mythology of Justice, Freedom, Equality and Fraternity".[1] Höchberg, says Marx, "has no doubt bought himself into the party" (he was a wealthy man and was prepared to help

[1] Marx to Sorge, Octobter 19th, 1877.

generously), "with the 'noblest' intentions, I assume, but I do not give a damn for intentions."[1] These are "people who do not want to learn anything fundamentally, educated gentlemen who try to schoolmaster the workers from the superior heights of their ignorant university-bred confusion."

"How few of the young literary men who fasten themselves on to the party give themselves the trouble to study economics or the history of the forms of society. If these gentlemen only knew how Marx thought his best things were still not good enough for the workers and how he regarded it as a crime to offer the workers anything less than the best."[2]

"Even the workers themselves, when they give up work and become professional literary men, always set some theoretical mischief going and are always ready to attach themselves to muddleheads from the alleged 'learned caste'." Utopian socialism, especially, which Marx for tens of years had been clearing out of the heads of socialists, this foolish "playing with fancy pictures of the future structure of society, is now raging in a much more futile form", since what was understandable and deeply significant before the rise of modern industry and the political awakening of the working class, is now when conditions point to constructive advance "only silly-silly stale and basically reactionary".[3]

The Höchberg affair worried Marx greatly. His long letter to Bebel and Liebknecht certainly ranks among the most important documents in which his political line is revealed. Three of the German leaders visited him in these days in what eventually proved to be a successful endeavour to clear up the difficulties over the Zürich *Social Democrat* and to discuss the problems of the party. They were Bebel, who brought Bernstein with him, and Hirsch who was at that time editing the journal from London. The visit achieved its various aims and in the end Bernstein was appointed provisional editor and carried out his tasks to everyone's satisfaction. Every week thousands of copies were despatched to Germany and, in spite of all the efforts of the police, were distributed among the Social Democrats.

But after Engels' death Bernstein reverted to reformism and swung the German party entirely in that direction. He taught that a painless

[1] *ibid.*
[2] Engels to Schmidt, August 5th, 1890.
[3] Marx and Engels to Bebel, Liebknecht and others, September 1879.

transition to socialism was possible, that the basic contradiction within capitalism could be overcome, and all that was needed was the securing of limited reforms one by one which would transform society into a real democracy. At the end of his life, however, Bernstein was himself partially to repudiate these "revisionist" views.

One of the founders and chief leaders of German Social Democracy was Wilhelm Liebknecht, who was the chief organiser of the union with the Lassalleans. He constantly discussed with Marx the problems of policy which arose during his leadership. Although Marx always regarded him with great affection he thought him a muddlehead. He was a journalist, an energetic organiser and speaker, but away from the controlling influence of Marx and Engels he was very liable to fall into opportunism. Marx frequently had cause to criticise him.

"Wilhelm is anxious to make up for the deficiencies in our theories, to have an answer ready for every philistine objection, to have a picture of the future society ready-made in his mind because the philistine might question him about it, and at the same time to be as independent as possible in theoretical matters, an endeavour in which he has been more successful than he realised, owing to his complete lack of any theory."[1] He enjoyed a degree of intimacy with Marx and his circle which few others achieved. He never resented criticism and it was the authority of Marx that made his position in the party a strong one.

The anti-socialist laws continued in force from 1878 to 1890, but the appalling difficulties of these years failed to destroy the socialist movement entirely. They proved in fact to be the prologue to a socialist renaissance in the political life of Germany.

The work of the party went on, mostly underground. In 1882 a conference was held at Zürich at which the bold step was taken of convening a party congress abroad. This took place at Copenhagen a few days after the death of Marx in 1883. In the general election a year later, the socialist party, though banned, won twenty-four seats. A new and excellent theoretical journal, *Neue Zeit*, appeared, edited by Karl Kautsky, a young Czech. When the Emperor Wilhelm I died, his successor Wilhelm II got rid of Bismarck and reversed his policies. In January 1890 the Reichstag repealed the law against social democracy. The new monarch had no more love for socialism

[1] Engels to Marx, May 28th, 1876.

than Bismarck, but he contemplated quite other ways of dealing with it.

The Social Democrats held the first Congress to take place in Germany under conditions of legality at Erfurt in October 1891. Here genuine Marxist policies were put forward by Kautsky, Bebel and Liebknecht. Marx was dead. Engels was now regarded as his successor and as the representative of everything he stood for.

The new programme recognised that the struggle of the workers against capitalism had to be industrial as well as political, and thus moved away from the Lassallean position of the Gotha programme. It insisted that it was the task of the Party to give the workers a consciousness of their mission, to emancipate the whole of society by converting private property into social property, and capitalist into socialist production. It also declared, what the Gotha Programme had forgotten, that the class struggle was international.

Nevertheless, Engels had a serious criticism to make. It had one great fault: "What actually ought to be said *is not there*. . . . People talk themselves and the party into the belief that the present society will grow into socialism without asking themselves if for this it is not equally necessary that society should grow out of its old social constitution and burst its old shell just as violently as a crab bursts out of its old shell."[1]

Germany was in 1891 by no means a constitutional democracy and it was still necessary to break the fetters of the semi-absolutist political order. The struggle for the democratic republic was of vital importance just because the working class could only come to power through its means, and because for Marx democracy was the specific form of the dictatorship of the proletariat.

In the final programme only a small degree of consideration was paid to Engels' criticism and the importance of the state power as the instrument of transition to socialism was not understood. But the party went forward and after thirty years of intensive effort it seemed that the Marxists had at long last the biggest working-class party in the world marching squarely behind them.

But it soon became apparent that the nominal conversion of the party to Marxist doctrine had left the two wings—reformist and revolutionary—both couching their arguments and defending their policies in Marxist terms and by appeals to the Marxist classics. The revisionist policies, now advocated by Bernstein, prevailed, however,

[1] Engels, Criticism of the Erfurt Programme.

and the party accepted its role as a successful and comparatively respectable parliamentary body, rejecting the possibility, indeed the real risk, of further repression and of losing its more cautious middle-class supporters. But these controversies were beyond the power of Engels to influence. He died in 1895.

19

MARX AND BRITISH LABOUR

MARX came to England when the great wave of Chartism was receding. Yet it was still feared, its leaders George Julian Harney and Ernest Jones, were still on the scene, the ferment of working-class feeling had not subsided.

In 1834 Robert Owen had organised his Grand National Consolidated Trades Union which aimed at the socialist transformation of society. Over half a million persons enrolled themselves, but few understood or shared the aims of its leaders. The general strike was to be its chief weapon. It failed, but Owen persisted in his endeavour to set up workers' production co-operatives. Although by 1831 some thirty of these were in existence they did not prove to be the real road of reform. Largely under Owen's influence, the working-class movement was anti-parliamentary, hoping to attain by means of trade unions what had hitherto been only considered possible of attainment by legislation.

The failure of these purely industrial methods and the attempts at a general strike were followed by the great political upsurge of the Chartist Movement. The proletarian movement was bitterly disappointed with the limitations of the Reform Act of 1832, and drew up a charter demanding further reforms. It demanded universal suffrage, annual parliaments, and the abolition of the property qualification of members of parliament. But the aims of the movement went beyond these demands and envisaged radical social reform. The *Northern Star* boldly declared that "Socialism and Chartism pursue the same aims, they only differ in their methods".

The Chartists presented petition after petition to Parliament, signed by enormous numbers of people.[1] They were all rejected. Meantime, the movement became divided into "physical force" Chartists and those working only by agitation. The Government became more and more alarmed and repressive. In August 1839, 130 Chartist leaders were arrested. There were serious riots in many parts of the country and a

[1] The Second National Petition was signed by over 3,000,000 people.

considerable uprising in South Wales. Many leaders were imprisoned or sentenced to transportation for life.

The radical bourgeoisie, themselves demanding an extension of the franchise, eventually left the movement to pursue their own interests, including the repeal of the Corn Laws. The result was the decisive separation of the proletariat from the bourgeoisie. The movement declined after the presentation of the last petition in 1848 when the Government mobilised 100,000 troops and 170,000 special constables. From May to October 1848 a reign of terror swept over England. Altogether about ninety Chartist leaders were imprisoned.

As early as 1842 Marx was publishing articles in the *Rheinische Zeitung* on industrial development in England, on the poverty and unemployment which accompanied it, and the political unrest. But it was Engels who with his articles in the *Deutsche-Französischen Jahrbücher* really opened his eyes to the condition of England.

Engels identified himself with the Chartists on his first visit to England and worked closely with Julian Harney, an eloquent speaker, editor of the Red Republican in which the *Manifesto* first appeared in England, and Ernest Jones, the Chartist journalist. During his life in London Marx, too, kept up his relations with the Chartists, wrote articles in the *People's Paper*, their organ (1853), met them frequently, delivered lectures, argued with them, and enlisted their co-operation when the International came into being.

In the *Neue Rheinische Zeitung* of December 1848 Marx described England at that time as the rock against which the waves of revolution would break. "The relations of industry and commerce within each country are determined by their relation with other countries, by their relations with the world market. But England dominates the world market and England is dominated by the bourgeoisie." Thus, so long as England holds her paramount position, any social advance in France or anywhere else must meet with defeat. England could only be overthrown by a war which would offer the Chartists, the organised party of the English proletariat, the conditions necessary for revolution. Only when the Chartists were at the head of the English government, he declared, would the social revolution advance from the realm of utopia to the world of reality.[1]

But the militancy of the British working-class movement was declining; it was no longer the threatening force which challenged capitalism itself as in the days of Robert Owen and the rise of Chartism.

[1] *Neue Rheinische Zeitung*, December 1848.

This was partly because the unions of skilled workers were securing concessions, while the unskilled were left to their fate.[1] The unions, led by the workers who were members of the General Council of the International, Odger, Cremer, Applegarth and many others, were carrying on a vigorous struggle for a wider suffrage in alliance with the radicals. The minutes of the General Council reveal an amazing amount of trade union activity, guided and encouraged by Marx.

The years 1848-50 witnessed a considerable revival of political interest and activity, probably in consequence of the influx of the exiled foreign revolutionary leaders. This increasingly took an international character. The workers in London were familiar with the names of the revolutionary leaders in France, Prussia, Austria and Hungary. They gave their warm sympathy and support to the Polish uprising of 1830, and took the keenest interest in the victories of Paris and Berlin in February and March 1848. They followed the course of the campaign in Hungary. When the revolutions were defeated, one after the other, many of the leaders fled and sought asylum in England and the United States. And in England support for the cause they had fought for was strong and well organised, especially among the London workers.

Marx never forgot that "a people which enslaves another people forges its own chains". The struggle for the emancipation of the British working class was, he saw, inseparable from that of the subject nations which Britain was exploiting. That was especially the case as far as Ireland was concerned, where the long struggle against British rule was still proceeding. The General Council resolved that for the speeding of the revolution in England "the first blow must be struck in Ireland".

Marx had received a long and detailed account of the Irish situation from Engels in 1856, and he followed the course of events in Ireland closely. In 1865 the International took up the case of the Fenian prisoners held in London after the Fenian insurrection. Marx came to the conclusion that it was "in the direct and absolute interest of the English working class to get rid of their present connections with Ireland".[2] It would, he declared, never accomplish anything until this had been achieved. It might, he believed, even strike a decisive

[1] The first of the unskilled or general workers' unions to be formed was organised by Will Thorne among the gas workers, with the help of Eleanor Marx, in 1889.

[2] Marx to Engels, December 10th, 1869.

blow against the English ruling class. "Hence the task of the International is everywhere to put the conflict between England and Ireland in the foreground." The special task of the Central Council in London was "to awaken a consciousness in the English workers that for them the national emancipation of Ireland is the first condition of their own emancipation".[1]

It is sometimes asserted that Marx failed to appreciate the significance of nationalism and the uprising of colonial people. This was never so. Not only did he take up the cause of Ireland, but since 1853 he had been giving special attention to the national liberation movement in India.[2] In that year he wrote a series of articles on India, including *The British Rule in India* and *The Future Outcome of British Rule in India*. "Nowhere more than in India," he declared, "do we meet with social destitution in the midst of plenty. The productive powers of India are paralysed." During the next four years he wrote twenty further articles on India, in which he dealt with the iniquities of British rule and the great uprising of the Indian people in 1857 known as "The Indian Mutiny". He foresaw considerable social and economic changes introduced by the imperial power, but it was clear to him that these would never go far enough to free the paralysed productive forces to the extent demanded by the needs of the Indian people. "All the English bourgeoisie may be forced to do will neither emancipate nor materially mend the social conditions of the mass of the people, depending not only on the development of the productive powers, but on their appropriation by the people. But what they will not fail to do is to lay down the material premises for both. Has the bourgeoisie ever done more? Has it ever effected a progress without dragging individuals and peoples through blood and dirt, through misery and degradation?"

Indian poverty and the paralysis of the productive forces illustrated Marx's basic theory of the inevitable results of "the whole system of production as it is now constituted in which that production rests on the supreme rule of capital. The bourgeois period of history has to create the material basis of the new world—on the one hand the universal intercourse founded upon the mutual dependency of mankind, and the means of that intercourse, on the other the development of the productive power of man and the transformation of material production into a scientific domination of natural agencies. Bourgeois in-

[1] Marx to Meyer, April 9th, 1870.

[2] Between 1853 and 1857 no less than twenty-three articles by Marx and eight by Engels were devoted to the subject of India.

dustry and commerce create these material conditions of a new world in the same way as geological revolutions have created the surface of the earth. When a great social revolution shall have mastered the results of the bourgeois epoch, the workers of the world and the modern powers of production, and subjected them to the common control of the most advanced people, then only will human progress cease to resemble that hideous pagan idol, who would not drink the nectar but from the skulls of the slain." In a memorable phrase Marx declared in a letter to Engels in January 1858 that "India is now our best ally".

Not only was he aware of the fact that a colonial uprising might be the beginning of capitalist collapse, but he was keenly aware of the importance of each nation within the International facing its own problems and securing its own emancipation. He continued to assert, however, that this was as much an international problem, in which the events in one country may hinder or accelerate emancipation in another, and in which working-class unity across all frontiers plays its indispensable role, as it was also a national question for each national working class to grapple with in its own way.

For several years, then, Marx played an important role in the development of the British working-class movement and was in the closest touch with all the trade union and political leaders of the time. It was then that, in opposition to John Weston, the carpenter, he insisted that trade union action was capable of raising the wages of labour above a subsistence level, just as monopoly could raise prices.

Later we find him combating the view of Bakunin, who saw the intelligentsia and representatives of bourgeois democracy, and not the working class, as the revolutionary element in society. Marx strongly opposed this view, as he did the even more impossible features of Bakunin's irresponsible policies and behaviour, and continued his humdrum but necessary task of furthering the enlightenment and organisation of the workers and above all of convincing the trade union movement that the "constitution of the working class into a political party is indispensable in order to ensure the triumph of the social revolution and its ultimate end—the abolition of classes".[1]

Unable to secure the franchise in the thirties and forties and therefore excluded from the field of actual politics, defeated by the collapse of Chartism, the workers were busy building up their trade unions. But Marx was right, the very tasks of industrial organisation forced

[1] Resolution of the London Conference of the International. September 1871.

them into the political field. Industrial organisation had developed to a stage where it came into collision with the political and juridical framework of capitalist society. This was plainly seen in the legal means open to the employers to deal with strikes and cripple union activity. The International Working Men's Association played an active part in stimulating political agitation and aroused a number of unions to participate in the fight for electoral reform. An extension of the franchise was won in 1867, and in 1871 a Bill was passed which secured union funds, but still the criminal law prevented militant action. In 1874 thirteen trade union candidates stood for Parliament and two were elected—the first workers to be returned to the House of Commons. In the following year a series of Acts were placed on the Statute Book, which gave immensely wider scope for trade union activity and constituted a considerable victory for the political side of the movement.

Engels, who not only worked with Marx during all these years but, after his death, continued to influence and guide the British labour movement to a remarkable degree, looked far beyond these partial victories to "the dominion of the working class" as the inevitable culmination of democracy. "A real democratic party is impossible unless it to be a working-man's party. . . . We live in a world where everybody is bound to take care of himself. Yet the English working class allows the landlord, capitalism and retail trading classes, with their tail of lawyers, newspaper writers, etc., to take care of the interests. No wonder reforms in the interests of the workmen come so slow and in such miserable dribbles. The workpeople of England have but to will, and they are the masters to carry every reform, social and political, which their situation requires."[1] But for many years the trade unions fell into political inactivity. They exerted their economic power on behalf of measures for the protection of the craft interest, but stopped short at the measure of legal recognition and protection conceded to them, and were content to allow one or the other of the political parties to govern. For many years Liberalism was to be the political creed of the trade union leaders; after the Paris Commune there was almost a stampede of moderates out of the International. After 1875 their political activities lapsed.

Marx was well aware of the difficulty of enlightening and organising the working class. He did not really imagine that they were ready at

[1] Engels, *The Labour Standard*, July 23rd, 1881.

his clarion call to leap to arms for the revolution. Towards the end of his life, when socialism was making tremendous strides in Germany, he saw England as still lagging behind, virtually impervious to his teaching. "Prolonged prosperity," he said, "has demoralised the workers." Bourgeois respectability had grown deep into their bones. "This most bourgeois of all nations is apparently aiming at the possession of a bourgeois aristocracy and a bourgeois proletariat as well as a bourgeoisie."[1]

Writing to Liebknecht in 1878 Marx complained that "the English working class has been gradually more and more deeply demoralised by the period of corruption since 1848 and has at last got to the point when they were nothing more than the tail of the Liberal Party. Their direction has gone completely over into the hands of the corrupt trade union leaders."[2]

It is remarkable to find even at this early date an explanation of this bourgeois infection of the workers as due to their sharing in the profits of capitalist colonial exploitation and England's monopoly of the world market. "Participation in the domination of the world market was and is the basis of the political nullity of the English workers. They will be shaken up only by the loss of this industrial monopoly." But at present "there is not a real proletarian movement here".[3]

Marx as early as 1850 had no illusions about the profound corruption of the working class by capitalism. "In order to work out their emancipation, and with it that higher form of life which present-day society inevitably opposes, the protracted struggle must pass through a whole series of historical processes, in the course of which men and circumstances alike will be changed."[4]

When in the same year the split in the Communist League occurred, Marx repudiated the demand of the old guard for an immediate revolution. The workers, said Marx, "must go through fifteen, twenty, perhaps even fifty years of war and civil war, not only in order to alter existing conditions, but even to make themselves fit to take over political power".

This completely realistic view of the workers was characteristic of Marx. It did not lessen his belief that since their interests required the transformation of society from capitalism to socialism, the pressure of circumstances, effective leadership of their trade unions, unremitting

[1] Engels to Marx, October 7th, 1852.
[2] Marx to Liebknecht, February 11th, 1878.
[3] Engels to Bebel, August 30th, 1883, and to Kautsky, September 12th, 1882.
[4] Marx: *Civil War in France*.

struggle against the frustrations and deprivations inflicted upon them by capitalism, and the awakening and guidance of their political consciousness by communists, would eventually arouse them to a higher degree of political consciousness and militancy.

It is interesting to note that he regarded the political awakening of women as necessary for this victory. "Anybody who knows anything of human history," he said in a letter to Kugelmann, "knows that great social changes are impossible without the feminine ferment." Social progress, he added, can be measured exactly by the position of women in society.

Nevertheless, as events moved forward, he had considerable hopes of genuine democratic advance both in France and especially in England, where the extension of the franchise and long-established constitutional methods gave exceptional opportunities to the working class movement. In Germany in 1849 economic conditions were not ripe and the proletariat undeveloped. Now, particularly in France and England, there was a large and increasingly class-conscious proletariat organised industrially and rapidly becoming aware of the necessity for independent political organisation too. Moreover, thirty years of Marxism had done something to give the movement theoretical understanding, and Marxist parties existed to give the necessary leadership in more than one industrial country.

Marx never threw aside the task of piecemeal reform and day-to-day struggle for immediate demands. He increasingly saw the possibility of resisting the downward tendency to worsening conditions, of improved factory legislation and shorter hours—not of course without intense struggle, which by its very nature and by its success would be a political education and would develop the unity and militancy of the working class. Nor did Marx, as some revolutionaries did, imagine that this would blunt the revolutionary consciousness.

This immediately raises the question as to whether the transition to socialism can be effected within the bourgeois state, utilising only its existing institutions and democratic procedures? This became the policy of Bernstein, who had frequently met and consulted with Marx, and the French "Possibilists". Marx never took this view, but always saw the sequence of working-class victories as leading to a real transfer of political power from the bourgeoisie to the working class. Only after this victory would it be possible to create a socialist society.

Marx saw many evidences of modifications within capitalism preparing the way for its supersession: the development of co-operative societies; the rapidly increasing separation of capitalist ownership, receiving the profit, and actual management and control, receiving the salary of superintendence; and the formation of larger and larger industrial concerns and monopolies.[1] He asserts that the development of corporate enterprise radically alters both the character of the ownership of the means of production and the role of the owners in the productive process. "Within the capitalist mode of production this is the transcendence of the capitalist mode of production—self-annulling contradictions which clearly represent a mere point of transition to a new form of production."[2]

Co-operation introduced a decisive change in ownership and in management. It represents the development of non-capitalist production within capitalist society. Although the British Co-operative Movement is essentially concerned with retail trade, there are numerous and effective Production Co-operatives associated with the Co-operative Wholesale Society. These have greatly increased since Marx's time and he was particularly interested in them. In such concerns, he says, "the antagonistic character of the labour of superintendence disappears, since the manager is paid by the labourers instead of representing capital against them".[3] They show the way in which, at a certain level of development of the material forces of production and of the corresponding social form of production, a new mode of production opens within and develops out of the old mode of production. Even though the employment of labour cannot but exemplify the shortcomings of the prevailing system, "the labourers themselves represent within the old form the first beginnings of the new".[4] Marx saw in the growth of monopoly the most important qualitative change within capitalism, bringing nearer and preparing the ground for the further change of the whole capitalist system into socialism. As Engels said, "Competition has been replaced by monopoly in England, and the road has been paved, most gratifyingly, for the future expropriation by the whole of society, the nation."[5]

"This", Marx declared, "is the abolition of the capitalist mode of production within capitalist production itself, a self-destructive

[1] *Capital*, Vol. III, 455 ff.
[2] *loc. cit.* and 519.
[3] *Capital*, Vol. III, 456.
[4] *Capital*, Vol. III, 521.
[5] Engels, Note to Chapter XXVII of *Capital*, Vol. III.

contradiction, which represents on its face a mere phase of transition to a new form of production."[1]

Marx and Engels considered it to be their special task to watch the development of the movement in connection with the course of international politics and industrial developments throughout the world. The part they played, however, was not that of theoreticians only, but of practical fighters. From the Chartist movement in the forties down to the Eight Hour movement in the nineties, Engels was actively participating in every struggle of the British workers.

After his earlier activity up to 1848, Engels returned to England to enter the family business in Manchester. He watched with deep attention the development of the English proletariat for more than half a century. In 1881 the trade unionist, Shipton, founded a weekly paper *The Labour Standard*, which advocated the formation of an independent political workers' movement in England, and Engels wrote a series of striking articles for it. He took up again the wages question which Marx had discussed with the International in 1865. It was still being asserted that the "iron law of wages" made it impossible under capitalism for wages to rise above subsistence. Engels declared that there was a certain latitude "within which the rate of wages may be modified by the results of the struggle between the two contending parties. . . . The great merit of trades unions, in this struggle, is that they tend to raise the standard of life." It is certainly true that increasing business competition brings great pressure on the employer to lower wages, for a reduction in wages remains the safest and readiest means of raising profits. "Against this constant, unceasing pressure unorganised labour has no effective means of resistance." Hence the tremendous importance of the unions.

But Engels went on to say that, even when they succeed in improving wages and conditions, this is not emancipation. For all their hard struggle the trade unions have not succeeded in freeing the working class from the bondage in which capital holds it. They have not become the owners of the produce of their own labours. They have never even tried to take such a step, and it is not the highness or lowness of wages which constitutes the economic degradation of the working class. This degradation is comprised in the fact that labour is in a condition of subordination to capital. How can this be remedied? Only when the economic struggle becomes a political struggle.

In 1872 Engels wrote a series of articles on *The Housing Question.*

[1] *loc. cit.*

Left to private enterprise and supply and demand, it can never be solved. "One thing is certain: even now there are sufficient habitable buildings in the large towns to relieve materially the real shortage of accommodation if sensible use were made of them." But this would require the expropriation of such property. When the workers won political power this measure could be easily carried out.

In 1891, in his criticism of the Erfurt Programme of the German Social-Democratic Party, Engels returned once again to the theory of the inevitable worsening of the condition of the workers. "The organisation of the working class," he said, "and their steadily growing resistance can act as a check on the growth of their misery. It is the uncertainty of their life which *is* certainly increasing."

In these years his home became a centre where Engels met many of the new men of the socialist and radical movements, Will Thorne, an able representative of the new unskilled union of Gasworkers and General Labourers, John Burns, Belfort Bax, Harry Quelch, Cunninghame Grahame and an endless stream of continental socialists.

Engels' knowledge of the English movement was extraordinarily profound, but both he and Marx exercised their leadership and influence with tact and prudence. Engels writing to Bernstein in 1881 says, "Marx has such achievements to his credit in the spheres of theory and practice, that the best people in all the various working-class movements have complete confidence in him. At critical moments they turn to him for advice, and they usually find that his advice is the best. We have constant contact with them, as far as there is opportunity. But any attempt to influence people against their will would only hurt us and destroy the old confidence which dates back to the International."

Marx never forced his opinion on those who came to him, but gave it if he was asked for advice. His mission, he felt, was to follow the course of the movement throughout the world and advance whenever he could every policy and move which would win over the working-class movement, and lead to the ultimate abolition of the proletariat. He not only believed that this was to the advantage of the whole human race, but that the continuance of the class conflict meant that the ruling classes themselves were even more intellectually and morally crippled than the oppressed classes.

Marxist parties of growing size and importance were to be found in Germany and France in the lifetime of Marx, but this was not the case in England. In 1881, H. M. Hyndman, a wealthy radical stock-broker, read *Capital* and was much inspired by it. He lost no time in making the personal acquaintance of its author and visited Marx frequently. Hyndman was a patrician of aristocratic appearance, agree-able, easy-going and expansive. He greatly enjoyed meeting and talking to men of genius, and Marx appeared to him to be exceptionally talented. He says of him, "The first impression of Marx as I saw him was that of a powerful, shaggy, untamed old man, ready, not to say eager, to enter into conflict, and rather suspicious himself of immediate attack. . . . When speaking with fierce indignation of the policy of the Liberal Party, the old warrior's brows wrinkled, the broad strong nose and face were obviously moved by passion, and he poured out a stream of vigorous denunciation, which displayed alike the heat of his tem-perament, and the marvellous command he possessed over our language."[1]

After absorbing a great deal of Marx's thought, Hyndman wrote an exposition of it which he entitled *England for All* (1881). In the Preface he stated that "for the ideas and much of the matter contained in Chapters 2 and 3 I am indebted to the work of a great thinker and original writer", whose works he hoped "would soon become acces-sible to the public". Hyndman thus concealed the name of Marx, who was furious.

Hyndman then set to work to organise a Marxist political party. A conference took place in June 1881 and the Democratic Federation was formed, shortly to become the Social Democratic Federation. Its membership increased slowly, but the most prominent socialists of the country joined its ranks, among them being Ernest Belfort Bax, a philosophical writer of ability, William Morris, Eleanor Marx and Harry Quelch, editor of its paper.[2]

Hyndman was an extraordinary character. Lenin described him a "a bourgeois philistine, who, belonging to the best of his class, even-tually struggles through to socialism but never quite sheds bourgeois conceptions and prejudices." He was a very self-satisfied and garrulous man of overweening ambition, and impatient to play the dictator. He had a more thorough knowledge of *Capital* than any other English Marxist, with the exception of Aveling, but had made no attempt

[1] H. M. Hyndman, *Record of an Adventurous Life*.

[2] Harry Quelch founded the *Twentieth Century Press* in Clerkenwell Green, which published *Justice* and many other socialist pamphlets and books. The building is now the home of the Marx Memorial Library.

to grasp Marx's theory of history. In his hands Marxism became a rigid orthodoxy and always remained so for many of his followers.[1] Engels came to regard him as a "careerist who in his chase after success discredits himself more every day. He is a wretched caricature of Lassalle."

Hyndman actually put up two candidates for Parliament with Tory money (the Tory aim being to split the Liberal vote) and then offered his support to Chamberlain if he were guaranteed a Birmingham seat. Marx never regarded the S.D.F. as a real proletarian movement.

Belfort Bax was a man of many-sided culture who had a good knowledge of German philosophy. An outspoken atheist and republican, he was one of the intellectuals who early in the eighties did something to restore to socialism its rights in the world of letters. He warmly championed Marx and wrote a book on *The Ethic of Socialism*. But with all his talents and good intentions he was unpredictable. He vigorously defended the view that men constitute the down-trodden sex, while women are privileged to excess. They used to say of him, "Why is Bax always so unanswerably in the right and so hopelessly in the wrong?" "A bookworm who has gone into journalism and has lost his balance somewhat in doing it," was Engels' summing up of him.

The Social Democratic Federation split a year after the death of Marx. Morris, Belfort-Bax, Eleanor Marx and Aveling then formed the Socialist League, an exceedingly small organisation which fell into anarchist hands.[2]

William Morris was a better Marxist than Hyndman. He had passed from art to socialism because he saw that under capitalism there could be no art and no happiness for the great majority. He saw clearly that so long as men are held in thrall by the industrial system, there could be no good art and no good life for the mass of the people. He put before the world his passionate conviction of the baseness and the

[1] He was a chauvinist who posed as an ardent patriot, and this decided the trend of his political thinking in 1914 when he supported the war; and in 1917 when he opposed the Russian Revolution.

[2] After various secessions the S.D.F. became the Social Democratic Party (S.D.P.) in 1908, and in 1911 merged with other Left-wing socialist groups, including Blatchford's *Clarion* group, to form the British Socialist Party (B.S.P.). When the First World War broke out the B.S.P. soon revealed a strong divergence between Hyndman's "will to victory" group, a minority, and those who declared the war to be imperialist. Hyndman and his supporters left. In 1920 the B.S.P. joined with other parties to form the Communist Party of Great Britain (C.P.G.B.).

iniquity of industrialism and did not flinch from the class struggle as the way to a socialist society. His knowledge of scientific Marxist theory was defective, but he clearly understood the inevitability and the necessity for the class struggle, and his faith in the workers never failed. His lecture on "Communism" concludes with words of which Marx himself would not disapprove: "Intelligence enough to conceive, courage enough to will, power enough to compel. If our ideas of a new society are anything more than a dream, these three qualities must animate the due effective majority of the working-people, and then, I say, the thing will be done."

20

MARX AND AMERICA

COMMUNISM came to America with the stream of German immigrants and refugees who poured into the country in the second half of the nineteenth century. They were entering at the rate of several thousand a year during the eighteen-thirties, but after the defeat of the German Revolution of 1848 this stream became a torrent of over 200,000 annually. Each successive defeat and wave of suppression brought more refugees—both democrats and socialists; from France after 1870, from Poland, from Russia and from Italy. But it was the Germans who remained the most decisive force in spreading the teaching of Marx in the United States through the rest of the nineteenth century. Many of them were well known to Marx, and some of them had been his comrades in the Rhineland in 1848.

Marx and Engels followed events in America with the closest attention. They commented with penetrating insight on the struggle to free American industrial capital and American labour from the fetters of slavery, on the use of large-scale industry, and on the land question. They were acquainted with the first movements towards the organisation of the American labour movement, in which their own friends and disciples played an important part. In spite of their remoteness from these events, they were remarkably well informed, and from the moment their exiled comrades began to arrive in "the land of the free" they maintained close contact by correspondence.[1]

The best informed of these old friends was Weydemeyer, who had been a Prussian military officer, to whom Marx frequently wrote. He became a colonel of a regiment in the Northern Army in the Civil War. He had known Marx in Brussels and attended his lectures there. August Willich, who was also a former Prussian officer, and had taken an active part in the revolution of 1848, came to London after its defeat and was the leader of the "left" group in the Communist League. Subsequently, he emigrated to America and distinguished himself

[1] *Letters to Americans*, 1848–1895, by Karl Marx and Friedrich Engels.

as a General ln the Civil War. Friedrich Sorge, another active participant in the 1848 uprising, played an important part in the early struggles to organise the labour movement. He was the leader of the North American section of the First International and its General Secretary when it moved to New York (1872). Marx and Engels thought highly of him, as their long and interesting correspondence with him indicates.

A very different man was Hermann Kriege, a former pupil of Feuerbach and an associate of Weitling, who went to America in 1845. Kriege, in his paper, *People's Tribune*, declared that American capitalism was totally different from that of Europe because of the vast areas of undeveloped land. If this were distributed among the poor, revolutionary socialism would be unnecessary. "An end will be put to poverty in America at one stroke." This became the first topic on which Marx contributed criticism and advice. In 1846 he replied to Kriege in the Westphalen *Dampfboot*, a monthly journal published in Germany at that time: "It is not within the powers of legislators to hinder by means of decrees, as desired by Kriege, the development of the (land) system into an industrial system", which would indeed be a backward step in the already industrialised eastern areas of the United States.

What Marx objected to was not the attack on agrarian reform, but the wild assertions that capitalism could be avoided, and that in this single reform was the solution of the whole social problem. The same question emerges in every backward agricultural country when it begins to advance. It arose in Russia in 1905, and Lenin quoted this article and enlarged upon it in his controversy with a section of the Narodniki and the Social Revolutionaries who were advocating similar policies.[1] Marx castigates Kriege for advancing this petty-bourgeois utopia as the ideal of revolutionary activity, and for his total failure to understand the real foundation of the modern economic system and its development; but he fully approved of communists supporting the American organisation which advocated these measures (The National Reformers) in view of the revolutionary aspect of the attack on private property in land. He regarded it as a peculiar initial form of the proletarian movement, but taken as the be-all and end-all of reform it could not succeed. It is the ideal of bankrupt shopkeepers who have come to America to become once again prosperous petty bourgeois. It will lead not to fraternity, but to some landowners prospering at the expense of others who will become mere labourers; the land

[1] Lenin: *Marx on the American "Black Redistribution"* (April 1905).

will inevitably be drawn into commerce. Capitalism cannot be avoided, and is historically progressive, since it brings nearer new and higher forms of the communist movement. As Lenin put it, "We are marching far beyond the end of any peasant movement; we are marching to the very end of the division of society into classes."

In 1881 Marx had once again to take up the agrarian question, this time to refute the single tax theories of the American reformer Henry George, whose theories received wide support both in America and in England.[1] George believed that the whole social problem would be solved if land rent were paid to the state, for the sole form of exploitation was in rent. Wage labour and capitalist production were not to be touched under this scheme, and yet surely, Marx argued, in the extraction of surplus value from labour is the very essence of exploitation, rent being merely one form in which it is appropriated. "How did it happen (if rent is the source of poverty) that in the United States, where, relatively, the land was accessible to the great masses of the people and still is to a certain extent, capitalist economy and the corresponding enslavement of the working class have developed more rapidly and more shamelessly than in any other country?"[2]

The land question was bound to be of the first importance in a country like America, with vast undeveloped areas of fertile land; but industry was already developing rapidly in the Eastern States, and Marx and Engels were deeply concerned with the economic and labour problems that rapidly made their appearance. They recognised the radical difference between America and Western Europe, both Germany and Britain. It was "the ideal of all bourgeois: a country rich, vast, expanding, with purely bourgeois institutions, unleavened by feudal remnant and monarchical traditions, and without a permanent or hereditary proletariat".[3] In this respect it was totally different from Germany, where there was no democratic constitution, and a powerful feudalism was still in the saddle. It was different also from Russia, which Marx studied intensively, where "the financial, commercial and industrial superstructure was similar to that at the time of Louis XIV, while in the United States capitalism was already well advanced and concentrated and a money economy firmly established".[4]

[1] Henry George, *Progress and Poverty*, 1879. The Single Tax movement is still in existence and conducts a vigorous propaganda in London and elsewhere.

[2] Marx to Sorge, June 20th, 1881. [3] Engels to Florence Kelley, 1886.

[4] Marx to Danielson, April 10th, 1879.

In comparison with the Old World, the New World had an abundant supply of free and cheap land easily accessible, and taken up by pioneer farmers. Although a great deal of it was acquired by speculators, no landed aristocracy comparable to that in Russia and France had appeared.

As early as 1844 Engels noted the tremendous forward strides of American capitalism. "America with its inexhaustible resources, with its unmeasured coal and iron fields, with its unexampled wealth of water power and its navigable rivers, but especially with its energetical active population"[1] had already developed an industry that was in certain sections competing with that of England.

But America was not going to escape those periodic economic crises which were inevitable to capitalism, or the fundamental clash of opposing interests; in fact, "capitalist economy and the corresponding enslavement of the working class have developed more *rapidly* and *shamelessly* than in any other society".[2] "Add to this the total indifference of a society which has grown up on a purely capitalist basis towards the human lives which succumb in the competitive struggle for capitalism. There are always plenty more—Italians, Dutchmen, Hungarians, Jews—available."[3]

Marx realised that the labour movement also had certain peculiarities and defects, both as regards the Americans themselves and the German immigrant socialists; the exigencies of practical labour and the rapid advance of industry produced a contempt for theory. Bourgeois prejudices were firmly rooted in the working class, which had never known feudalism and had grown up on a bourgeois basis of industrial enterprise and independence from the beginning. Since America had taken its origin in a revolt against British monarchical rule it imagined itself to be progressive, and essentially more democratic than Britain. There was thus a certain backwardness of thought. Only great events could change this. "It is the revolutionising of all established industries by industry as it develops that also revolutionises people's minds."[4] The more rapid the industrial development of a country, the speedier would be the emergence of a working-class movement essential to the struggle for socialism.

The German socialists were both an asset and a liability. It was they who brought socialism to America and were instrumental in bringing

[1] Engels, *The Condition of the Working Class.*
[2] Marx to Sorge, June 30th, 1881. [3] Engels to Schluter, March 30th, 1892.
[4] Engels to Sorge, December 31st, 1892.

into existence the first labour and socialist organisations; but some of them, like Willich, were entirely concerned with organising the German socialists for the purpose of furthering the revolution in Germany; others took refuge in utopianism or various forms of anarchism, while Kriege advocated his policy of land reform. Many never learned any language except German and kept themselves apart from the American workers; they became dogmatic and sectarian, and despised the American workers as politically ignorant. Engels rebuked the German Marxists because they had not understood how to use their theory as a lever which could set the American masses in motion, but treated it in a doctrinaire and dogmatic way as something to be learned by heart—a creed and not a guide to action. But "our theory", said Engels, "is not dogmatic, but an exposition of a process of evolution, and that process involves successive phases. . . . Do not make the inevitable confusion of the first start worse confounded by forcing down people's throats things which at present they cannot possibly understand."[1] Begin where you find people today; limiting your theory to the actual starting-point of the struggle as you find it. Sectarianism effectively separated the German worker from the main stream of organised labour and made it easier for employers to use the technique of divide and rule. In setting one nationality off against another, America capitalism had no rivals.

Weydemeyer and Sorge were men of a different calibre. Weydemeyer really understood Marxism and did much to clarify the ideas of the American socialists. Marx considered him "one of our best men". In the terrible years of his early exile in London, both Karl and Jenny Marx found a sympathetic friend in Weydemeyer. In 1850 Jenny wrote to him: "The thing that hits me hardest of all and makes my heart bleed is that my husband is worried by so many petty troubles. . . . He has never lost his confidence in the future, not even in his worst moments, and he has always kept up his good spirits and was happy if he saw me in a good humour and our dear children making a fuss of me."

In August 1851 Marx writes to Weydemeyer: "You can imagine that my situation is gloomy. My wife will go under if it lasts much longer. The continual troubles and the petty day-to-day struggle to make ends meet are wearing her out. And on top of all this there is the infamy of my opponents."

When Weydemeyer left for America, Marx racked his brains to

[1] Engels to Sorge, December 28th, 1886.

think of some suitable occupation which he might follow. "Once you are there, what guarantee is there that you won't lose yourself in the Far West? We have so very few really good men and we must be economical with our forces." However, Marx found it a very good thing to have a capable representative of the communist cause in America. Weydemeyer set to work to issue a weekly under the title of *Die Revolution* and Marx mobilised all available talent for the task, including the poet Freiligrath; for his share Marx promised to write on the *coup d'état* of Louis Bonaparte. Funds ran out in America, but a Frankfurt tailor who visited America that summer (1852) placed all his savings, forty dollars, at the disposal of Weydemeyer. A thousand copies of *The Eighteenth Brumaire of Louis Napoleon* were printed, and but for the Frankfurt tailor it would not have been published at all. About 300 copies went to Europe and were distributed by friends in England and in Germany.

Some of Marx's letters to Weydemeyer are of great theoretical or personal interest. In 1852 we find him writing that "no credit is due to me for discovering either the existence of classes in modern society or the struggle between them. Bourgeois historians had described the historical development of this struggle of the classes long before me, and bourgeois economists had portrayed their economic anatomy. What I did that was new was to prove: (1) that the existence of classes is bound up only with specific historical phase in the development of production; (2) that the class struggle necessarily leads to the dictatorship of the proletariat; (3) that this dictatorship itself only constitutes the transition to the abolition of all classes and to a classless society."[1]

Friedrich Sorge was a man of iron will and great ability. He was the relentless opponent in America of the views of Lassalle, and the organising force behind the American section of the International. Marx's earlier letters to him are entirely concerned with the business of the International—Conference Resolutions, copies of the Official Statistics and Regulations, and instructions for the organisation of the New York Central Committee. In 1862 he writes, "We have issued a French translation of *The Address on the Civil War in France*, price 2½*d.* per copy. If wanted in the U.S., please write." As time passes, the letters grow warmer in tone and important questions of tactics and theory appear. He informs Sorge of the publication of the French and Russian translations of *Capital*. The Russian translation, he says, is a "masterly job". In 1874 he is being sent to Karlsbad for his "damned liver

[1] Marx to Weydemeyer, March 5th, 1852.

complaint". "Being unable to work," he says, "is indeed a death sentence for any man who is not a beast." In 1877 he is again writing to Sorge about Russia. The war with the Turks had just broken out and Marx declares that "all sections of Russian society are in full decomposition economically, morally and intellectually".

He also wrote to Weydemeyer and Sorge on the mistakes of the socialist leaders in Germany, to show how the lessons of these errors were to be applied in America. Sorge had to combat the ideas of Lassalle which so many German socialists had brought to America—especially his project for securing socialism by getting the government to finance co-operative societies, and the consequent slackening of the everyday struggles of the workers and the neglect of trade unions.

Under the influence of Sorge and the other Marxists the importance of trade unions and active economic struggle was recognised. The various labour journals and organisations gradually passed from Lassallean to Marxist control. Gompers, at that time a radical young trade unionist, later to become the reactionary and autocratic leader of the American Federation of Labor, was closely associated with the Marxists in this historic struggle.

Later, Marx is explaining the French situation to Sorge. Here Proudhon and anarchism were still influential. But the anarchists, says Marx, "do not consist of actual workers as their rank-and-file soldiers", and their influence cannot therefore count for much.

Bakunin was by no means without influence in America, and Engels, writing to Theodor Cuno in 1872, brilliantly outlines the Marxist reply to the anarchist case. Bakunin was for complete abstention from all politics and the abolition of the state—capitalism would then disappear. "But the mass of the workers," says Engels, "will never allow themselves to be persuaded that the public affairs of their country are not also their own affairs; they are by nature *political* and whoever tries to convince them that they should leave politics alone will in the end be left in the lurch."[1]

Marxists were associated with three very early working-class and socialist organisations in America: the First International, of which Sorge was the last General Secretary; the Proletarian League, founded in New York in June 1852 on the initiative of Weydemeyer and Sorge—the first definitely Marxist organisation on American soil, composed of seventeen of the most advanced Marxists in New York City, and the Communist Club of New York.

[1] Engels to Cuno, January 24th, 1872.

In March 1853 the Marxists issued a call through the trade unions of German-speaking workers for the formation of one large workers' union, and the American Labour Union was launched. This organisation, before it disappeared, brought into existence the General Trade Union of New York City, with 2,000 members representing some forty trades.

A few years later we find Weydemeyer helping to organize The Communist Club of New York, which established communications with similar but smaller groups in other cities. The centre of the movement shifted to Chicago, and it was here that the well-known publishing concern of Charles H. Kerr brought out practically all the early Marxist classics, including the English translation of three volumes of *Capital.*[1]

In 1866 the first attempt was made to set up a general national organisation of American labour. Weydemeyer worked hard for it and it came into existence as the National Labour Union in Baltimore on August 26th. Its leader was William H. Sylvis, a friend of Weydemeyer and Sorge and a supporter of the International. During its six years of existence it led important struggles and campaigned vigorously for the eight-hour day. Marxists took an active part in its activities. They were militant builders of trade unions and advocates of working-class political action. They were also active on the Negro question, demanding the repeal of all laws discriminating against Negroes. The organisation reached its highest point in 1869, with a membership of 600,000, but thereafter rapidly declined, largely because Lassallean influences weakened its belief in trade union action and turned its attention to the solution of all economic questions by currency reform and credit manipulation. In 1870 Sorge wrote to Marx: "The National Labour Union, which had such brilliant prospects in the beginning of its career, was poisoned by Greenbackism (dollar and currency cranks) and is slowly but surely dying." It played its part in the early development of the American labour movement and was followed by the far more powerful and influential Knights of Labour and the American Federation of Labor, the well-known A.F.L.

The impact of Marx in American life was by no means restricted to the labour movement. For over ten years he contributed articles on political affairs to the *New York Daily Tribune*, edited by the distinguished liberal, Horace Greeley, which had at this period a circulation of over 200,000 copies, then probably the greatest of any newspaper

[1] For many years the Kerr publications of the most important works of Marx and Engels were the only ones available in England.

in the world. Greeley's policy was to extend a special hospitality to new ideas and he even ran a series of articles on the socialist theories of Fourier. Greeley was a man of progressive sympathies in many directions and a leading spirit in the anti-slavery movement. Americans regarded themselves as ahead of the world in the achievement of democratic rights. They had won their constitutional victory in the War of Independence against Britain in 1776, some years before the French Revolution, and in 1848 their sympathies went out to the liberal revolutions which disturbed Europe. Dana, Greeley's managing editor, was looking for new readers for the *Daily Tribune*, especially from the ranks of the German immigrant population in and around New York, and he invited Marx, whom he vividly remembered, from the Cologne days, to write a series of articles on German affairs especially on the revolution and the fighting which had taken place during the rising.[1] Marx was in dire poverty and he eagerly caught at the offer, which would not only be of the greatest use to him, but would give him an excellent opportunity for disseminating his own views on America. He was to be paid £1 per article, but in fact many of his articles never appeared, and when financial stringency overtook New York, the number of articles was drastically reduced. The series came to an end in 1862 when Dana informed Marx that the internal American situation—the Civil War was still raging—would require all the room there was in the paper.

When the Civil War broke out Marx wrote a series of articles defending the Federalists and dealing forcefully with the Confederate arguments and those of their supporters in England. His contributions emphasised the attitude of Europe in general as well as England to the Union cause and dealt with the cotton crisis that followed the naval blockade of the Southern ports, the threatened invasion of Mexico, and the diplomatic crisis occasioned by the arrest of the steamship *Trent* with Southern delegates aboard on its way to England. In 1862 Marx was also requested to contribute to *Die Presse* of Vienna, and in these articles he continued to comment on the Civil War, now entering the phase when Lincoln declared for the emancipation of the slaves. It was on August 9th, 1862, that he informed his readers that "Negro slavery would not outlive the Civil War". The Emancipation Proclamation was made on January 1st, 1863.[2]

[1] A collection of these articles appeared in 1917 under the title *Gesammelte Schriften von Karl Marx und Friedrich Engels* in two volumes by Dietz, Stuttgart.

[2] For the articles and correspondence mentioned, see Marx and Engels, *The Civil War in the United States.*

Marx realised before the outbreak of hostilities the significance of the racial issue. "In my opinion the biggest things that are happening in the world today are on the one hand the movement of the slaves in America started by the death of John Brown, and on the other the movement of the serfs in Russia."[1]

It was evident to him that the eventual emancipation of the American working class depended upon the destruction of Negro slavery. "Labour cannot emancipate itself in the white skin where the black is branded." The development of any sort of independent working-class movement would be held back "so long as slavery continued to exist in any part of the Republic". This was indeed true, if only because slavery threw into disrepute the dignity of manual work, though it also hindered the development of industrialisation and therefore the growth of the labour movement.

Turning to his articles in the *Daily Tribune* and *Die Presse*, we find Marx at his controversial best. Press and government in Britain were striving with every kind of sophistical argument and subtle misrepresentation to put the North in the wrong and arouse sympathy for the South. They said: If the war were really for the abolition of slavery we would of course support it on humanitarian grounds, but it is not; it is for the conquest of the South. Marx replied that the North had never claimed that it was a war against slavery, but neither was it a war of conquest, for it was the South which had undertaken the war, while the North took arms with the utmost reluctance in order to save the Union. The South moreover had itself proclaimed the perpetuation and extension of slavery to be the only and main end of the rebellion. Had not the new constitution of the Confederation for the first time in American history recognised slavery as a good thing in itself?

The British press then tried another line of argument and asked why the North would not welcome the secession of the South instead of putting it down. Marx replied that it was not a question of the autonomy of the existing slave states, with which the North had not interfered, but the emphatic demand of the South for the inclusion of vast new border states in the area devoted to slavery. Victory for the South would mean not the dissolution of the Union, but its reorganisation on the basis of slavery, under the recognised control of the slave-holding oligarchy. "The war of the Southern Confederacy is, therefore, not a war of defence, but a war of conquest,

[1] The serfs were emancipated in 1861.

a war of conquest for the extension and perpetuation of slavery. The whole movement was and is based, as one sees, on the *slave question*: not in the sense of whether the slaves within the existing slave states should be emancipated or not, but whether the twenty million free men of the North should subordinate themselves any longer to an oligarchy of three hundred thousand slave holders."

The British press then diverted the whole question to the issue of tariffs—the South had been cruelly exploited, they argued, by the protective tariff of the North. It was really a war for "free trade"! That was ridiculous, Marx replied. They had had free trade from 1846 to 1861.

Then came the *Trent* Case, when two Southern envoys, Mason and Slidell, on their way to Europe to secure support, were taken off their ship by a Union warship. Hotheads in Britain called for war. Marx in his articles for *Die Presse* gave a full account of the controversy, in which crowded anti-war meetings resisted the war-mongers. Common sense prevailed. There was no declaration of war. A cause more likely to create sympathy for the South was of course the difficulty in getting cotton for the Lancashire mills owing to the blockade of the Southern ports. Marx saw clearly that "the government was only waiting for the intervention cry from below, the pressure from *without*, to put an end to the American blockade and English misery. Under these circumstances, the obstinacy with which the working class kept silent or broke its silence only to raise its voice against intervention and *for* the United States was admirable."[1] Marx went on to describe a great workers' meeting in Marylebone, the most populous district of London, denouncing by a unanimous vote Mason and Slidell as "the confessed agents of the tyrannical faction that is at once in rebellion against the American republic and the sworn enemy of the social and political rights of the working class in all countries". Marx and Engels were responsible for another great meeting, held in the St. James's Hall (March 26th, 1863), attended by 3,000 people, at which Henry Adams, son of the American ambassador, was present. The meeting passed a resolution declaring "that the success of free institutions in America was a political question of deep consequence in England and that they would not tolerate any interference unfavourable to the North".

After the war was over the International reverted to the role of the British working class in their Address to the National Labour Union

[1] *Die Presse*, February 2nd, 1862.

which declared that, "It was not the wisdom of the ruling class, but the heroic resistance to their criminal folly by the working classes of England that saved Europe from plunging into an infamous crusade for the perpetuation and propagation of slavery on the other side of the Atlantic."

The International, which was under the leadership of Marx, organised further meetings in London in 1864 in support of the North and sent a message of warm congratulation to Abraham Lincoln on his re-election to office.

A shrewd estimation of Lincoln's character and policy was contributed to *Die Presse*. "President Lincoln never ventures a step forward before the tide of circumstances and the call of general public opinion forbids further delay. But once 'Old Abe' has convinced himself that such a turning point has been reached, he then surprises friend and foe alike."

As the war went on Marx urged the North to wage a revolutionary war, to arm the Negroes, to abolish slavery. He clearly perceived that the war could not be won without the destruction of the South's "peculiar institution", as they called it, which so signally contradicted the Declaration of Independence.

Marx, of course, was aware of the economic roots of the war as being "nothing but a struggle between two social systems, between the system of slavery and the system of free labour". Many years later Charles Beard described it as "a struggle between two divergent economic and social systems—one a single crop agricultural order based on slavery, and the other a diversified system of agrarian and industrial production based on free labour".[1]

Something should be said on the letters and articles which Engels wrote on the strategic issues of the Civil War. Engels was an expert on such questions and had played a courageous and competent part in the fighting in Germany in 1848. He was convinced that the Northern generals would not emerge from the war victorious unless they drove through Georgia from Atlanta to the sea. He declared in the Vienna *Presse* that once Georgia was conquered in this way "the Confederacy would be cut into two sections which would have lost all connection with one another". This was the course eventually followed by Sherman, and it was decisive. Engels was severely critical of the Union commanders, especially McClellan, whom he held up to scorn for his endless delaying tactics. Grant he recognised as an able general,

[1] Charles Beard, *The Rise of American Civilisation* (1927).

and when he captured Richmond in 1865 Engels compared his campaign with that of Napoleon at Jena.

When, after victory was achieved, Lincoln was assasinated, the International sent an Address of Sympathy to President Johnson. They hoped, indeed, that he would take a strong line with the Confederate leaders and open the way to the enfranchisement of the Negroes. They were disappointed. Johnson gave in both to the big capitalist interests in the North and to the old slave oligarchy in the South. Marx wrote to Engels in 1865, "The reaction has already begun in America and will soon be greatly strengthened if the hitherto prevailing slackness does not quickly cease". Engels replied that it did indeed appear that Johnson's hatred for the Negroes was apparent in his whole policy. "If things go on like this, in six months all the old villains of secession will be sitting in Congress in Washington. Without coloured suffrage nothing can be done there, and Johnson leaves it to the vanquished ex-slaveholders to decide upon the matter. It is too absurd."[1]

As Marx and Engels anticipated, the ex-slaveholders regained ascendancy. There was no enfranchisement for the Negroes and the great landed estates were preserved. The war for freedom, in spite of everything, was not yet won. Marx's last word was that the United States had not yet entered the revolutionary phase. That was yet to come.[2]

[1] Engels to Marx, July 15th, 1865. [2] Marx to Engels, April 23rd, 1866.

21

MARX AND RUSSIA

In his Foreword to the first volume of *Capital* Marx declared that the war for the abolition of slavery sounded the tocsin for the new labour movement in Western Europe. In Russia the burning question of the day was the abolition of serfdom. It was the period of "great reforms", and of the rise of those underground revolutionary societies chief among which was the Land and Freedom Society. All this tended to show how really international the world had become. No one was more conscious of the fact than Marx, whose interest and intervention in affairs extended from India and China to America, from the internecine struggles of Western Europe to the coming revolution in Russia.

But the concern of Marx with Russia long preceded his revolutionary hopes for the Russian people. From the distant days of the German revolution of 1848 Marx's consistent policy had been that the defeat of Russian Tsarism, the bulwark of reaction in Europe, would not only hasten the revolution in Russia, for which the elements existed on a large scale, but with it the revolution throughout Europe.

This well illustrates not only the wide scope of Marx's activities and the close interdependence in his theory and practice of international politics and the development of the labour movement, but also his conception of the strategy and tactics of the campaign for a socialist world. So far from narrowing his activities to the immediate policies of socialist parties, he was prepared to suspend them when the agenda of history confronted him with such historic tasks as the defence of the Union in America or the fight for constitutional liberty in Germany. This was far from being mere opportunism. It was the fight for socialism itself that demanded the temporary postponement of immediate socialist objectives to win a victory on a wider field, and often with the strangest of allies—allies destined in the future to become the main enemy of the cause he held most dear.

Thus it was that in 1848 the *Neue Rheinische Zeitung*, which Marx was editing in Cologne and through which he sought to inspire and direct the German revolution, dealt overwhelmingly with the immediate political aspects of things—the struggle for the Constitution, and not with working-class problems at all. Marx was then concerned solely with the agitation in favour of the creation of the democratic revolutionary forces which would free Germany from the crippling remnant of its obsolete feudal system. This was what Lenin called 'the next link in the chain". But very rapidly the whole situation might change—as it did in Germany—and a sharp turn in tactics would be demanded, in which case persistence in the original course would be folly.

Therefore the whole course of Marx's revolutionary activity is interwoven with international politics and inseparable from it.

This is clearly shown in his estimation of the role of Russia in the struggle first for democracy and then for socialism. Russia was the main enemy of liberalism, constitutionalism and progress in Europe, but there was a new Russia emerging from the disintegration of Tsarism, which was the hope of the future. "The impulse for the European revolution can scarcely come from anywhere but Russia. In Russia the movement is advancing faster than in all the rest of Europe."[1]

When the Napoleonic Wars ended with the Holy Alliance against all revolutionary movements, Tsar Alexander I and Metternich were its leading figures. Against them were ranged the democratic forces of France and of those areas of Germany (the Rhineland and the Palatinate) which had been for a long time in the hands of France. Westward into Germany and France came the exiled Polish revolutionaries who had risen against the Tsar, and all over Western Europe poets, politicians and rebels of all sorts struggled against reaction in every form. And it was Russia that was considered the mainstay of this reaction. Yet even in Russia the same forces which fought for liberalism were stirring, and in 1825 the Decembrist movement attempted an armed insurrection. We have to think of the young Marx, along with Börne, Heine, Becker and many others, as caught up in and sharing in this widespread liberal movement, which found expression in the Polish rebellion of 1831, the French uprisings of 1830 and 1848, the German revolution itself of 1848, and the uprisings all over Austria of Hungarians, Czechs and the people of Vienna itself.

When the revolutionary wave reached Vienna in 1848, Russia instantly intervened. Nicholas I offered help to Germany and Austria. The Hungarian revolution was defeated with the aid of Russian forces. The Prussian King gladly accepted Russian money. In June the defeat

[1] Marx to Engels, December 13th, 1859.

of the Paris proletariat presaged the defeat of the great revolutionary upsurge everywhere in Europe. Marx urged war with Russia as the only means of saving it. The French revolution had taken new life when foreign powers had attempted to overthrow it. Resistance to the war of the reactionaries in the revolution of 1848 would have the same result. Marx vigorously championed in the pages of the *Neue Rheinische Zeitung* every revolutionary tendency against the established order. He demanded the re-establishment of an independent Poland. He supported the widely based movement for the unification of Germany.

The revolution was defeated, largely owing to the pusillanimous conduct of the bourgeoisie. There was a period of decline; but in 1853 things were moving again. The chief reactionary powers were falling out. Russia, seeking some rewards for her services in suppressing the revolution, had designs on the Balkans and Turkey—undoubtedly it was Constantinople and the Dardanelles that were the prizes she desired. France and Britain, with other lesser powers, supported Turkey and in 1854 the Crimean War broke out. Marx and Engels welcomed it.[1] The defeat of Russia would stir the revolutionary energies of Germany and overthrow the main prop of European reaction. But this did not mean that Britain, France and Turkey were declared to be the saviours of civilisation and progress. When Marx found such allies he combined firm support on the main issue with merciless criticism of their inconsistencies and treacheries. Only thus would common victory over the main enemy lead to the next phase of the struggle—against the reactionary elements among these former allies themselves. England and France came in for as much denunciation as Russia.

Marx clearly saw other consequences of the Russian defeat, of more direct concern to the working class and the peasantry of Europe. Russia was shaken; there was profound unrest everywhere. It was clear that a state based on the antiquated system of serfdom was incapable of fighting a modern war against capitalist states of a more advanced political character.

Reforms were promised. Russia was forced to consider the emancipation of the serfs. The economic crisis of 1857 gave encouragement to the whole socialist movement. It shook even Russia and spurred her along the path to liberal reforms.

In 1859, when France was at war with Austria, Russia withheld all aid to her former ally. Lassalle, who desired to curry favour with the

[1] Marx-Engels, *The Eastern Question* (a reprint of letters written 1853-56 dealing with the events of the Crimean War).

Prussian Government, argued that Russia could be ignored; France was a liberal power; the real enemy was Austria. Let Germany side with France (and Russia) and crush Austria. Marx saw in this a real bit of political chicanery. Louis Napoleon a progressive force! And what crawling flattery Lassalle displayed in his support for Prussian military ambition! On the contrary, if necessity arose, Germany should come to the help of Austria against France, relying on Russian complicity. That would not be at all welcome to the Prussian autocrats. It would indeed be a war of revolution against reaction and could rapidly bring about an upsurge of liberal and revolutionary enthusiasm, and lead the way to the long overdue German socialist revolution.

Meanwhile revolution was stirring in Russia, of which a considerable part of Poland was an oppressed province. Serfdom had been abolished but more radical reforms were being demanded. In 1863 Poland revolted, and all Western Europe supported her. Great meetings of support were held everywhere and the International placed the cause of Poland high on its list, nor would Marx allow its removal as irrelevant to everyday working-class demands. The undermining and destruction of Tsardom, the liberation of all the revolutionary forces in Russia was the path to revolution in Europe.

Surprisingly, perhaps, Marx supported Germany in the Franco-German war, though he opposed all annexations or indemnities. A complete victory for France would require Russian aid and once again the Tsar would become the arbiter of the destinies of Europe. Meanwhile, it would be the dismemberment of France that would force France into the arms of Russia. "There will then only remain two courses open to her. She must at all risks become the avowed tool of Russian aggrandisement, or, after some short respite, again make ready for another 'defensive war'—a war of races."

Marx made a thorough study of the diplomatic history of the period of Russian ascendancy in the Baltic in the eighteenth century. He found it difficult to understand how British statesmen and diplomatic representatives betrayed Sweden, pursued a policy of masterly deception, and ignominiously allowed themselves to further every political move which advanced the power of Russia and conceded to her every strategic advantage, while British interests were undermined or surrendered.

"The overwhelming influence of Russia has taken Europe at different epochs by surprise, startled the peoples of the West and been submitted to as a fatality, or resisted only by convulsions. But alongside the fascination exercised by Russia, there runs an ever-reviving scepticism, dogging her like a shadow, growing with her growth, mingling shrill notes of irony with the cries of agonising peoples, and marking her very grandeur as a historic attitude taken up to dazzle and to cheat. Other empires have met with similar doubts in their infancy; Russia has become a colossus without outliving them. She affords the only instance in history of an immense empire, the very existence of whose power, even after world-wide achievements, has never ceased to be treated like a matter of faith rather than a matter of fact. From the outset of the eighteenth century to our days, no author, whether he intended to exalt or to check Russia, thought to dispense with first proving her existence.

"How did this power, or this phantom of power, contrive to assume such dimensions as to rouse on the one side the passionate assertion, and on the other the angry denial of its threatening the world with a rehearsal of universal monarchy?"[1]

Marx then reviews the history of Russia from the raids of Oleg on Byzantium down to the successful manœuvres by which Ivan I and III used the very power of their overlord the Tartar Khan to weaken his power and attain their own supremacy and the triumph of Russia, just as centuries later Catherine I and Peter the Great used Britain to achieve an even more remarkable and menacing power in Europe.

What of the other Russia? Marx always discerned in any situation not only what was disintegrating and dying away, but what was new and coming into being—this was his legacy from Hegel. In Russia there was a new birth as well as the inevitable decay of a dying autocracy. If Tsardom was the eternal enemy, the progressive forces in the West had "gained an ally in the Russian serf. The struggle which has now broken out in Russia between the ruling classes of the rural population and the ruled is already undermining the whole system of Russian foreign policy. The system was only possible so long as Russia had no internal political development. But that time is past. The industrial and agricultural development which the government and the aristocracy have promoted in every possible way has thrived to such a degree that it can no longer be reconciled with the existing social conditions. Their abolition is a necessity on the one hand and an impossibility—unless they are changed by force—on the other."[2]

Russia could not indefinitely continue as a purely agricultural

[1] Marx, *Secret Diplomatic History of the Eighteenth Century.*
[2] Marx: *Savoy, Nice and the Rhine.*

country. Industry must in due course find its place in her economy. "From the day Russia introduced railways," said Engels, "the introduction of modern means of production was a foregone conclusion." The first railway in Russia ran from St. Petersburg to the imperial palace of Tsarskue Silo, a distance of fifteen miles. It was built in 1838. When Nikolas I died in 1855 there were still only 650 miles of railway in the whole of his vast empire. When his successor Alexander II died in 1881 there were over 14,000 miles in operation. Engineering and heavy industry began about 1861 and received a new impetus after the defeat in the Crimean War. But these new industries, said Engels, destroy their own home market by ruining the domestic industry of the peasantry, so that the peasants' purchasing power is reduced to a minimum. "Capitalist production is full of internal contradictions which develop and become evident in proportion as it develops. This tendency to destroy its own market at the same time that it creates it, is one of them."[1]

With this arises the necessity of forcibly opening new markets. "Capitalist production works its own ruin. . . . I am sure the conservative people who have introduced capitalism into Russia will be one day terribly astonished at the consequences of their own doings."[2]

Marx followed the development of industrial and social progress in Russia very carefully. Here he demonstrates once again his ability to grapple with actual conditions, to comprehend concrete reality, despite his reputed concern only for basic theoretical principles. At the beginning of 1870 he began to study Russian and was soon able to read it fluently. This came about, he tells us, when he received an important book from St. Petersburg. *The Condition of the Working Class in Russia* by Flerovsky. He writes: "I also wanted to familiarise myself with the excellent economic works of Chernyshevsky (who was rewarded by being sentenced to the Siberian mines for the past seven years). The result was worth the effort that a man of my age must make to master a language, differing so greatly from the classical, Germanic and Romance languages. The intellectual movement now taking place in Russia testifies to the fact that fermentation is occurring deep below the surface. Minds are always connected by invisible threads with the body of the people."[3]

Chernyshevsky (1828-89) was a leading member of the Narodniki or Populists and their principal theorist. He wrote extensively on

[1] Engels to Danielson. September 22nd, 1892. [2] *ibid.*
[3] Marx to Meyer, January 21st, 1871.

philosophical subjects but is best known by his utopian novel *What is to be Done?* the chief character of which reflects all the idealism of the high-minded social reformer and his hatred of those who oppress the peasantry. In it he depicts the ideal of a man of moral strength and integrity who risks all in his struggle against serfdom.

The Narodniki (Narod = people) idealised the "people", by which they meant the peasantry, at a time when industrial workers were relatively few in numbers. They were romantic idealists, chiefly students and "repentant noblemen". They held the view that there was a soul of goodness and regard for the common life in the peasant and in the village *mir* or commune, that could save Russia. There was no need for Russia to become capitalist, for the *mir* could become the basis of a communist social order. They were for the overthrow of serfdom, Tsarism and the autocracy. Chernyshevsky supported these theories with a form of Hegelian philosophy and a vigorous materialism, seeing in society a developmental process passing inevitably from serfdom to communism. He believed that so far from human nature being always the same it is entirely moulded by institutions, and that institutions are changed and reformed from age to age.

Marx studied Chernyshevsky's works on peasant reform with special attention and declared that they did "great honour to Russia", while Lenin, later, said of him that he was "the only really great Russian writer who from the fifties until 1888 was able to keep on the level of an integral philosophical materialism and avoid the rubbish of positivists and other muddleheads'.[1]

Flerovsky's book Marx declared to be "the first work to tell the truth about Russian economic conditions. The man is a determined enemy of what he calls 'Russian optimism'. . . . This is the most important book which has appeared since the *Condition of the Working Class.*"[2]

Another Russian, much better known in England, was Alexander Herzen (1812-70), who lived in exile in Western Europe after 1846. He was an aristocrat, a romantic individualist, even anarchistic, and romanticised the Russian peasant to an extreme degree. Marx speaks of "the imaginative lies of Citizen Herzen".

London and Paris saw the coming and going of refugees and exiles from all over Europe and especially from Russia and Poland. In 1843 Jenny Marx writes that when they were living in rue Vanneau, Faubourg St. Germain, they frequently met not only Heine and Ruge,

[1] Lenin, *Materialism and Empirio-criticism.*
[2] Marx to Engels, February 10th, 1870.

but also the Russians Tolstoi,[1] Bakunin and Annenkov, a literary figure who lived a great deal abroad. Annenkov met Marx again in Brussels, where he was present at the stormy interview with Weitling. Marx wrote him a long letter on Proudhon, which is the best and clearest summary of Marx's criticism of Proudhon's theories.

Lopatin was another Russian who got to know Marx in London. Marx described him as "a very wide-awake critical mind, a cheerful character as stoical as a Russian peasant, who puts up with anything he finds". They discussed Chernyshevsky's works and Marx told him that Chernyshevsky was the only contemporary economist who had really original ideas. His praise was so enthusiastic that Lopatin returned to Russia and engaged in a desperate attempt to bring off Chernyshevsky's escape from exile; in this he failed and found himself in prison in Irkutsk. He escaped and reached Paris safely in 1873. Later we find him discussing the Russian situation with Engels, who told him that "Russia is the France of the present century. To her belongs rightfully and lawfully the revolutionary initiative of a new social organisation."

When the chemist and astronomer Nikolai Alexandrovich Morozov, who died in 1946, visited Marx in 1880, he says that he did not notice in him any of the moroseness or unapproachableness that he had been warned about. He was received cordially and entered into a long discussion on the politics of the *Narodya Volya* (the People's Will, organisation of the Narodniki). When Morozov was on his way back to Russia, unaware of the assassination of Alexander II, he was arrested on the frontier and imprisoned in the fortress of St. Peter and St. Paul and then in the Schlusselburg, from which he was not released until 1905. His last act before leaving Geneva was to give a copy of *The Communist Manifesto* to Plekhanov to be translated into Russian. Marx declared the translation when it appeared to be "by far the best I have seen".

There were many other Russians who got to know Marx—Rusanov, Voden, Kravchiskaya and Kovalesky, the historian and jurist, a liberal politically, who got to know him at the height of his controversy with Bakunin and Dühring. He met Kovalevsky not only in London but at Karlsbad, where Marx was sent by his doctor for his liver complaint. Here they walked in the mountains almost every day, and he became one of Marx's "scientific friends", as he called them.

In 1870 the Russian colony in Geneva applied to join the

[1] This was not Leo Tolstoi, but Grigory Mikhailovich Tolstoi, a landowner from Kazan.

International, writing to Marx direct and inviting him to be their representative on the General Council. They wrote in terms of great humility and admiration and Marx observed: "What I will never forgive these fellows is that they turn me into a *Venerable*. They obviously think I am between eighty and a hundred years old." In his reply he was careful to direct their attention to Flerovsky's book and to emphasise the fact that the chief task of Russian members of the International was to work for the liberation of Poland which would create an effective barrier between Western Europe and Tsarist Russia, the sworn enemy of democratic freedom.

Finally a group of Marxists appeared among the Russian revolutionaries, but this was two years after the death of Marx. Engels wrote to Vera Ivanova Zasulich, later an active member of the Marxist Emancipation of Labour Group in St. Petersburg, to congratulate the Russians. "I am proud to know that there is a party among the youth of Russia which frankly and without ambiguity accepts the great economic and historic theories of Marx and which has decisively broken with all the anarchist and slightly Slavophile traditions of its predecessors. Marx himself would have been equally proud of this had he lived a little longer."[1]

After Marx had mastered Russian he read not only Chernyshevsky, but the literary critic Dobrulyubov, the novels of Shchedrin, Turgenev and Gogol, and the works of Lermontov and Pushkin. He then commenced an exhaustive study of Russian agrarian conditions and the system of communal landholding—Engels speaks of "two cubic metres of books on Russian statistics". For the last fifteen years of his life he was largely occupied in this exhaustive study of Russian conditions. Engels once remarked to him, "It would give me pleasure to burn up the Russian publications on the condition of agriculture, which for several years have kept you from finishing *Capital*." As a matter of fact it was partly for the purpose of completing the second and third volumes that Marx engaged in this laborious research. Explaining, in a letter to Kugelmann of June 27th, 1870, why there had arisen some delay in completing the second volume, he says that in dealing with the land question "it became essential to go to the original sources in studying the relations of Russian landed property".

Large parcels of books continued to arrive from Russia, and various reports of investigating commissions on Rural Economy and Taxation, historical monographs and scientific works. He spent a good deal of

[1] Engels to Vera Zasulich, April 23rd, 1885.

time studying Russian geology and agronomy in order to complete the sections on land rent in Volume Three. It was of course the origin and constitution of the village commune or *mir* which particularly attracted his attention, and he was in correspondence with his Russian friends on the controversies on this topic which Russian scholars were engaged in at the time.

It will be clear that with these extensive contacts both with the Russian exiles and with many friends and correspondents in Russia, the question of a translation of *Capital* would be bound to arise. Only a few weeks after its publication copies of the German edition arrived in St. Petersburg and Moscow, where Marx's work found attentive readers among the progressive intelligentsia. The distinguished chemist Timiriazev was one of the first to see it, in the autumn of 1867. He found it in the study of his friend Professor Ilienkov, the agricultural chemist, who proceeded to give him on the spot practically a whole lecture on the volume. It also fell into the hands of Nikolai Danielson, an enthusiastic Narodniki, who in spite of his total disagreement with Marx on all basic issues at once set about the task of getting it translated. Bakunin was the first to be commissioned for this task, but got no further than the first few pages. Then the task was handed over to Lopatin, a close friend of Marx, who said of him, "There are few people whom I love and respect as I do him". Lopatin set to work and made numerous suggestions for its revision and amendation, most of which were accepted. But then he felt compelled to return to Russia to secure the liberation of Chernyshevsky and his work came to an end. Danielson therefore decided to finish the work himself and maintained a regular correspondence with Marx while doing so.

In March 1872 the Russian edition of *Capital* was published. Marx said that the translation was masterly. The three thousand copies sold rapidly, and it was reviewed very favourably and at considerable length in the *European Messenger* of St. Petersburg, Marx quoted considerable portions of this review in the Preface to the Second German Edition.

It might be supposed that the Tsarist censorship would have forbidden the publication of *Capital*, but they considered it to be written in an insufficiently accessible form to do any harm, and as the labour movement was weak they anticipated no serious threat from the working class. The report of the censors is interesting.

"Although in his convictions the author is undoubtedly a socialist and the whole book reveals a definitely socialist character, yet, noting that its treatment cannot be called accessible to everyone, and that, on the other hand, its form is that of a scientific-mathematical argumentation, the committee recognises that for this book prosecution in the courts is impossible."

Later, however, when the labour movement had become a serious factor in the revolutionary struggle, every effort was made to suppress it, and for being in possession of it men were sent to penal servitude.

Capital, says Mehring, "was more widely read and received greater recognition in Russia than anywhere else, particularly in the younger world of science and literature where Marx won many supporters and not a few personal friends. However, the two main tendencies of the Russian mass movement, as far as one can speak of such a thing at that time, the Party of the People's Will and the Party of Black Distribution,[1] still found his ideas completely foreign. The chief question at issue for them was formulated by Marx as follows: "Can the Russian peasant community, an already very degenerate form of primitive common ownership of the land, develop directly into a higher communist form of land ownership, or must it first of all go through the same process of dissolution seen in the historical development of the Western European countries?"[2]

The answer to this question appears in the Preface to a new Russian translation of *The Communist Manifesto* published in 1882. Marx says: "If the Russian revolution gives the signal for a workers' revolution in the West, so that both revolutions supplement each other, then the existing form of communal property in Russia can serve as the starting point of a communist development."

Marx was always ready to join forces for a limited objective with every militant agrarian or peasant movement, even though he made no secret of the inadequacy in his view of their total programme and never ceased to criticise their neglect of the class struggle or their hopeless attempts to realise their desires in little more than dreams and hopes.

Nor did Marx accept the position that capitalist development could be avoided. No more in Russia than anywhere else was it possible to develop a higher social form directly out of primitive agrarian communism.

But if capitalism was bound to come in Russia, under what conditions would it arise and what would be the probable consequences?

[1] The Black Distribution was a proposal similar to that of Kriege in America to solve the social problem by the distribution of limited plots of land to all citizens.

[2] Franz Mehring, *Karl Marx*.

Some Russians, the Narodniki, feared that it might prove an unmitigated disaster. Most of them held to the utopian notion that Russia had no need to become capitalist, that the peasant commune could become the basis of a communist social order. Others feared the coming of capitalism because since it would develop out of a primitive social system it would involve a terrible dislocation of a society and appalling hardships. The Right-wing socialists, however, thought that the evils associated with the transition to socialism could be considerably lessened or overcome.

There was however a third possibility, that of "Russians finding a path of development for their country which will be different from that which Western Europe pursued and still pursues—whether she can, without experiencing the tortures of the capitalist régime, appropriate all its fruits by developing the particular historic conditions proper to her—the finest chance ever offered by history to a nation to escape the fatal vicissitudes of capitalism."[1]

But did not Marx predict that the revolution would occur first of all in the highly industrial countries of the West rather than in more backward Russia? On the contrary, he saw the English working class as becoming more and more demoralised until it was likely to be little more than the tool of the Liberal Party. There was no more proletarian movement there.[2] In Germany the united Social-Democratic Party had seriously compromised with the Lassalleans in their Gotha Programme. The Höchberg article on "The Socialist Movement in Germany"[3] had clearly adumbrated the future revisionist policies of Bernstein who was one of its authors. Marx and Engels were looking in another direction: "This time the revolution will begin in the East, hitherto the unbroken bulwark and reserve army of the counter-revolution."[4]

"All sections of Russian society are in full decomposition, economically, morally and intellectually. The Russians are approaching their 1789. The revolution *must* break out there in a given time—it *may* break out there any day—the country is like a charged mine. . . . The most important thing is that the impulse should be given in Russia, that the revolution should break out there. There where the position is so strained, where the revolutionary elements are accumulated to

[1] Marx to the Editor of *Notes on the Fatherland*, 1877.
[2] Engels to Kautsky, September 12th, 1882.
[3] Zürich *Yearbook for Socialist Science and Politics*, 1879.
[4] Marx to Sorge, September 27th, 1877.

such a degree, where the economic situation of the enormous mass of the people becomes daily more impossible, where every stage of social development is represented, from the primitive commune to modern large scale industry and high finance, and where all these contradictions are violently held together by an unexampled despotism there, when 1789 has once been launched, 1793[1] will not be long in following."[2]

[1] 1789—the French Revolution; 1793—the Jacobins seize power.

[2] Engels to Vera Zasulich, April 23rd, 1885.

22

LAST YEARS

MARX had sacrificed his health and his family to his unending labours. After working thirteen hours a day and sometimes all night, attending to the day-to-day affairs of the International, turning from his more important work to write pamphlets, to engage in theoretical controversies, to write letters to his friends and disciples in every part of the world, his health began to show signs of serious impairment in 1873. He suffered much from his head, and only the efforts of his doctors and visits to Karlsbad enabled him to get back to work. The fact that Engels was now living in London relieved Marx of a good deal of responsibility and made these visits to the continent possible. In 1870 Engels, who had for some years been a partner in Ermen and Engels in Manchester, retired and came to live in Regent's Park Road, quite near to Marx.

Marx resumed his work and for some years played an important role in guiding the new Marxist parties in Germany and France. He was in correspondence with almost all the socialist leaders in different countries and they frequently came to him for advice.

As the years went by it gradually became clear to him, as illness more and more interrupted his work on the remaining volumes of *Capital*, that he would never be able to complete the second and third volumes unless he could be completely restored to health, and this was most unlikely.

Even at this time, when he recovered somewhat, he was back at his desk, never went to bed until very late, and was up the next morning between eight and nine, drinking black coffee and reading the newspapers. Work was such a passion with him that he often forgot his meals. He smoked incessantly and used to say that all he got from *Capital* would not suffice to pay for the cigars he had smoked while writing it.

In the midst of his political and economic work he found mental refreshment in classical literature from every country. Perhaps one of of the most unlikely interests of Marx was mathematics, to which he often turned when distracted by trouble. He wrote a work on the infinitesimal calculus which contemporary mathematicians still find illuminating.[1]

In 1859 he was immensely excited by the publication of Darwin's *Origin of Species*. He and his circle of more intimate friends discussed its significance for months. Marx sent Darwin a copy of *Capital* on its publication, and it may still be seen in Darwin's house at Downe.

Paul Lafargue, who had married his daughter Laura, worked very closely with Marx. He tells us that he was the only person to whom Marx ever dictated any of his work. In his reminiscences we find an account of Marx's household in the seventies and he describes Marx's study, which was at the back of the house on the first floor, flooded with light from a broad window that looked out into the park.

"Opposite the window and on either side of the fireplace the walls were lined with bookcases filled with books and stacked up to the ceiling with newspapers and manuscripts. Opposite the fireplace on one side of the window were two tables piled up with books and newspapers; in the middle of the room, well in the light, stood a small plain desk (three feet by two) and a wooden armchair; between the armchair and the bookcase, opposite the window, was a leather sofa on which Marx used to lie down for a rest from time to time. On the mantelpiece were more books, cigars, matches, tobacco pouches, paperweights and photographs of Marx's daughters and wife.

"Marx never allowed anybody to put his books or papers in order —or rather in disorder. The disorder in which they lay was only apparent, everything was really in its intended place so that it was easy for him to lay his hand on the book or notebook he needed. Even during conversations he often paused to show in the book a quotation or figure he had just mentioned. He and his study were one: the books and papers in it were as much under his control as his own limbs.

"Marx had no use for formal symmetry in the arrangement of his books: volumes of different sizes and pamphlets stood next to one another. He arranged them according to their contents, not their size. Books were tools for his mind, not articles of luxury. He paid no heed to size or binding, quality of paper or type; he would turn down the corners of the pages, make pencil marks in the margin and underline whole lines. He never wrote on books, but sometimes he could not refrain from an exclamation or question mark when the author went

[1] See Professor Dirk Struik in *A Century of Marxism*.

too far. His system of underlining made it easy for him to find any passage in any book. He had a habit of going through the notebooks and reading the passages underlined in the books after intervals of many years in order to keep them fresh in his memory. He had an extraordinarily reliable memory which he had cultivated from his youth according to Hegel's advice by learning by heart verse in a foreign language he did not know.

"Marx was a tireless worker. He would rest by pacing up and down the room. A strip was worn out from the door to the window as sharply defined as a track across a meadow. He was so absorbed in his work that he often forgot his meals. He had to be called several times before he came down to the dining-room and hardly had he eaten his last mouthful when he was back in his study. His physical constitution had to be good to put up with this unusual way of life and exhausting mental work. The only physical exercise he ever pursued regularly was walking; he could ramble or climb hills for hours, chatting and smoking, and not feel tired. One can say that he even worked walking in his room, only sitting down for short periods to write what he thought out while walking. He liked to walk up and down while talking, stopping from time to time when the explanation became more animated or the conversation serious."[1]

During these years his third daughter, Eleanor, was his most devoted helper. As a child she was "the idolised darling of the whole house". When she became older she became her father's secretary and companion. More than her sisters, she was closely associated with the labour movement and helped Will Thorne in the organisation of one of the first unskilled workers' unions, the Gasworkers' and General Labourers' Union. She actually taught Will Thorne to read and write. She took an active part in the London dock strike of 1889. Beatrice Webb describes her as she appeared in 1883. "In person she is comely, dressed in a slovenly, picturesque way, with curly black hair flying about in all directions. Fine eyes full of life and sympathy."

For many years she lived with Dr. Edward Aveling, a brilliant but erratic figure who worked hard for the socialist movement. He had as good an understanding of Marxism as any man in England and together with Samuel Moore translated the first volume of *Capital*. He also translated Engel's *Socialism: Utopian and Scientific* (from *Anti-Dühring*) and with Eleanor wrote a book on *The Working Class Movement in America*, and a compendium entitled *The Student's Marx*.

[1] Paul Lafargue, *Reminiscences of Marx*.

She and Aveling took an active part not only in speaking and lecturing but in the preparation of some of Marx's works for publication, among them the well-known economic lectures on *Value, Price and Profit, The Life of Palmerston* and *The Eastern Question* and *The Secret Diplomatic History of the Eighteenth Century*. They were both members of Hyndman's Democratic Federation and later of Morris's Socialist League.

Unfortunately, Aveling's character revealed the gravest defects. He had no conscience about money and was completely without scruples. Startlingly ugly, people used to say of him that "nobody could be as bad as Aveling looked". It is generally supposed that he was the model for Louis Dubedat, the slippery but talented artist of Bernard Shaw's *Doctor's Dilemma*. There is no doubt that he treated Eleanor despicably, but as in Shaw's play, the deliberate blindness of Dubedat's wife in respect of all that was said to the detriment of her husband is precisely the counterpart of the obstinacy with which Eleanor Marx, despite all her experiences, continued to believe in him. In one of her last letters, when at last she began to realise the kind of man he was, she writes, "It's a bad time for me. I fear there is little to hope for, and the pain and suffering are great. Why we all go on like this I do not understand. I am ready to go and would do so with joy, but so long as he needs me I am bound to remain."

As one by one the Marxist parties came into existence, and on the Continent looked like becoming a significant political force, questions of their programmes and political strategy and tactics came to the fore. The possibility of immediate revolution had receded, and what was needed was a policy for Marxist parties proceeding towards a revolutionary situation that lay some distance ahead.

At a banquet given to celebrate the anniversary of the *People's Paper* on April 14th, 1856, Marx made a speech in which he outlined the development of the British working-class movement from the time of the Chartists to his own time. He saw in Chartism the rise of the whole working class against the bourgeoisie and behind its straightforward aims for annual parliaments and so on, revolutionary implications, social as well as political. It was the class movement of the workers against capitalist exploitation. The rise of the working-class movement was the result of the coming into existence of industrial and scientific forces of surprising significance, and with them definite and menacing evils. "All movements and progress seem to result in endowing material forces with intellectual life and in stultifying human life into a material force." This finds expression in the growing antagonism between these vast forces and the way in which men are associated together in operating them—the relation of capitalist owner working for profit and wage earner hired to produce saleable commodities. Under these conditions the forces of production are not utilised to full advantage. "If the new fangled forces of society are to work satisfactorily they need to be mastered by new fangled men—the workers themselves." They are as much a creation of the modern age as machinery, and they have their indispensable part to play in the social revolution produced by modern industry. Of the present social system "history is the judge; its executioner the proletariat".

Marx sees first a movement of social unrest and protest, with utopian socialists regarding the workers only with pity and dreaming of an ideal social order free from injustice and exploitation. But as industrialism develops the socialist sects are outmoded, valuable though they were once when the workers were not yet ripe for an independent historic movement; it becomes necessary for the movement to formulate political aims and for its social struggle to become political struggle, organised and led by an independent political party of the workers.

The attainment of constitutional democracy, while not in itself the last victory, does achieve the form in which the class struggle can and must be fought to a conclusion and total victory.

We can trace in Marx's thoughts a sharp change from the tactics of permanent revolution he advocated in relation to the German revolution of 1848, to the concept of the majority revolution which was the final form of his revolutionary programme.

In 1848 he thought that the struggle of the bourgeoisie for political rights could be carried forward to a higher stage by mobilising, after the first victory for bourgeois demands, the smaller bourgeoise and the workers, and then after still further victories for that alliance against the wealthier bourgeoisie, a final struggle in which the proletariat achieves a victory which aims at the higher good of the whole of society.

Marx and Engels subsequently confessed that neither industrial development nor the proletarian movement were well enough developed in 1848 for this to happen. In his Preface to *The Class Struggles in France*, Engels, looking back on the 1848 situation, declared that "the economic development was not ripe for the removal of capitalist production" and then proceeds to set forth the tactics and strategy of the proletarian struggle in the new period. As this was worked out by Marx and Engels it envisaged the growth of the trade union movement, and the development of socialist ideas and socialist parties, both arising from growing discontent with conditions under capitalism. The working-class movement would make the fullest use of the extensions of suffrage and the democratisation of political institutions to extend the class struggle in this field and secure reforms. But the aim must be the creation of a distinct political party and the conquest of political power.

An important distinction from "reformism" here appears. Marx never supposed that electoral victory was synonymous with revolution, that by its means alone socialism could be achieved. But under the changed conditions of developing capitalism it had become possible under certain conditions, to transform political democracy "from an instrument of deception—as up to now it has been—into an instrument of emancipation".

How did Marx envisage this transformation? Did he mean that through the operation of constitutional means the transition to socialism might be peacefully effected? Both Marx and Engels denied that the existing political system in Germany, which was without a a democratic constitution, would allow such a peaceful transition to socialism. But in his speech to the Amsterdam branch of the International in 1872 Marx asserted that a peaceful transition to socialism was possible for some countries. After arguing that to establish a socialist society it is necessary for the working class to conquer political power, he adds: "Of course, I must not be understood to imply that the means to this end will be everywhere the same. We know that special regard must be paid to the institutions, customs, and traditions of various lands; and we do not deny that there are certain countries, such as the United States and England, in which the workers may hope to secure their ends by peaceful means. . . . Even so, we have to recognise that in most Continental countries force will have to be the lever of revolution." And Engels, in his criticism of the Erfurt Programme of the German Social Democrat Party in 1891, declared that peaceful change was possible in France, America or England, where the constitution allowed the legislature to do what it liked provided it was backed by a majority of the nation.

Marx did not fail to qualify this hope for a peaceful transition in England. In an interview with the correspondent of the New York *World* (July 18th, 1871) he said: "The English bourgeoisie has always displayed readiness to accept the decision of the majority so long as it had the monopoly of the vote. But believe me, the moment when it finds itself in a minority on questions which it considers vitally important, we shall have here a new slave-owners' war."

The importance of the democratic republic was not that in itself it provided all the means by which the transition to socialism might be effected, but that it was the form in which the workers could wage the widest and freest struggle for political power—not excepting the electoral struggle, but by no means limiting the struggle to that and nothing more. Once political power is secured, what then? Marx insisted that the fullest use of it must immediately be made to break up the old state machine, and the state power must be fully used for *holding in subjugation*[1] the antagonists of the proletariat. At the time of the Paris Commune Marx had seen the importance of abandoning any attempt "to transfer the bureacratic military machine from one hand to another". On the contrary, it would be necessary "to *smash* it, and that is essential for every real people's revolution on the Continent".[2] Was this policy also necessary for socialists outside the Continent? Presumably it would be if the military-bureacratic machine assumed the dimensions and power of that on the Continent. But if the seizure of power went through without insurrection, as Marx and Engels thought it might, could the new government then take radical measures for the transformation of society without facing rebellion by the exploiters? Much would depend, of course, on the determination and unity of the workers. Marx was not optimistic, but Engels repeats that "he told me (and how often!) that in his opinion we would get off cheaply if we could buy out the whole lot of them".[3] But as Engels remarks, "He hardly expected the English ruling classes to submit without a pro-slavery rebellion to this peaceful and legal revolution".[4]

It would indeed be folly to count on their acquiescence in so vast a social transformation in which their pecuniary interests would be

[1] The word Marx used was *Niederhaltung*.

[2] Letter to Kugelmann, April 12th, 1871.

[3] Engels, *The Peasant War in Germany*. Lenin interpreted this to mean that in the England of the seventies a policy of compensation might ensure a peaceful transition. In that situation, he writes in *Left-Wing Communism*, "it was perfectly admissible to think of paying the capitalists well, of giving them ransom, *if* the circumstances were such as to impel the capitalists, providing they were bought off, to submit peacefully and to pass over to socialism in a cultured, organised manner."

[4] Engels, *Preface* to the English translation of *Capital*.

threatened with extinction. No ruling class has ever been known to abdicate. "It is an old and historically established maxim that obsolete social forces still in possession of all the attributes of power and continuing to exist long after the basis of their existence has rotted away, once more summon all their strength before the agony of death; pass from the defensive to the offensive, challenge instead of giving way, and seek to draw the most extreme conclusions from premises which have not only been put in question but already condemned."[1]

The acquiescence of a minority is usually withheld—is almost inevitably withheld—when the issue involves the substitution of a new social system for an old one. A dying social system may defy death long after senility has overtaken it and may well seek to hide its wasted strength in some last desperate effort of bitter violence.

From 1877 onwards the life of Marx was moving to a close. Almost imperceptibly at first, things at Maitland Park Road were changing. His daughters were now young women, the elder two married and with children of their own. Eleanor was her father's secretary and assistant. During these years the matters that chiefly occupied his attention were the programmes and policies of the growing Marxist parties in Germany and France, and in England his increasingly disagreeable relation with H. M. Hyndman. Marx's doctrines as embodied in his more important works were only accessible at this time to those Englishmen who read either German or French, but in 1880 Marx was delighted by an article written by Belfort Bax in the December issue of a British journal called *Modern Thought*. It was one of a series entitled "Leaders of Modern Thought" and on the walls and hoardings of the West End appeared advertisements for the article on KARL MARX by Belfort Bax. In spite of the fact that a good deal of the biographical material was inaccurate and the account of his economic theories extremely confused, Marx valued it as the first English publication of its kind. He wrote enthusiastically to Sorge in America to tell him about it. He was at that time watching by the bedside of his dying wife and he tells Sorge that this first recognition of the significance of Marx for modern thought greatly cheered her last hours.

Marx was heartened in his last years by visits from Wilhelm Liebknecht, now a Deputy in the Reichstag, editor of the Party journal, and busy with endless meetings and political organisation. In fact he

[1] Marx, Hyde Park, London, June 25th, 1855.

was successfully building the mass party which Marx had always hoped for. Still deeply attached to Marx, he consulted him whenever any important question of principle or policy arose. The ties that bound him to Marx were not just those of the politician to his leader or the disciple to his teacher; they were of warm personal affection.[1]

Edward Bernstein in those last years had been restored to favour and friendship. He had been entirely convinced of the basic Marxist position at last by Engels' *Anti-Dühring* and was editing the *Social Democrat* very competently and in a thoroughly revolutionary spirit. Visiting Marx in his home in 1880 in company with Bebel, he described the typical middle-class suburban villa in Maitland Park Road, with the basement kitchen and breakfast room and Marx's study on the first floor at the back of the house. Marx greeted them with extreme cordiality. "He spoke in the quiet lucid tone of a patriarch, and was quite unlike the picture which I had formed of him, not a suppressed, highly excitable man, but a white haired scholar whose dark eyes held a friendly smile and whose speech was full of charity."[2]

When Bernstein said as much to Engels, Engels replied: "Well, the Moor can thunder quite properly even now."

There were also plans for a journal of a more theoretical type than the *Social Democrat*. Marx thought of it as "a really scientific socialist journal which would provide an opportunity for criticism or counter-criticism in which we could discuss theoretical points, expose the utter ignorance of professors and lecturers and at the same time enlighten the minds of the general public—working class or bourgeois". Marx could find no one really competent for the task, for once again it was Höchberg, the wealthy young philanthropist "a good fellow but terribly naïve" who launched *Die Zukunft*. Marx insisted that in any such journal ruthless criticism based on scientific understanding was essential, and that this would be impossible not only because Höchberg's collaborators were insufficiently equipped, but because they assumed total ignorance on the part of their readers. Imagine, he said, a journal of chemistry where the readers' ignorance of chemistry is constantly assumed as the fundamental presupposition! Marx therefore refused to support the journal.

Marx knew very well the endless difficulties in the way of getting the right material published either in books or by means of journals.

[1] See Liebknecht's *Reminiscences* and also *Wilhelm Liebknecht; Briefwechsel mit Karl Marx und Friedrich Engels*. Edited by George Eckert (The Hague).

[2] Edward Bernstein, *My Years of Exile*.

On the one hand it was often impossible to get the right editor when the money was forthcoming from confused but generous men like Höchberg and when the right man and the right material were available, publishers, police and booksellers, all of them "interested representatives of all the tendencies I am attacking" united to raise every kind of obstacle. Even the socialists were "angry with me for opposing their utopian declarations", as he consistently did.

His thought was never doctrinaire, always realistic. In a letter to his Russian translator, Danielson, he mentions the inevitable objections which his type of thinking and writing met with—the boycotting. "If you break through the webs of routine thoughts, you are always sure to be boycotted in the first instance; it is the only arm of defence which in their first perplexity the routineers know how to use."[1]

In his dealings with these disciples and collaborators, with unreliable intellectuals and confused but loyal disciples, Marx showed a really remarkable psychological insight; as he did in his exposure of the "false consciousness", the ideological defences, of the defenders of capitalism.

No one ever had so deadly a sense of the infinite capacity of human nature for remaining oblivious or indifferent to the pain we inflict on others when we have a chance to get something out of them for ourselves, or the real conviction with which men hide the realities of their social life from themselves. They will regard the actions of socialists and reformers not only as treason to their interests but as treason to society; for they will inevitably identify the social order they have created and by which they profit with the principle of order itself, and their own interests with the general interests of all men; then they will regard the threat of a competing political order as synonymous with the peril of chaos. A social or political system, a ruling class or an economic organisation, may be persuaded to mend some of its incidental defects; but it can hardly be persuaded to recognise that its day is done.

But the party grew in numbers and strength. The name of Marx was known everywhere in Europe and in the United States. His influence and authority in the socialist movement were immense. But whilst the clouds gradually lifted from the social and political horizon the dusk sank deeper and deeper on him and his house. In the autumn of 1878 Marx wrote to Serge to tell him that his wife was "very unwell". A year later he tells him that she is dangerously ill with incurable cancer. When Bernstein and Bebel visited Marx,

[1] Letter to Danielson, February 19th, 1881.

although she was desperately ill, she got up to preside at the dinner table for her guests and talked with them about their work in Germany. Then she was obliged to leave them and return to her sick-room. In the summer of 1881 she made the heroic effort of going to Paris to visit her married daughters Jenny and Laura. Marx writes to Jenny in the same year, "It is dull since you went away—without you and Johnny and Harra and Mr. 'Tea'. I often run to the window when I hear children's voices, forgetting for the moment that the little chaps are across the channel."[1] Marx was a great lover of children. Once he said, "After all, we can forgive Christianity much because it taught us the worship of the child".

We have one of the last pictures of Marx and his wife at that time in Eleanor's memoirs. "Mother lay in the big front room and the Moor (who was recovering from a violent attack of pleurisy) in the little room next to it. The two who had grown so used to each other, whose lives had completely intertwined, could no longer be in the same room together. . . . The Moor got over his illness once again. I shall never forget the morning when he felt himself strong enough to get up and go into Mother's room. It was as though they were young again together—she a loving girl and he an ardent youth starting out together through life, and not an old man shattered by ill-health and a dying old lady taking leave of each other for ever."

The great love and admiration which Marx had for his wife are revealed in the letter he wrote when he revisited Trier, his birthplace and hers, at the time of his mother's death. "I have been making a daily pilgrimage to the old Westphalen house, because it reminds me of happy youth, and used to shelter my sweetheart. And every day people ask me right and left about the 'most beautiful girl' in Trier, the 'Queen of the Ball'. It's damned agreeable for a man to find that his wife lives on as an 'enchanted princess' in the imagination of a whole town."

Jenny Marx died on December 2nd, 1881, and Marx survived her by only fifteen months. In January 1883 he suffered a last blow when his daughter Jenny died in Paris. His broken health kept him away from London most of the time, often at Ventnor in the Isle of Wight. Engels writes to the effect that medical skill might have kept him alive for some years longer, but Marx could never have borne a merely

[1] Marx to his daughter Jenny, April 11th, 1881. Johnny, Harra, Mr. "Tea", were the Longuet's children, of whom Marx was very fond.

vegetative existence. "To live with the vast uncompleted work before him, with the Tantulus-thirst to finish it, and without the power to do so—that would have been a thousand times more bitter to him than the gentle death which overtook him. He used to say, with Epicurus, that 'death is not a misfortune for him who dies, but for him who survives'." For years Engels had seen his great comrade's energy beginning to flag; he no longer had the strength to master the great mass of material which he had gathered and organised. He had, in fact, done far more than anyone, even Engels knew, to complete his work. After his death, Bebel expressed surprise that Marx had kept Engels in ignorance of the stage the work had reached. "It was simply because if I had known," Engels answered, "I would have given him no peace night or day until it was finished and printed."

In his letter to Sorge, Engels described Marx's last moments: "Every morning for the last six weeks I had a terrible feeling of dread that I might find the curtains drawn when I turned the corner of the street. Yesterday afternoon (March 14th, 1883) at 2.30—which is the best time for visiting him—I arrived to find the house in tears. It seemed that the end was near. I asked what had happened, tried to get to the bottom of the matter, to offer comfort. There had been only a slight haemorrhage but suddenly he had begun to sink rapidly. Our good old Lenchen, who had looked after him better than a mother cares for her child, went upstairs to him and then came down. He was half asleep, she said, I might come in. When we entered he lay there asleep, but never to wake again. His pulse and breathing had stopped. In those two minutes he had passed away, peacefully and without pain." He had got up from his bed and gone to his study and sat down in his work chair at his desk. There they found him.

Engels went on: "Mankind is shorter by a head, and the greatest head of our time at that. The proletarian movement goes on, but gone is its central figure. . . . The final victory is certain, but circuitous paths, temporary and local errors—things which even now are so unavoidable—will become more common than ever. Well, we must see it through. What else are we here for? And we are not near losing courage yet."

Engels wrote to Liebknecht on March 14th: "Although I have seen him this evening laid out in his bed, the rigidity of death in his face, I cannot fully realise that this brilliant mind has ceased to impregnate the proletarian movement of both worlds with its mighty thoughts. We all owe what we are to him; and the movement as it is today is the creation of his theoretical and practical work. If it had not been for him we should still all be groping in a maze of confusion".

On March 17th Karl Marx was buried in the grave of his wife in Highgate Cemetery, where some years later their faithful servant, Helene Demuth (Lenchen) was buried with them. Engels spoke at the graveside. His memorable eulogy contains these words: "As Darwin discovered the law of evolution in organic nature, so Marx discovered the law of evolution in human history. . . . His name will live through the centuries and so will his work."

His favourite daughter and devoted companion, Eleanor Marx, seems the most fitting person to sum up his character.

"To those who are students of human nature it will not seem strange that this man, who was such a fighter, should at the same time be the kindliest and gentlest of men. They will understand that he could hate so fiercely only because he could love so profoundly; that if his trenchant pen could as surely imprison a soul in Hell as Dante himself it was because he was so true and tender, that if his sarcastic humour could bite like a corrosive acid, that same humour could be as balm to those in trouble and afflicted."

CHRONOLOGY OF EVENTS IN THE LIFE OF KARL MARX TOGETHER WITH HIS BOOKS, ARTICLES AND OTHER WRITINGS

1818 May 5th	Karl Marx born at Trier in the Rhineland.
1835 October 15th	Marx enters Bonn University (Faculty of Law).
1836 October 22nd	Marx enters Berlin University (Faculty of Law) and meets the Young Hegelians.
1841 April	Marx submits his thesis on *Differences between the Natural Philosophy of Democritus and the Natural Philosophy of Epicurus* to Jena University and receives the diploma of Doctor of Philosophy.
1842 January	Marx writes the article, *Notes on the Latest Prussian Censorship Instructions*, subsequently published in 1843 in Arnold Ruge's *Anekdota*.
April	Marx begins to contribute to the *Rheinische Zeitung*.
October	Marx goes to Cologne and becomes editor of the *Rheinische Zeitung*. First meeting with Engels here.
1842-43	*Kritik des Hegelschen Staatsrecht* (Critique of Hegel's *Philosophy of Law*).
1843 January	Prussian Government imposes rigorous censorship on *Rheinische Zeitung* and orders its suppression from April 1st.
March 17th	Marx resigns the editorship.
June 19th	Marx marries Jenny von Westphalen and goes to Kreuznach.
October	Marx in Paris where, with Arnold Ruge, he edits the *Deutsche-Französischen Jahrbücher*, published February 1844, to

	which he contributed *Introduction to the Critique of Hegel's Philosophy of Law*, and *On the Jewish Question*.
	Engels contributes his *Outline of a Critique of Political Economy* and *The Position of England: Thomas Carlyle's Past and Present* to the *Jahrbücher*.
1844	Marx contributes article to *Vorwärts*, Paris, and writes *The Economic and Philosophical Manuscripts*.
	In June, Marx welcomes the rising of the Silesian Weavers, as demonstrating the political advance of the working class, in an article for the *D.F.J.*
1844 September	Meeting of Marx and Engels in Paris. Marx and Engels at work on *The Holy Family* and Engels on *The Condition of the Working Class in England in 1844*.
1845 January	Marx expelled from Paris by the French Government under pressure from Prussia.
February	Marx in Brussels. Publication of *The Holy Family*.
Spring	Marx writes his *Theses on Feuerbach*. Engels joins Marx in Brussels.
May	Engels' *Condition of the Working Class in England*, is published in Leipzig.
July	Marx and Engels in England to study English economic and political life and literature. Meet leading Chartists and League of the Just.
December	Marx renounces Prussian citizenship to avoid deportation.
1845-46	Marx and Engels write *The German Ideology*.
	Correspondence Committees set up in London, Paris and Germany for the organisation of progressive and working-class movements. Circulars despatched from the Brussels Committee, written

	by Marx and Engels, exposing the German "True Socialists".
	Marx contacts Weitling in Brussels. Engels organises the Paris Committee.
1846 December	Marx's letter to Annenkov criticising Proudhon and expounding briefly the materialist conception of history.
1847	Marx writes *The Poverty of Philosophy*.
1847 February	J. Moll of the London Committee of the League of the Just visits Marx and Engels in Brussels to invite their membership and help.
June	Engels attends the Congress of the League of the Just in London, which decides to call itself the Communist League.
November-December	Marx and Engels at the Second Congress of the Communist League in London. Marx is instructed to prepare a programme.
December	Marx lectures on *Wage, Labour and Capital* to the German Workers' Society in Brussels.
1847-48	Marx contributes articles to the *Deutsch-Brusseler Zeitung*.
1848 February	Publication in London of Marx and Engels' *Manifesto of the Communist Party* in German.
March	Marx expelled from Belgium and arrives in Paris where the February Revolution has taken place.
	Marx elected Chairman of the Communist League; Schapper Secretary; Engels, Moll and Bauer Executive Committee members.
	Marx and Engels draw up the programme for the Communist Party in Germany in connection with the revolution there.
April 6th	Marx and Engels leave Paris for Germany

	to take part in the Revolution. Marx edits *Neue Rheinische Zeitung* in Cologne (No. 1 published June 1st, 1848) and writes (1848-49) numerous articles. Marx
1848 August	visits Berlin and Vienna where he gives several lectures.
1849 February 8th	Marx tried in Cologne for "incitation to revolt", defends himself in court and is acquitted.
May 19th	Marx expelled from Prussia. *Neue Rheinische Zeitung* ceases publication.
	Marx in Paris from which he is then banned.
August	Marx arrives in London.
1850	Engels takes up work in the office of his family firm, Ermen and Engels, in Manchester.
	First English translation of *The Communist Manifesto* by Helen Macfarlane, printed in Julian Harney's *Red Republican.*
1850 March	Marx and Engels write the *Address of the Central Committee to the Communist League.*
	Six numbers of *Neue Rheinische Zeitung-Politsche-Ökonomische Revue* produced by Marx and Engels including *The Class Struggles in France, 1848-1850* and Engels' *The Peasant War in Germany* and many other articles and reviews.
	Marx secures a majority in the Central Committee of the Communist League against adventurist risings in Germany.
1851-62	Marx and Engels contribute articles to *New York Daily Tribune* including *Revolution and Counter Revolution in Germany* and articles on *The Eastern Question, Palmerston, Secret Diplomatic History of the Eighteenth Century.*
1852 March	Marx writes *The Eighteenth Brumaire*

	of Louis Bonaparte, and his pamphlet *Revelations about the Cologne Communist Trial.*
1852 November	On Marx's proposal, the Communist League declares itself dissolved.
1855	Articles in the *Neue Oder-Zeitung*, Breslau.
1857	*Grundrisse der Kritique der Politischen Ökonomie* and the Introduction subsequently published with the *Critique* (see next entry).
1859 June	*A Contribution to the Critique of Political Economy*, with the Introduction of 1857, published.
1860	Marx writes *Herr Vogt.*
1861-62	Marx and Engels write articles on the American Civil War for the Vienna *Die Presse.*
1862	Marx criticises Lassalle's "Workers' Programme".
1864 September	Foundation of the International Working Men's Association (First International).
	Marx writes the *Inaugural Address* and the Provisional *Rules* of the International Working Men's Association.
1865 February	National Reform League, (campaigning for manhood suffrage) set up on the initiative of the General Council on Marx's suggestion.
June	Marx writes *Value, Price and Profit*, an address to the General Council (since known as *Wages, Price and Profit.*)
September	First Conference of the International in London.
1866 July	Marx writes instructions for the delegates of the General Council to the Geneva Congress of the International, notably a statement on trade unions.
1866 September 3rd-8th	First Congress of the International in Geneva.

1867 April	Marx takes the first volume of *Capital* to the publisher in Hamburg.
September	Second Congress of the International in Lausanne.
September 14th	Publication of *Das Kapital:* Vol. I, *Capital: A Critical Analysis of Capitalist Production*, in Hamburg.
November	General Council's discussion on Ireland.
1868	Third Congress of the International in Brussels.
1869	Marx begins an extensive study of Russian economics and agrees to represent the Russian section of the First International (in Geneva) on the General Council.
	Congress of the German Social Democratic Workers' Party in Eisenach.
	Fourth Congress of the International in Basle.
1869 November	Marx opens discussion at General Council exposing Gladstone's police rule in Ireland.
1870 July	On the outbreak of the Franco-Prussian War Marx writes the *First Address of the General Council* on the Franco-Prussian War.
September 9th	After the defeat of the French Army at Sedan and the setting up of the republic in France, Marx writes the *Second Address of the General Council* on the Franco-Prussian War.
September 18th	Engels leaves Manchester and settles in London. He is elected to the General Council of the International.
1871 March	Establishment of the Paris Commune. Marx and Engels organise demonstrations of workers in various countries in its defence. Their speeches at the General Council and Marx's *Letters to Kugelmann* explain the significance of the Commune.

1871 May	The General Council adopts the address on *The Civil War in France* written by Marx.
September	Second London Conference of the International. Conflict with Bakunin. Marx secures adoption of a resolution declaring the need for the workers to form their own political party and win political power.
1872 April	Publication of the Russian translation of *Capital*, Vol. I.
	Fifth Congress of the International at The Hague.
	Expulsion of Bakunin.
	Speech of Marx in Amsterdam.
1875	Union of the two sections of the German Social Democrats, the Eisenachers and Lassalleans at the Gotha Congress.
	Marx writes his *Critique of the Gotha Programme*.
1878 July	Publication in a separate edition of Engels' *Anti-Dühring*, printed in Vorwärts in 1877–78.
October	Proclamation of Anti-Socialist Law in Germany.
1879 September	Letter on opportunist policy to Bebel, Liebknecht and Bracke.
1880	Engels publishes *Socialism: Utopian and Scientific* consisting of three chapters of *Anti-Dühring* and an Introduction.
1880 April	Marx and Engels help Guesde and Lafargue to draw up the programme of the programme of the French Worker's Party.
1881 December 2nd	Death of Marx's wife.
1882 January	Marx and Engels write the Foreword to the Russian edition of *The Communist Manifesto* in which they describe Russia as a forward section of the revolutionary movement in Europe.

1882	February-October	Marx in ill-health. He goes for treatment to Algiers, France and Switzerland.
1883	January 11th	Death of Marx's eldest daughter, Jenny Longuet.
	March 4th	Death of Karl Marx.
	March 17th	Marx buried at Highgate Cemetery. Engels' speech at the graveside.
1885		Engels prepares and publishes *Capital*, Vol. II.
1887		Publication of the English translation of *Capital*. Vol. I, by Samuel Moore and Edward Aveling.
1888	January	Authorised English translation of *The Communist Manifesto* by Samuel Moore, edited by Engels, published.
	February	Engels publishes *Ludwig Feuerbach and the End of Classical German Philosophy* (written in 1886).
1891		Engels' criticism of the Party programme to be discussed in the *Erfurt Social Democratic Congress*.
1894		Engels publishes *Capital*, Volume III.
1895		Engels writes the Introduction to the new edition of Marx's *Class Struggle in France, 1848-1850*.
1895	August 5th	Friedrich Engels dies.
1905-10		Marx's *Theorien über den Mehrwert* (Theories of Surplus Value) published by K. Kautsky in Stuttgart.

INDEX